D1132258

an

With kindest regards

Joan & Arthur

COAL MINING
IN
COUNTY
DURHAM

produced by Durham County
Environmental Education
Curriculum Study Group.

County Hall

May 1993

The rapid decline of the coal mining industry in County Durham and the clearing and improvement of the colliery sites prompted this project. Its objectives are:-

- to promote ideas which could stimulate interest in, and exploration of, the school environment
- to research the history and social life of the neighbourhood
- to provide resource material for school use
- to encourage schools to build up a store of local resources for their own use in future years
- to supply references from which further work can progress to the desired level

The project has taken three years to complete. Members of the Environmental Education Curriculum Group and their friends have gathered vast amounts of useful material which the editorial team shaped for publication. All who have made any contribution to this publication, which follows a twenty year tradition of publications by teachers of this county are to be congratulated on a worthy result.

Keith Mitchell.

Keith Mitchell

Director of Education

County Hall

May 1993

I am delighted to commend this book about my own industry
to our schoolchildren, to all people within County Durham and
further afield. From the foothills of the Pennines to the coast
and beyond, from the Tyne, almost to the Tees, coalmining has
developed over the centuries.

The industry has had hard times, times of relative prosperity
and more recently has been concentrated on a few coastal pits,
but most of the County has evidence of some coalmining either
in the landscape or in memories of the inhabitants of its towns
and villages.

This project will help to ensure that the basic industrial heritage
of this area is not forgotten, but will be appreciated and
understood by future generations of the young people of
County Durham.

Mick Terrans

Cllr Terrans

Chairman of Durham County Council

CONTENTS

WALKING IN
COLLIERY VILLAGES

A series of interesting excursions into the past

CONTENTS

KEY : FOR ALL MAPS

	ROADS : MOTORWAY / A / B		SEA : LOW TIDE
	SETTLEMENT	●	SITE
	RIVER : STREAM / : SOURCE		BECK : BRIDGE / : CULVERT
	PUBLIC FOOTPATH		BOUNDARY
	BRIDLEWAY		CHURCH
	ROUTE : DIRECTION	□ ■	SPECIAL BUILDING
	RAILWAY		: FOOT-BRIDGE / : VIADUCT
○	COLLIERY	▷	VIEW POINT
D	DRIFT MINE	⑦	STOPPING PLACE
	INDUSTRIAL SITE	ⓒ : Ⓟ	CAR PARK / START
	TIP	▷	PHOTOGRAPH
	QUARRY		
1 Km N	SCALE / NORTH		

THE PIT ROAD

It is quiet on the pit road over the hill
Where once the gaitered legs
Shaped bishops in the gloom
The crump of bartered boots is faintly heard
In ghostly winds which blow there still

There is small happiness in this grey earth
And accidents of joy are rare
To keep one here. Whistle if you can
In echoes of the tankey tones
Before the wheels stood grinning
With a soulless mirth

My father died among the aching years
And when the force wind combs
The hairy dust, I hear again
The hobbled hardness of his foot
Fall on the metal of the old pit road
Winding along my tears

Only the ash remains of older pits in elephan-
tine capes
Only the ash remains, once recognised and
loved in human form
The dead face emptied of its life and worth
Only the ash remains on mother earth

And yet I hope that there is more than this
That there are energies which flicker on
When all I know has vanished in the rains.

● Bill Dowding, a prolific writer, here turns his hand to verse to describe in emotional terms his thoughts on the Pit Road.

EVENWOOD

● Evenwood CE Primary School had a project gathering local information and planning a walk in this area: leader P Hodgson

Coal was worked continuously in the Evenwood area from the 14th Century, and probably earlier still. Evidence of coal mining in the Evenwood area goes back to 1383, when a mine was leased to John de Merley and three other persons for a term of six years at £22 per annum rent, and mines at 'Raly, Caldhirst..... and in the barony of Evenwood' formed part of a lease of 1424 which has been described as the most important in the Bishopric during the fifteenth century. Coal mining continued throughout the 16th and 17th centuries. However, the coal of South Durham could not compete with that of Tyne and Wear until the cost of transporting it could be radically reduced. It was not until the coming of the railways in the mid-1820's that the desired price revolution occurred.

Coal is the reason for the growth of Evenwood and Ramshaw during the 19th century. During the later part of the eighteenth century, Norwood Colliery, the most important in the Evenwood area, was owned by the Earl of Strathmore and he was extremely active in fighting for a rail link from Stockton and Darlington into the Gaunless valley to serve this colliery. Finally in 1825 the Darlington and Stockton railway line was opened which paved the way for Branch lines to be opened and consequently work began on the Hagger Leazes line.

The line followed the river Gaunless. It ran from St. Helens to Spring Gardens, past the mill to Ramshaw although the line actually ran through Evenwood. The line was officially opened in 1830. The Hagger Leazes line was very profitable. Flour was carried from the mill at Evenwood and lead was brought by pack horse from Weardale but of course the main freight was coal.

By 1851, the Hagger Leazes branch of the Stockton and Darlington railway had been working for 20 years or so and in 1852 the following collieries were working along the Hagger Leazes branch railway; Copley Colliery or Smout Pit, Jane Pit, (East Butterknowle Colliery) and Millfield Grange; Lands Colliery;

Storey Lodge Colliery; Norwood Colliery; Evenwood New Winning; Evenwood Colliery (more commonly known as Thrushwood); Tees-Hetton Colliery; Gordon Colliery and West Auckland Colliery. By far the largest enterprise in the district was the complex combining Norwood Colliery and Evenwood Colliery. The Railey Fell Pit covered a huge area largely to the north of modern day Ramshaw. It was in these local pits where most of the population found employment.

In 1891 the North Bitchburn Coal Company bought the Evenwood and Thrushwood Collieries for £55,000. This company sank the Randolph Pit in 1893. The Randolph Colliery was later under the control of Pease and Partners Ltd. and the Randolph Coal Co. Ltd. from January 1933 until January 1947 when together with its coking plant it became part of the National Coal Board, Northern Division No.4 area. The NCB sank the Hutton Drift at Randolph in 1953 and invested in a new Coking Plant but various seams were abandoned over a period, with final colliery closure in 1962. The Norwood Colliery at Ramshaw closed 1904 and the Railey Fell complex of drift mines and tubways finally closed in 1939.

ACCIDENTS IN THE PITS; EVENWOOD AREA; UP TO 1918 (Not An Exhaustive List)

FATALITIES:

1865 George Richardson aged 32 at Evenwood Colliery when a shaft cage fell on him.

1867 John Stonebank youth Evenwood Colliery serious accident.

1867 William Cummins aged 47 Norwood Colliery fall of coal.

1874 Robert Richardson aged 35 Evenwood Colliery fall of stones.

1887 George Sanderson aged 24 Evenwood Colliery fall of stones.

1894 George White aged 22 Norwood Colliery fall of stones.

1896 John Robert Taylor aged 38 Randolph Colliery head between tub and roof, this was the first fatality at the pit.

1896 William Adams Robinson aged 52 Norwood Colliery; caught between cage and shaft.

1903 Watson Hutchinson aged 14 Gordon House Colliery; fall of stones.

1906 John Dowson aged 67 Randolph Colliery; fall of stones.

1906 Harry Towers aged 14 Randolph Colliery; fall of stones.

1910 John T. Robinson aged 28 Randolph Colliery; crushed by a truck.

1910 Arthur Hutchinson age unknown Randolph Colliery; found dead in stables may not have been accidental

1911 Albert McConnell aged 14 Randolph Colliery; crushed by tub.

1914 John Hope age unknown Randolph Colliery caught head against balk.

1916 Ralph Brown aged 55 Randolph Colliery; fall of roof.

1918 Thompson Hope age unknown Randolph Colliery crushed by tubs.

EVENWOOD WALKABOUT

1. Evenwood and Ramshaw Community Centre - carpark - formerly the National School opened 1865 on a site given by John Bowes. The school closed in 1974 when the new Junior School along the new road was opened.

2. A view northwards towards a row of single storey red brick, grey slated bungalows (now called Devonshire Place) formerly the Randolph Aged Miners' Homes. Opened 24th January 1925.

3. The recreation ground - locally known as the welfare ground - the home of Evenwood Town A.F.C. who play in the Northern League Division Two and Evenwood Cricket Club who play in the Durham County League Division One. The welfare ground was laid out by the Randolph Colliery Welfare about 1925 - the ground originally included football and cricket pitches, bowling green, two tennis courts. The recreation ground was handed over to the parish council in 1974.

4. Cragwood - a walk into the wood will find the abandoned site of Evenwood Colliery 1835 - 1895. Evidence of the pit heap, shafts, drifts and tramways can be found.

5. Viewpoint - looking north over the Gaunless Valley and a large tract of land known locally as ''Railey Fell''.

6. Norwood Colliery and Cokeworks. Working prior to 1833 closed 1904. (Worked privately in the 1960s and early 1970s by Wardle and Company.

7. West Tees/Railey Fell Colliery, working prior to 1852 closed 1939. Many drift mines and tramways served this complex - a complicated history.

8. The Oaks - site of colliery housing - front, back and cross rows (4 in all) constructed prior to 1857 and demolished in the mid 1950s. Residents were rehoused in the new council houses at Newholme Crescent and Shirley Close.

9. Viewpoint looking north over the former railway lines.

10. Hagger Leazes Branch (Stockton and Darlington Railway Company) 1830 - 1963.

11. Barnard Castle Branch (South Durham and Lancashire Railway) 1863 - 1962. Station Terrace can be seen - the site of the first Evenwood Station. To the west the station buildings and station master's house still stand. Opened 1884, closed to traffic 1957. Known as Evenwood Station although located in Ramshaw.

12. Evenwood Mill - now demolished. The Mill Cottages are being refurbished (April 1991).

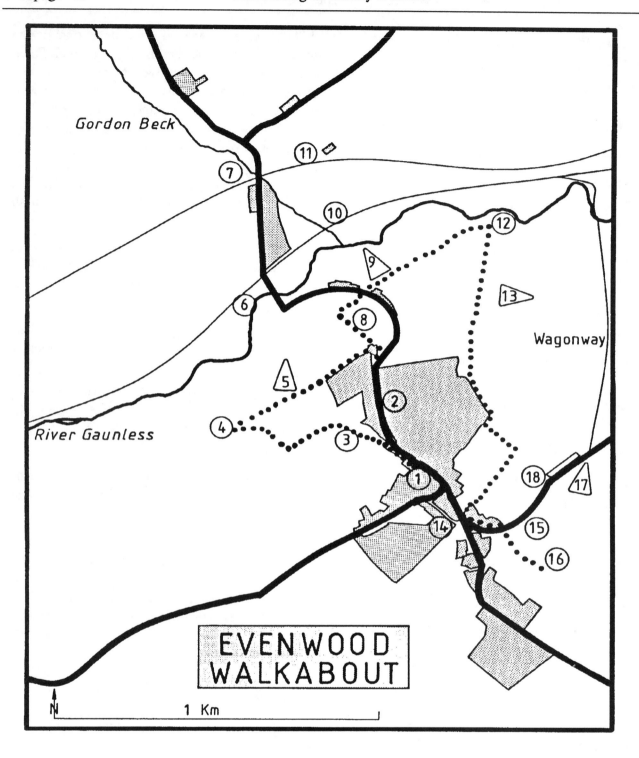

EVENWOOD
WALKABOUT

1 Km

13. Viewpoint: Thrushwood opencast site, currently working, scheduled to be completed 1992. They will excavate the sites of Thrushwood and Tees Hetton Collieries, Copeland Colliery, Ramshaw No. 2 Colliery and the huge Randolph North Pit Heap. The Randolph Incline, 1260 yards long, linking Randolph Colliery and Coke Works to the Hagger Leazes Branch Railway will also be excavated. The incline was worked by a stationary engine and took wagons (6 at a time) down to the railway. Operations ceased August 1968.

14. Randolph Institute South View - now the doctor's surgery - was opened 1897.

15. Randolph Cokeworks - probably the most famous landmark in South West Durham until 1984 - particularly the glow from the flame and the cloud of steam rising every 40 minutes or so.

16. RANDOLPH COLLIERY:

North Bitchburn Coal Company sank Randolph in 1893. It worked until 1962. It was also under the control of Pease and Partners Limited and the Randolph Coal Company Limited (1933 - 1947). Following nationalisation it was vested into the National Coal Board Northern Division No. 4 Area. The Low Main, Marshall Green, Harvey, Victoria, Brockwell and Busty Seams were worked. The Hutton Drift was sunk 1953 and abandoned 1962 it was located to the north of the main colliery. The conical pitheap, Randolph South, was another famous landmark until it was reclaimed in 1987. A brick- works was opened in the 1930's and following nationalisation, retained by W. Summerson and closed 1958.

17. Viewpoint: A view to the north east overlooks what remains of the Thrushwood pitheap and the Thrushwood opencast site (April 1991).

18. Copeland Row - originally known as Tees Hetton Row was built prior to 1873 to house miners working for the local mining companies. Other colliery rows were Chapel Street and Randolph Terrace.

The children and staff of Evenwood School, would like to express their thanks to Mr Kevin Richardson and Mr Brian Carter, without whose help this project would not have been as detailed. We would also like to thank Miss Nancy Bell who provided additional material for the project.

BUTTERKNOWLE

WALK 1

A circular walk along tracks and field paths to the River Gaunless, following an old railway track and along the village street from Diamond Bank.

Distance : 3 miles (5 kms)

Time Required : about 1 hour 30 minutes

Starting point: Quarry Lane picnic site, just beyond the west end of Butterknowle village (G.R. 100256).

O.S. Map: 1:50,000 *Barnard Castle.*

Landranger 92

This route has been waymarked with arrows in places to guide you.

Turn right out of the picnic site into Quarry Lane and follow this to main road which you cross.

Turn left for few yards and take track on the right, opposite a terrace of houses. Continue down the track for 1/2 mile (1km).

You will pass several farms and buildings along the track. The second on the right is where Brian Fletcher, the jockey, lived - he rode three Grand National winners, including Red Rum.

At the end of the track, carry straight on through the gate and follow the hedge to another gate in left hand corner - go through this and keep to the top of the bank to a stone wall and pine tree. Turn right here and drop down to a gate in the stone wall, with the River Gaunless beyond. Go through the gate, cross the river on stones - be prepared to get your feet wet here - and bear right up the bank opposite, through bracken to the corner of a stone wall. A wooded gill is on your right. Keep the wall on your left and aim for the bridge over the old Bishop Auckland to Barnard Castle railway line.

Do not cross the bridge, but carry on left down the bank on to an old railway line and continue with good views over the Gaunless valley towards Butterknowle and beyond.

● Lynesack and Softley Parish Council produced these walks in association with Teesdale Patchwork Project and kindly permitted David Noble to re draft them for this publication.

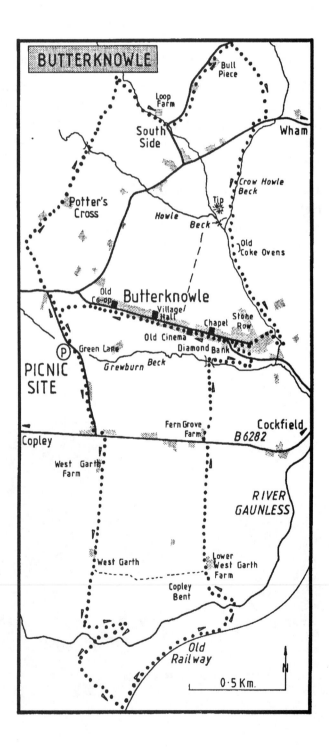

The railway line was built in the early 19th century, mainly to exploit the coal deposits in this area, most of which would have been taken over the Stockton and Darlington Railway for shipment from the River Tees at Middlesbrough. The early pits were fairly small but more recently mining in the area has been by larger opencast methods. The spoil heaps of old pits can usually still be seen, but most opencast workings are completely restored to retain the original landscape.

Where the track bends to the right of the farm, carry on for a short distance and, before crossing a bridge, drop down the bank on the left and aim for a footbridge over the River Gaunless at the bottom of the slope.

Cross the footbridge and bear left through a field and up a bank to the gate at the top. Go through this and keep alongside the wall to a track in front of a barn.

Turn right here and along the concrete drive beside a farmhouse for about 1/2 mile (1 km) to the main road

Cross the road and go down the drive of Fern Grove Farm immediately opposite. Keep to the right of the farmhouse and go through a gate and then a stile in the wooden fence.

BUTTERKNOWLE MINER c 1900

Keep to the left hand edge of the field and down the steps to cross the Grewburn Beck.

Turn right immediately over a stile and follow a path up the bank through the remains of old Diamond Colliery to a kissing gate. Go through this and turn sharp left to another gate on to the road at Diamond Bank.

Very near here you should see a stone slab in the wall behind the pavement, marked with an arrow. This is the site, where in 1884, a local policeman, Sergeant Smith was murdered.

Turn left up the hill and follow the main village street of Butterknowle past the Wesleyan Chapel on your right.

100 yards further on, on your left, you pass a workshop and warehouse. These used to be the miners' hall and the Kino Cinema. Further along, on the right hand side of the street, is the old Co-operative store.

At the end of the village, where the road bends, take the footpath on the left past the front of two houses to come out into Quarry Lane.

Turn left here to the picnic site where you started your walk.

DIAMOND COLLIERY

Walk 2

A circular walk on tracks to Potters Cross and field paths to South Side, a short road section and then a pleasant path along the Crow Howle Beck, past old mining and industrial remains to Stone Row and the village street.

Distance : 3 miles (5 kms)

Time required : about 1 hour 30 minutes

Boots or stout footwear recommended.

Starting point: Quarry Lane picnic site, just beyond the west end of Butterknowle village (G.R. 100256).

Turn left out of the picnic site into Quarry Lane and at the main road, cross over and take the wide track ahead.

This track forms part of the old burial route to Hamsterley church, about 4 miles to the north.

At the first big house, fork right along another track through two gates in front of a farm to a small group of attractive cottages at Potters Cross.

Here you join a small road which soon bends to the right - at this point, leave the road and go through a gate to pass along the front of the cottages on the left. Go through a second gate and keep straight across the field, through another gate and then across a stile to a footbridge over a small stream.

Keep ahead to another stile in fence and follow left hand edge of two fields and into a third.

Once in this field, turn right and follow fence to a stile next to a gate and on to a track past Loop Farm. This will lead you onto a road at South side.

Turn left here and follow the road for 1/4 mile, passing Bull Piece Farm on your right.

Just past the farm, where the road bends, go through a stile in the hedge on your right and follow the stiles along the edge of three fields to come out on another quiet country road.

Turn right along the road for about 50 yards and take the path on your left which leads you down alongside the Crow Howle Beck.

This is a very pleasant path which will

Bell pits (so called because of their shape)

Early mines in Butterknowle would be just like this.

eventually bring you out next to an old colliery spoil heap.

Just beyond this, up on the right, you will see the remains of the colliery blacksmith's shop.

Cross the stile ahead, but do not go as far as the bridge - turn left instead, to follow route of old railway line.

The track is the bed of the old Butterknowle - Haggerleases Railway branch line. This railway was built specifically to serve the Butterknowle and Marsfield colliery, the remains of coke ovens in the undergrowth on the left of the path. These are built of bricks made in Butterknowle, distinguished by a thumb print in each brick. The whole complex of industrial activity in this small valley, together with the railway, closed down in 1910.

Following this path, with the industrial remains on your left and the stream on your right, you will come to a large concrete bridge just before the first houses of Butterknowle.

Cross this bridge and climb the path up to the houses in Stone Row which were built by the Butterknowle Coal Company.

Continue ahead past the village school and along the main street.

Continue past the Wesleyan Chapel on your right and for another 100 yards, past a workshop and warehouse on the left.

These used to be the miners hall and the Kino Cinema.

Further along, on the right hand side of the street, is the old Co-operative store.

At the end of the village, where the road bends, take the footpath on the left past the front of two houses to come out into Quarry Lane.

Turn left here to the picnic site where you started your walk.

Diamond shaft (with pigeon cree) 1992

SHILDON

Before 1825 Shildon was little more than a farming hamlet. Coal had been mined in the area on a small scale since the Middle Ages but mining was more extensive in the Wear and Gaunless valleys to the west and north where coal seams were nearer the surface. The coal was carried by road using horse-drawn waggons. Shildon was sited on a ridge of hills separating this coal mining area from the coastal lowlands to the east. For the promoters of the Stockton and Darlington Railway it was this ridge that formed the greatest obstacle to bringing the trade of the coalfield to the mouth of the River Tees where the coal could be shipped to places such as London.

When the railway was opened in 1825 the waggons of coal were hauled and lowered over the ridge by cables wound by stationary steam engines sited on the summit, one near Brusselton for the main line and one near Shildon for the Black Boy Branch (opened 1827). Horses pulled the trains of waggons along the more level parts. Steam locomotives were also used on the line from Shildon to Stockton.

At the foot of the Brusselton east incline the railway settlement of New Shildon was built for the employees working on the railway and in

● This full account of Shildon incorporates a walk, background information, personal memories of Shildon in its hey day together with the incomparable illustrations of David Snell.

the Railway Company's workshops. Timothy Hackworth was appointed as Superintendent Engineer in charge of the railway. The success of the railway soon encouraged new coal mines and industries to be set up around Shildon, using the railway to transport their goods. Both Shildon and New Shildon grew rapidly, eventually joining to form the town of Shildon.

THE MINING TRAIL

The trail visits sites of coal mines and associated branch railways around Shildon. The main features are outlined on the route plan. Information boards in the town give further details. A useful day's excursion could include the trail and a visit to the Timothy Hackworth Museum where there are exhibits on local mining, railway and social history. The trail begins and ends at the museum. It is in five sections, each starting at an 'Investigation Site' (A-E on the plan). The complete route is 6.3km (3.9 miles).

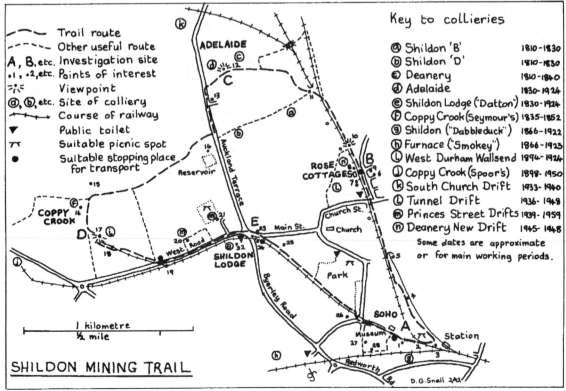

SHILDON MINING TRAIL

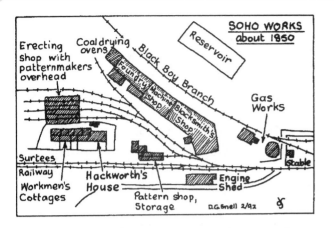

It can be shortened, for example, by starting at Site B (Rose Cottages) and returning there directly from point E (4.7km / 3 miles). Or visits to specific sites could be made.

SITE A; TIMOTHY HACKWORTH MUSEUM AND SOHO ENGINE WORKS

The first section traces the course of the Black Boy branch railway. From the museum follow the path towards the station, passing the site of Hackworth's engineering works (1) (Which building remains?), the Black Boy stables (2) (What work do you think the horses did on the railway?), and the coal drops ramp (3), used for loading coal onto the steam locomotives. There was also a gas works here built by the S&DR in 1841 for lighting the railway and works. Lighting was by gas in Shildon until the electric power station was built in the early 20th century, south of Shildon Lodge Colliery. The railway station area was still lit by gas in the late 1960's. (What fuel was used to make gas and electricity?) Some collieries had their own gas works. In 1859 a pit was opened at the Soho works, working four coal seams.

The Black Boy branch joined the main S&D line between the stables and the coal drops. It was opened on 10 July, 1827, to serve Black Boy Colliery (named after a local pub and partly owned by Jonathan Blackhouse, S&DR Company Treasurer) and other collieries in the Coundon and Eldon areas to the north.

Near the station bridge turn left along the path by the railway cutting leading to Shildon tunnel. The path passes an aqueduct (4), built when the cutting was made. (Why was this necessary? The water was a stream flowing through open countryside).

The tunnel (5), named the 'Prince of Wales Tunnel', was opened on 10th January 1842. (Find out which prince was born the previous month? Who was his mother?). It was built by the Shildon Tunnel Company, a subsidiary of the S&DR Company, to capture the trade of collieries in the Crook area, linking up with the Bishop Auckland and Weardale Railway. (What were the advantages of building a tunnel rather than using the Black Boy railway over the hill?). We will see the other end of the tunnel later. Look out for the tops of the brick ventilation shafts (how many?) along the trail. Beyond the first ventilation shaft the line is used for a market on Fridays. Cross the main road and, looking out for another tunnel ventilator, continue to Rose Cottages (Site B), passing, on the right, Market Place, Queen Street (6) and Foundry Street. On the left near Hackworth House Residential Home (7) was a sandstone quarry. (What buildings might the stone have been used for?).

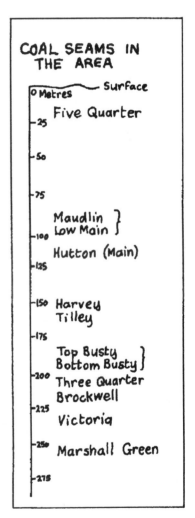

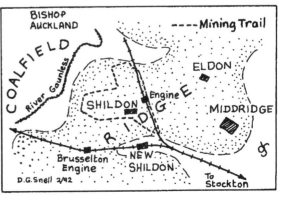

Freda Rutter was born at 7 Queen Street on 26th August 1920, living there until she was 11. She says, 'There was my Grandad, my Gran, my mam, my Uncle Bobbie and my Uncle Freddie. Freddie was the youngest, he was 14 when I was born. My uncle Marmaduke was married and left home before I was born. He lived in Station Street and worked at Datton Pit. My grandparents also had two other children, Ethel and Polly. They worked away in service. There was always bustle in the house, everyone busy. There was always one or other of the men coming in from the pit.

Our house had a stone floor with hooky and proddy mats that mam made. In the kitchen was a black kitchen range with a coal fire and boiler. There was always lots of broth and stew cooking on it. There was a big wooden table, some straight chairs and a rocking chair. Grandad, Bobbie and Freddie were miners. There were no baths at the pit so they came home black. They got bathed in a big tin bath in front of the kitchen fire. I had to go out the way. I would play in the wash house. In the end Bobbie came out of the pit because of bronchitis and asthma. He helped wash up and tidy the house.

In the sitting room was gran's rocking chair by the fire. She was ill for a lot of years and she slept in the rocking chair. When I was 11 she died in it. There was a couch and two armchairs and an organ that Freddie played. We used to sing. He also played a mouth organ. By the window was a little table with a plant on it and we had a gramaphone with a horn. I played it when I got up a bit. There was a bed like a sideboard with doors. The bed unfolded out and Grandad slept on it. I slept upstairs in the back bedroom with my mam in a double bed. Freddie and Bobbie slept in the front bedroom. Under the stairs was the pantry where we kept the food, dishes and pans, with a sink and a tap.

We had gas lights with mantles. A lamp hung from the sitting room ceiling. The glass globe had a hole in the bottom and two chains hanging down. Grandad was very tall. He pulled one chain to turn the gas on. The other turned it off. He lit the gas from the fire with a taper. They put electric in the house whilst I lived in Queen Street.

The yard at the back was open all the way along the row. Across the yard was the netty, the coal house and our wash house. Mam did not work because she looked after gran. She took in washing, especially during the 1926 strike when there was no money about. I used to help her. She did washing for a man in St. Paul's Terrace and for Murphy's show people when they were in town. Mam once took me into a caravan during Shildon show. In the wash house was a set pot with a fire for boiling water, a mangle, a poss tub and a big table for scrubbing clothes. The tin bath hung on the wall. The wash house was a good place to play with my friends, Peggy, Flo, Ada and Dolly, especially with the big table. We played sweet shops, and fish shops with a piece of candle in a cardboard box! I had an old fashioned doll's pram probably the only one in the street, and a doll's house and a doll's cot with lace round it. I always got a good Christmas Box. I had a lot of uncles, and aunties in service and they would club together'.

SITE B; ROSE COTTAGES

These were workers cottages (8) built by the Stockton and Darlington Railway company. Look for the S&DR property plaque on the wall. In front of the cottages was the winding engine for the Black Boy inclines over the Shildon ridge. (Why this spot?). There was a reservoir beyond the cottages. (What for?) Looking back, across the road, is Foundry street, and Phoenix Place (9). This was the site of Nicholas Downing's Phoenix Iron and Brass Foundry. It had its own railway sidings. (Why did the railway make it a suitable place to build a factory?)

When Freda Rutter was a girl the railway lines were still here. Her uncle Freddie played football along here and also quoits using iron rings. Freda also played along the old line and down onto the tunnel top. (What games would you play?) Freda says, 'We played hidey bow seek and chasey and games in a ring. We played tip cat with a piece of pointed wood. You hit the end with a stick to see how far you could get it. I had an iron booler and a hook. When we rolled it in the back lane we would get wrong because of the noise. We also played kick the tin. We would get wrong for that as well because of the racket. Me grandad chased us many a time. I had a top and whip, a skippy rope made from straw rope that fastened orange boxes, and some chucks. Grandad made me these from small pieces of wood. You threw them up to see how many you could catch on the back of your hand. You could buy them as well. We played itchy bay. You marked the yard with a piece of stone you could chalk with. It was like hop scotch. Don't tell anyone, but we sometimes played knocky nine doors. You tie a piece of string to a knocker, with a tin on the other end and then knock on the door. I got a penny every Saturday to go to the matinee at the Cosy Cinema. It was near where the new library is in Church Street. I sometimes got something extra to go to the colliery swimming baths down Eldon bank. It was an open-air pool with changing cubicles around the edge. It is now used as a scrap yard. I went to the council school in Thornhill Gardens. The thing I remember it for most was the maypole dancing on the first of May. I used to love it.

Every Sunday I went to the Primitive Methodist Sunday School, where the Co-op park is now. I also went with mam to the morning or night service."

Leaving the road, begin to descend the North incline. Stop by the narrow footpath on the left (west) (10). It leads past a tunnel ventilator.

The field is the site of two drift coal mines: Tunnel Drift (1936-1948) and Deanery New Drift (1945-1948). In a drift mine the coal was brought to the surface through a sloping or level tunnel, often using a tramway (narrow railway). (Can you think of any advantages/disadvantages compared with a vertical pit shaft?)

Looking north, down the track, the incline is straight with a constant slope using a cutting and an embankment. (Why was this necessary? - think of how the coal waggons were hauled up the incline). In the distance can be seen rows (how many?) of miners' houses, built near the sites of coal mines, including the Black Boy Colliery. At one time there were many more. Beyond is the Wear Valley.

Continue down the track. Black coal dust gives another clue to its original use. (How did it get here?). Pass a field with a ventilator in it. Leave the Black Boy railway by bearing left (west) along the route of a siding to cross over the tunnel entrance. Here, and alongside the cutting, are waste heaps (11). They contain a great deal of the yellowish clay which overlays the more solid rocks, rather than the grey shale of colliery waste which we will see later. (Where might the waste be from? An environmental issue here) Much of the tunnel spoil was used for the South Church embankment to the north.

The footpath by the field west from the tunnel top passes the sites of two old pre-railway collieries: Shildon 'B' Pit and Shildon 'D' Pit (1810 - 1830). No remains are visible.

The trail continues north alongside the cutting. About halfway from the tunnel to a footbridge over the railway turn left (west) over a stile. The footpath crosses a field and another stile, over the brow of the hill to the site of Adelaide colliery (12).

The footbridge provides a good view of the railway and tunnel. The disused span crossed the West Auckland Branch line (13th September, 1856) which swung round the hill to link with the main S & DR line beyond the Brusselton inclines which were then no longer used. They finally closed in 1858.

Site 'C': Deanery and Adelaid ('Shildon Bank') Collieries

This area (12) has been the site of extensive coal workings from the early 19th century, when Mr. Brown opened the Deanery Pit (c1810 - 1840), until the closure of Adelaide Colliery (1830 - 1924). Adelaide Colliery was owned by the Quaker Joseph Pease. His father, Edward, played a major role in starting the Stockton and Darlington Railway. Sidings linked the colliery to the Black Boy line and, later, the tunnel line. There were extensive coke ovens towards the bottom of the slope (What is coke made from?). In 1894 shafts were sunk to the Busty and Brockwell seams. 240 men and boys were employed at that time. The whole area has been reclaimed. (Loock for the bollards in the field marking the pit shafts. What is the land use now?)

There is a fine view of the market town of Bishop Auckland sheltered in the valley. Nearer is South Church. The colliery opened an infant school here in 1839, supported by the Society of Friends (Quakers). The garden nursery in the foreground is the site of South Church Drift (1933 - 1940). Rows of colliery houses can be seen on the hillsides, interspersed with older farms and newer industry. To the right (east) is a brickworks. Many bricks used in the area were made here: they bear the name 'ELDON'. The first Eldon brickworks was owned by Pease & Co. The railway embankment leading from the tunnel across the Gaunless valley is visible.

Freda sometimes walked to Bishop Auckland with Grandad and his pet spaniel, Jess. Or they would walk to Howden-le-Wear on the hills beyond Bishop Auckland to see Grandad's sister Polly. Sometimes they went to Leasingthorne, over the hill beyond Eldon. Freda says, 'I remember dragging elderberry branches back home. We used the berries to make elderberry wine. We would also walk to Darlington to see my Ant Polly. I only once went away as a child. That was on a Sunday School trip to Redcar by train. An odd time or two I went to Bishop Auckland by bus and to Darlington by train but we usually walked everywhere. One time we lost Jess in Darlington.' (How do you think Freda felt walking home?) 'She got back home before we did!'

'Grandad also kept canaries and once we had a cat, but it got the canary. My grandad got me three white Angora rabbits. I used to brush them and Grandad sent the wool away. At first we kept their hutch on a shelf in the coal house but they kept getting black! Then they lived in the wash house. They used to follow me across into the house.'

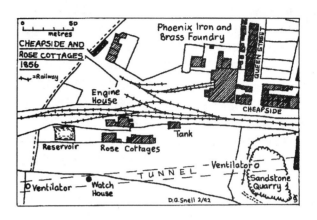

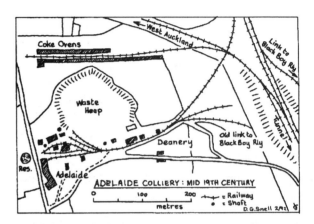

Continue along the footpath, leaving the field by the stile near the road, not the track gate. Turn left up the road, past the end of Busty Terrace (13), with its yellowish brick colliery houses. (How did it get its name?) Towards the top of the hill take the footpath on the right, across the road, just before the covered reservoir (14). This is the highest point in Shildon. An open reservoir was built here by the Weardale and Shildon Water Works set up in 1866 because of an acute water shortage due to the growth in population and the demands of the steam locomotives in New Shildon and steam-driven machinery in the mines. The local water was too hard. Water was brought from Waskerley (1871) and Tunstall (1879) Reservoirs in the Pennine hills, 20 & 25km away. (Why choose this spot? Why was so much water needed?)

Follow the path through the fields until it is well below the brow of the hill. Pause where the path turns left (south) through a stile in the fence. The depressions across the field to the right (north) are the remains of an early 20th century clay pit and brick works (15). (Where might the bricks have been used?) There were several local brick and tile works using the boulder clay that covers the surface in this area. The clay is yellowish, but it fires to make red brick and pantiles. Many of the older buildings in Shildon have been re-roofed, but look out for the original pantiles on outhouses. Some collieries made bricks from the fire clay found beneath the coal seams. This fired to a yellowish brick: look out for these too in some of the old walls. They often had the name of the colliery or its owner: "PEASE" bricks were used at Adelaide Pit; "B & V Co" at various pits.

Go over the stile and follow the edge of the field. The field to the west is the site of Luke Seymour's Coppy Crook Colliery (1835 - 1852) (16), and the mining hamlet of Coppy Crook Cottages. A shaft here was sunk to the Brockwell seam. Continue south along a permissive right of way, over a stile, turning left on to the waste heap (17).

Site 'D': Coppy Crook: West Durham Wallsend Colliery

This is the waste heap of West Durham Wallsend Colliery (1894 - 1924) (17). The No. 1 shaft was sunk to below the Maudlin Seam, but sinking stopped in May, 1895 because of water difficulties.

Fig. 10

From the waste heap is a good view south of the route of the Brussleton West Incline. (See sketch). Beyond the nearby house the roofs of Brusselton Cottages and the Engine House can be seen on the nearest hill. The engine drew the coal waggons up the S & DR incline from the Gaunless River valley on the right (where they were pulled by horses). The railway passes below Brusselton Farm,. by Low West Thickley Farm, and through the cutting to Brusselton Cottages. They were then lowered down the other side of the hill, away to the left. (Later study the technology: the descending train of waggons helped raise those ascending. What about the returning empty waggons? The inclines were single line and unequal lengths! How would you raise coal in a drift mine?) Try to locate the sites of old mines using the sketch - some waste heaps are still visible. Many of the fields have also been open-cast mined in the past. In comparatively recent times coal was

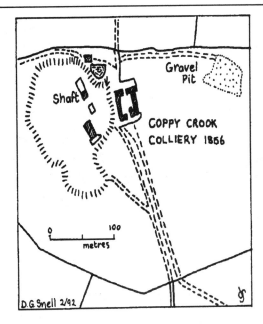

COPPY CROOK COLLIERY 1856

Gravel Pit

Shaft

0   100
metres

D.G.Snell 2/92

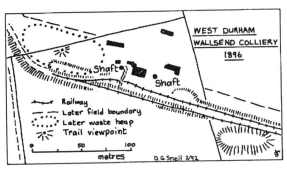

WEST DURHAM WALLSEND COLLIERY 1896

Shaft   Shaft

Railway
Later field boundary
Later waste heap
Trail viewpoint

0   50   100
metres   D.G.Snell 2/92

transported by aerial cable from Brusselton Colliery to the railway near Shildon, beyond Brusselton Cottages.

Return to the footpath, skirting the foot of the main waste heap, along the track of the railway (18) which carried coal from the colliery to join the "Surtees Railway" at Shildon. Look at the typical grey shale of the waste heap, found in layers with the coal.

Continue through the scrubland to the field boundary on the left (north). Follow the path across stiles to West Auckland Road, turning left past the cemetery. The railway line crossed the road and ran parallel with it on the right (19).

Fig. 11

Beyond the cemetery, on the left, were two terraces of mine houses, Bolckow and Vaughan Streets (20), named after Teesside iron founders who used the S & DR to supply their blast furnaces at Witton Park using Cleveland ironstone. The company worked several mines in

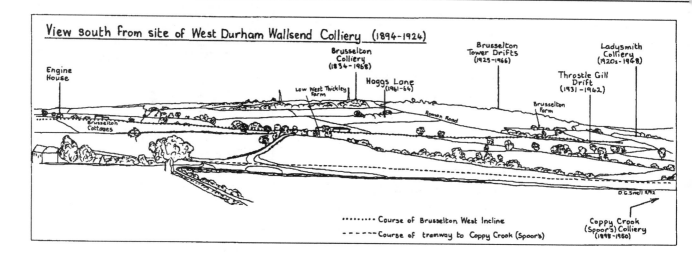

the area from about 1857 including Shildon Lodge and Furnace Pits. Bolckow Street has been replaced by new flats West Close), Vaughan Street remains (What colour bricks?). Behind was a drift mine opened by the Princes Street Colliery Company (1939 - 59). Further along on the left is Princes Street (21). The playing field at the far end is the site of a second drift worked at the same time.

On the right of West Road was Shildon Lodge Colliery ("Datton Pit") (22).

Freda Rutter's grandfather and uncles were miners at Datton Pit in the 1920's. As a teenager Freda lived in West Road with her mother, her stepfather, George, and her baby half brother, Dennis. "The house was number 30 on the corner of Princes Street opposite Datton Pit. The row has gone now. There were three houses, then five, than another three. It

only had two rooms, one up, one down. My mam and George slept at one end of the bedroom, our Dennis and I slept at the other, one each side of the fireplace, though Dennis was often at his grandparents just along the road: one of the houses where the railing is by the road, number 8. The houses are still there. Dennis's grandfather was Jack Parker. He was fore overman at Datton. I can remember watching the chimneys at the pit felled from the bedroom window. When I was 14 I left school. I didn't have a job so I went to the dole school in Bishop Auckland for training. Then I went away into service in Surrey".

Continue to the main road junction. It is safest to bear to the left a little way before crossing Auckland Terrace. Then return to the junction. Go round the corner into Main Street (Site "E") (23).

Site "E": Shildon Lodge Colliery ("Datton Pit")

From the bottom of Main Street (23) look back across the junction along West Road. Compare the scene with the photograph showing the pithead of Shildon Lodge Colliery. The filling station now occupies the land to the left and centre of the photograph. The stone garden wall in the extreme right foreground still exists, as do some of the buildings beyond (Which?). The big house in the distance is at the end of Princes Street.

Shildon Lodge Colliery was started on land owned by Robert Surtees, in 1830, using the "Surtees Railway" to link it to the S & DR near the junction with the Black Boy Branch.

Grandfather Rutter

The colliery was worked by Bolckow and Vaughan. Seams worked included Low Main, Harvey and Brockwell. The large tall building contained the winding gear that lowered the cages down the shaft, driven by a steam engine: the tall chimney to the left was for its boiler. Underground the workings linked up with those of other mines. The buildings by the road were the colliery offices, where the miners checked in and out, with the overmen's and manager's offices beyond. Behind the fence on the left was the railway. The "Grey Horse" and the crossing gates leading into Byerley Road are just off the photograph.

Freda's Uncle Marmaduke worked at Datton Pit. "He lived in Station Street. One day he was late for work. He rushed and got the last cage down. The draught from the tubs of coal blew the lamp out and he was run over by the tubs and killed. His daughter Annie was only two at the time. This was before I was born and before Freddie started work.

"During the 1926 strike Grandad and Freddie went to Coppy Crook digging for coal. What they got was no good. It wouldn't burn. The children had to go to soup kitchens from school at lunch time. I went to Old Shildon Club. I remember being put off by the dumplings floating in the stew. I would also stand in queues for my mother who would then take over to get our handout of food.

"When the pit closed Freddie biked to London looking for work. He didn't find any so he biked back again. He managed to get on the railway at Darlington Engine Works."

Cross Main Street to the old sandstone "Coach House" (24) (An information board gives more details of this area). Follow the course of the Surtees Railway. It bears right off Main Street behind the Coach House. Or return to Rose Cottages via Main Street and Church Street.

When Freda lived at Queen Street, Grandad and Freddie used to go to the Old Shildon Working Men's Club in Main Street. "Bobbie could manage to walk there too. Freddie liked to go to the dances".

"A funny thing happened to Grandad when he was going out one Christmas. We never had a tree but Gran made what she called a "mistletoe" from wooden barrel hoops and tissue paper. She hung decorations and toys on it like you do on a Christmas tree. Grandad put it up inside the back door. It had a boat hanging from it and one day it caught on Grandad's bowler hat as he went out. He wondered why everyone was calling to him as he

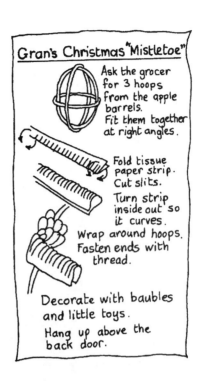

Gran's Christmas "Mistletoe"

Ask the grocer for 3 hoops from the apple barrels. Fit them together at right angles.

Fold tissue paper strip. Cut slits.

Turn strip inside out so it curves. Wrap around hoops. Fasten ends with thread.

Decorate with baubles and little toys.

Hang up above the back door.

walked down the road, he looked so funny! On Christmas Eve we would all sing carols and Freddie would play the organ or his mouth organ. Then I would hang one of my uncle's long socks under the mantle piece in the kitchen. Santa would leave me an apple, orange, nuts, a chocolate Father Christmas and a candy mouse or pig, pink with a string tail."

Follow the Surtees Railway. To the left, across the road from the terrace of houses, are the remnants of old sandstone quarries (25. (Look for the sandstone in the railway line wall). Further on, on the right past the park, by the Masonic Hall, is the site of a clay pit and brick and tile works (26).

Cross the road junction and return to the Timothy Hackworth Museum along Hackworth Close, or continue down Alma Road and Mill Street, the site of a steam powered corn mill (27) (Another use of coal). The route of the main S & DR, past the old school (28), now the Salvation Army Hall, built by the railway company in 1841, and continue to the museum.

BOWBURN AND SHINCLIFFE

BOWBURN

The colliery known as Bowburn in the village of that name (NZ 304379) was the second colliery to bear that title. The original Bowburn Colliery (NZ 31843676) was sunk in the 1840's close to the terminus at Coxhoe of the Clarence Railway's Durham City Branch to which it was connected by rail. It was a small concern which was worked in the 1850's firstly by Robson and Jackson, then later by the West Hetton Coal Company. The seams worked were the Main seam and the Five Quarter both were abandoned in 1857. The Mining Record Office Plans (F.25/25; 13912) show that the workings only covered a small area to the south west of the shaft, under what is now the Park Hill Estate. The only evidence of the colliery is the red-ash waste heap behind Clarence Villa near the Three Mile Bridge, Coxhoe.

The second Bowburn Colliery (NZ 304 379) was sunk in 1906, this newspaper report from the Northern Echo of 24th July 1906 tells the story:

"Much Interest was shown at Bowburn, near Coxhoe, yesterday, when Miss Bell, daughter of Sir Hugh Bell, commenced the work of sinking the shaft of the colliery which the firm of Bell Bros. starting. ...The new shaft is in close proximity to the main road from Coxhoe to Durham, and is being sunk to relieve the haulage at the adjoining colliery at Tursdale (NZ 301360) owned by the same firm, who also own Browney (NZ 250388) and Page Bank (NZ 233347) collieries.

It is intended to sink to a depth of 110 fathoms (200 metres) into the Brockwell seam passing through the Harvey and Busty seams. The latter is already being worked at Tursdale... but the haulage is expensive. The Tursdale colliery will

● Details of two neighbouring mid-Durham Collieries and a circular walk in the vicinity of Shincliffe compiled by Don Wilcock

continue working in the south-east direction in the Busty and Brockwell seams the new shaft taking the east and west districts.''

The first coals from the new colliery were drawn in July 1908 and the colliery was closed in July 1967.

After sinking the coal drawing shaft, Bell Bros. opened out Heugh Hall colliery (NZ 323379), which had been closed in the 1880's as a man-riding shaft until the Bowburn Upcast shaft (NZ 307381) was sunk c 1911.

Nothing now remains of the colliery, the colliery yard has been partially developed as an industrial site, the upcast shaft has a workshop on it, and the extensive waste heaps have been landscaped and planted with trees. All that remains is the colliery baths, and the colliery housing in two distinct areas, Bow and Burn Streets and Durham Road, Steavenson, Clarence and Wylam Streets, and with the Infant School attached.

Map 1, shows the colliery and the village in 1914, shortly after opening

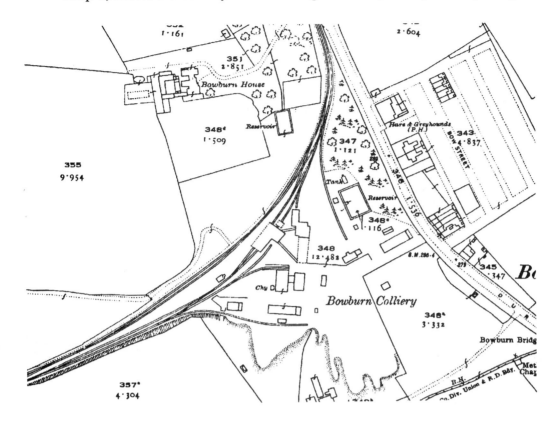

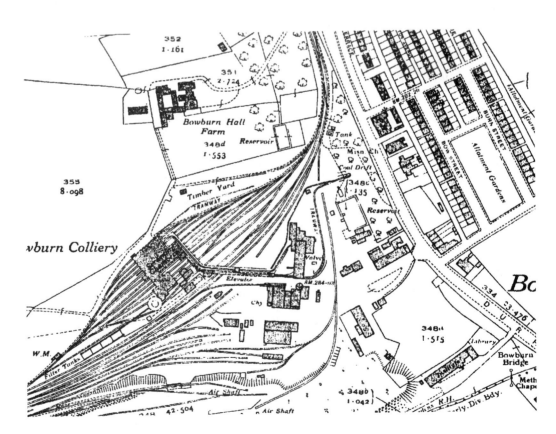

Map 2, is dated 1938 and shows the village before the War and before the
large estate was built in the period 1948 - 1954.

SHINCLIFFE

Coal mines are mentioned at Shincliffe in the Dean and Chapter's "Great Book" of 1721, to 1749. It is not known where these coal mines were but there is evidence of some working near the village in ground disturbance beside the footpath behind the old school at or near NZ 293407.

Shincliffe Colliery (NZ 299399) was sunk in 1837 at the top of Shincliffe Bank, and is sometimes referred to as *Bank Top* Colliery. It was originally sunk down to the Hutton seam and worked that seam exclusively, then in 1867 the shaft was deepened down to the Brockwell seam. The Low Main seam was worked with Houghall Colliery (NZ 282406) both collieries being under the same ownership almost from the beginning. The first owners of Shincliffe being Bell and Company until 1841, followed by Bell, Davidson, Morrison and Spark. Spark became the principal owner in the 1860's only to be joined in the mid 1860's by Joseph Love, who becomes the principal owner in the late 60's and remained so until the colliery was abandoned in May 1886.

The undermentioned Houses are situate within the Boundaries of the

No. of Schedule	ROAD, STREET, &c., and No. or NAME of HOUSE	HOUSES Inhabited	HOUSES Uninhabited (U.) or Building (B.)	NAME and Surname of each Person	RELATION to Head of Family	CONDITION	AGE Males	AGE Females	Rank, Profession, or OCCUPATION	WHERE BORN
72	14 Miners Cottages	1		John Embleton	Head	Mar	28		Coal Miner	Northumberland Newcastle
				Jane do	Wife	Mar		28		Yorkshire
				Ellen do	daur			8	Scholar	Durham Lanchester
				Henry do	Son		4		do	do
				Mabel do	daur			4 mo		do Shincliffe
73	15 do	1		John Ridley	Head	Mar	31		Coal Miner	do Ferry
				Jane do	Wife	Mar		30		do Chester le Street
				Sarah do	Daur			8	Scholar	do Winston
				Margaret do	Daur			7	Scholar	do Lanchester
				John do	Son		3			do do
				George do	Son		1			do Chester le Street
74	16 do	1		John Wainwright	Head	Mar	42		Coal Miner	Wales
				Jane do	Wife	Mar		41		Ireland
				Elles do	Son		12		Scholar	Durham Castle Eden
				Elizabeth J do	daur			9	do	do Bradford
				William do	Son		4			do
75	17 do	1		Richard Bromfield	Head	Mar	20		Coal Miner	do Hutton
				Mary do	Wife	Mar		19		do Framwellgate
76	18 do	1		John Overton	Head	Mar	60		Plat Layer	do Darlington
				Ann do	Wife	Mar		59		do Stanhope
77	19	1		Michael Sweney	Head	Mar	22		Coal Miner	Ireland
				Mary do	Wife	Mar		36		do
				Thomas do	Son		15			Durham Kelloe
				William do	daur		13			Newcastle
				Margaret do	daur			8		
ψ	Total of Houses.. 6				Total of Males and Females..		13	12		

* Draw the pen through such of the words as are inappropriate.

The colliery was connected to the Durham and Sunderland Railway via an incline due north the route of which remains as a footpath to and beyond the present Manor Farm, it is at this site, at one time called Waggonway Farm, there are remains of the engine house and of the waggonway man's cottage. South of the route, are remains of the associated brickwork kilns which are now in the care of the Parish Council.

There is no sign of the colliery, the Infant and Junior Schools stand on the site, what does remain are the colliery housing, as in Front Street and Overmans Row, and the village school, known as the Parochial school, now a private house. Also standing is the chapel, now a workshop, on a site presented by Joseph Love, the coal owner, and built with bricks, embossed "LOVE" supplied from the colliery brickworks.

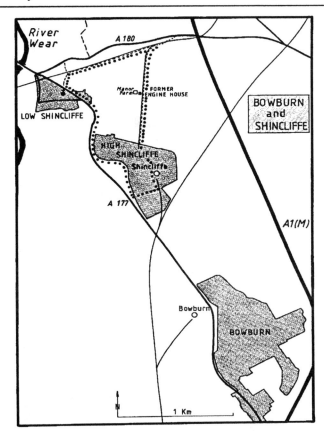

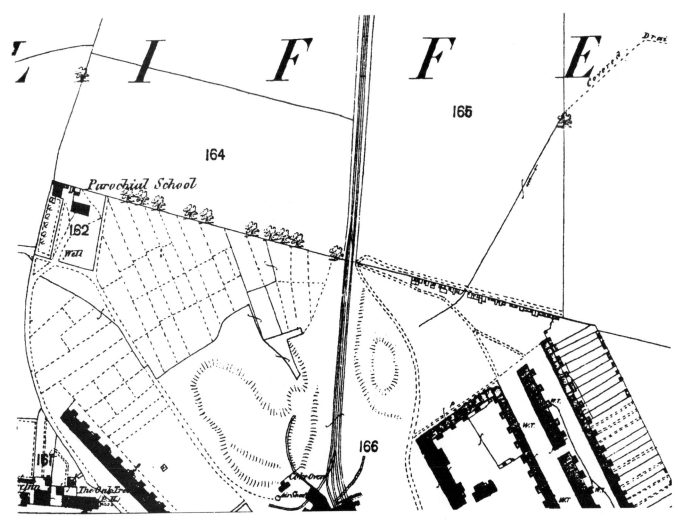

PITHILL, BEAMISH

● This walk around the Village of Pithill, now known as Beamish has been prepared by Mike Horne.

The walk starts and finishes at EDEN PLACE picnic area where there is ample space for parking and a large grassed area with tables for a packed lunch to be eaten. THERE ARE NO TOILET FACILITIES.

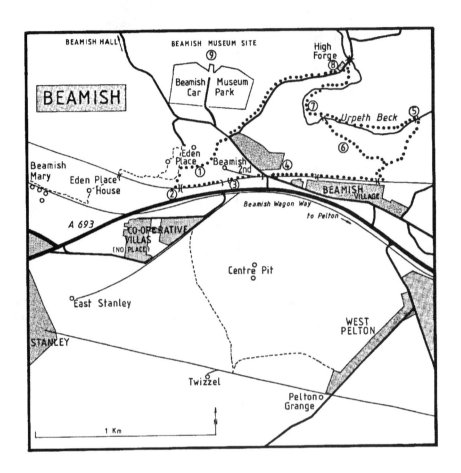

EDEN PLACE. The area you are standing on used to be a separate, thriving community of some 70 houses with a sports field and other amenities, it was built to serve the mine at **POINT 1**. This mine was known as Chophill or Beamish 2nd Pit. If you look to the South you will see the area known as No Place or Co-Operative Villas. This is a similar area, although larger than Eden Place and was built at about the same time to serve the Beamish Mary or 1st Pit.

At **POINT** 2. You join the Sustrans cycle path which links Consett in the west with eventually Sunderland in the East. This used to be a railway line built to link the Consett Iron and Steel works with the coast and the main rail system at Chester-le-Street.

As you walk down the line you are moving towards the East. At **POINT** 3. you pass under the bridge that was built to allow the coal wagons from 2nd Pit to cross the line and join the mineral line incline, the A 693 main road now covers this part of its route. There is very little evidence of this mineral line left to view.

Station Road Beamish

At **POINT 4** you are passing through the site of Beamish Station. This small station provided passenger services both up and down the line and had a small goods yard siding.

Carry on along the Cycle Track to the second bridge down the line from the Station site and join the footpath taking you down into the valley of Beamish Burn (River Team). Cross the burn by the footbridge, **POINT 5**, at the side of an old building to join the Bridle Path. This building used to be a Paper Mill using the power of the burn and coal from the local exposed coal measures (see point 6) to produce the paper.

As you move along the bridle path, westward, you will enter an area of woodland. On the right hand side of the path immediately on entering the wooded area you will see the remains of the entrance to Papermill Drift. This drift mine, opened in 1895, used to have all of its production of coal taken along the path you are now following. Some of it was used to power the steam pump at point 7 whilst the remainder was taken back underground via a vertical shaft at point 7 and carried underground to be lifted via a vertical shaft at the 2nd pit, Eden Place.

The Valley side to the South of you has exposed coal measures that can be viewed with care at **POINT 6**. This footpath is more easily found from the lower end, a footbridge, and then walking uphill. These measures were last worked, unofficially, during the mining strike of the 1980's. These easily worked, exposed measures were part of the reason that the valley in this area was so heavily ''Industrialised'' before the industrial revolution. There was so much small industry along this valley that plans were made in the 18th century to construct a canal to link the valley with the river Tyne but nothing ever came of these plans. If you look at the stream you will see a number of pieces of evidence of old mill races and other means of taking power from the stream.

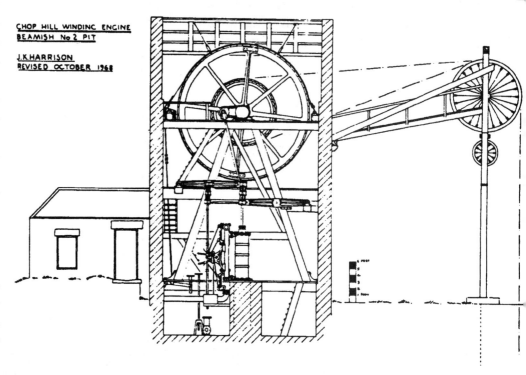

CHOP HILL WINDING ENGINE
BEAMISH No 2 PIT

J.K.HARRISON
REVISED OCTOBER 1968

POINT 7. In the undergrowth here you can discover the remains of the old Pump House and its associated buildings. There was a pump on this site first recorded in 1838 through to 1926. These pumps were used to take water from the surrounding underground workings.

The first was a Hydraulic pump using water taken by gravity from the higher seams to power the pumping of water from the lower seams. This was replaced by a steam powered pump which was certainly in position and working by 1857, as it is shown on the 1857 Ordnance Survey Map of the area. This area had a boiler house, pump house and a small cottage. The pump was manned and working 24 hours a day with 3 men each working an 8 hour shift. The first time the engine was allowed to come to a halt was in 1926 in the General

Unofficial Drift Mine - 1926 General Strike

Strike. It was then discovered that the water levels in the local mines did not rise, they were self draining, how many years had been wasted in pumping the water?

As you carry on along the bridle path you will cross the stream by a footbridge, note the constructed ford on your right hand side. From the footbridge to the road the surface of the path is made up of slag from the forges at High Forge, pick up a piece of the material and note how heavy it is in contrast to other stone.

At **POINT 8** - HIGH FORGE the houses to the East of the Stream once housed the workers from the forges to the west of the stream. Again this industrial site used power from the stream and coal from the local sources to work iron into finished products. The Forge site is at present being excavated and reconstructed by Beamish Museum to eventually be a working exhibit.

Carefully make your way back to the Eden Place site. The wall to your right, North, marks a part of the boundary to the old Beamish Estate which is now occupied by Beamish Museum which has a very large collection of mining archives, artifacts and buildings in their display area.

POINT 9 The Museum. Visit the coal mine to add practical experience to the walk

CROXDALE

● This route will guide visitors to the area and is ably described as a personal memory of Mrs Andrew

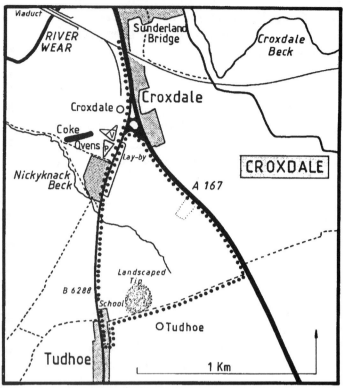

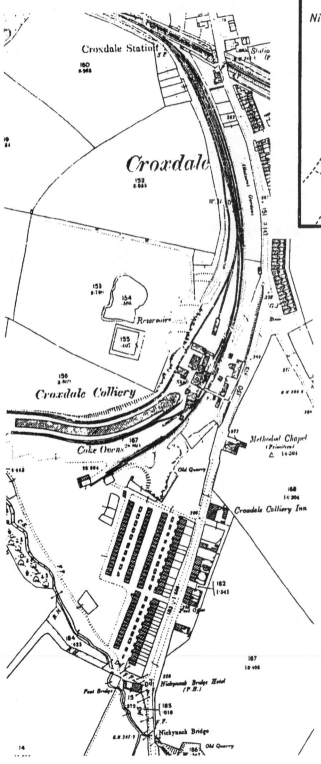

There is a small lay by on the B6288 60m from the roundabout.

The site of the Croxdale Colliery and associated works can be viewed from the pavement or from the field adjacent to the playing field. Using the 1:10,000 maps the location of the pit buildings, coke works and rail/wagon ways are easy to see. The pit heap is now a coniferous wood just over the hill. The rows of stone houses built for the pit workers line the A167 and occupy terraces by the playing field. The area shows how well the reclamation was done. Nothing remains of the extensive works indicated on the map.

For the rest of the walk, proceed in the direction of Tudhoe and when just past the school (Tudhoe Colliery Primary School) take the track leading behind the school, which goes through the area of reclaimed pit heap of the Tudhoe Colliery. This track leads to the A167 where the wide grass verge offers a safe return to the cemetery gates from where a paved path leads back to the roundabout.

Croxdale Colliery opened about 1873 and the tall red chimney had the figures "1875" in white bricks. It belonged to a company called the Weardale Iron, Steel and Coal Company. There were four seams of coal (which means four levels). Their Names were Brockwell, Victoria, Busty and Hutton. It employed at the beginning 400 men and boys many of them were only about 14 years old). They got 600 tons of coal out a day. What happened was that there were so many men employed that houses had to be built. These were fairly quickly done with stone from quarries, one along the Hett road and one straight opposite my bungalow. It's a straggling village with Johnson Terrace, Rogerson Terrace, Cross Street, and finally the colliery -indeed they were all colliery houses.

Lots of families came. My father was shaft man (later enginewright) and my uncle Tom an engineer. The pit was now the main source of employment. As a young girl I was fascinated by what went on and loved to go to the pit wall. Some wooden steps led down to the blacksmith's shop, the lamp cabin where the miners hung their lamps and the offices where the pit manager and officials worked. The pitmen collected their lamps across a gangway to the cage which took them down into the pit. They worked shifts 6 'til 2, 2 'til 10, and 10 'til 6. Looking after the cages and the shaft was part of my dad's work. the pulley wheels were at the top and when the wheels moved the cages moved up and down. If the cage got stuck my dad had to go down the steel rope to free the cage. We lived in Rogerson Terrace and on the days when my dad went down the rope we were worried for if he fell he could have been killed.

The pony's job was to pull the tubs of coal to the shaft bottom: poor little ponies, many of them never saw daylight. The miners took their bait with them- this was often a bottle of water and jam and bread. They did have a short break called 'bait' time. Leaving the stables the men walked and then as the seams got smaller this was called going 'in-by' and they often were bent double. On and on they went until sometimes they were lying flat, working wet and as low as two feet.

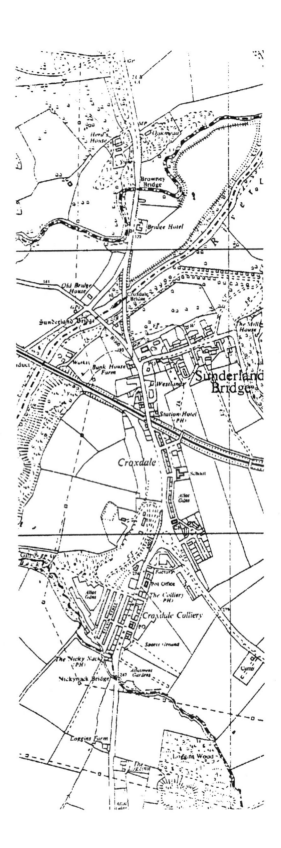

My dad had to wear special clothes which my mother, a clever dressmaker, made. The suit was made out of special creamy white material with a black stripe running through. They were called fustian. He had a special leather hat on, like a helmet but with a fairly long leather cape at the back. This was because water often dripped onto his back.

Miners had a dirty job, saw little sunshine and also had little money for working very hard. The manager, I would say, was not a very kind man. He never called a man by his christian name and expected every ounce of work they could give. When the man got to the bottom of the pit they dug and hewed the coal which had to be brought out of the pit- done by filling the coal into tubs which were then taken up in the cages. I know what I'm talking about for on quite a few occasions I went down the pit with my dad on Sundays. When you got out of the cage at the shaft bottom you walked underground. The men either carried their lamps or had them fitted onto their heads so that they could see. Not far from the pit bottom you passed the stables where the pit ponies lived in stalls. The ponies had names printed on their stalls and the man often gave them 'tit-bits' to eat.

My reason for going down the pit was that I thought pit men had a horrid job and I want to know what they had to put up with.

Back to the pit and what happened to the coal When it reached the top..... It was poured down a kind of chute - a bit like a slide with sides up - and put into trucks. The trucks, when full, were pulled along railway lines to be weighed at the weigh cabin - the weight and destination put on a ticket, pulled by a little engine called the "Yankie" and then on to the main line to go either north or south wherever it was needed.

The colliery, sunk in "1873 to 1875", continued until 1937 when the owners thought it wasn't making plenty money and then it was closed. In 1939 after a lot of dismantling the Royal Engineers came to blow the chimney down. It didn't go down at the first attempt and needed to be done twice. Some old families may have pictures of this, I know there is one in the Colliery Inn at Croxdale showing it falling down.

While the pit was working we also had coke ovens working - these looked like old fashioned bee-hives and some of the coal was made into coke. When we were small we liked to play round the coke oven and often at night tramps slept there for they were warm. However, the coke ovens finally went too. While the pit was working if you went for a walk through Croxdale Woods you passed by a huge pipe where water from the pit used to flow into Croxdale beck which finally joined the River Wear. We spent many happy hours jumping over the beck and playing in the woods. These were happy days for children for there was one part of the River Wear where we used to go for picnics. Lots of children both boys and girls learned to swim there (my own husband and son).There were always grown up people about so children were not in any danger. This was a popular place and people came from both sides of the river.

I've spent a long time talking about the pit but other things were going on in Croxdale. The Ten houses, as we call them, were built from the quarry down Hett Lane. The quarry was owned by Mr. Foster but an old man called Mr. Metcalfe cut the stones (the real name of Ten houses is Foster's Terrace). Do you know what I remember about this quarry? - weasles running in and out of the stones! I went once along a pathway at the bottom of the quarry to see if we

could find St. Herbert's well. There was certainly a heap of stones there with a red mark. Croxdale Colliery was made up of Front Street, Salvin Streets (2) and Wood View. In the front street was the Colliery Inn, Siddles the butcher, the Workmans Club, a fish and chip shop, the Post Office, a private house run by Mrs. Cowans and a shop which had various owners, Barnetts, Browns and Billinghams. When Miss Cowan gave up the Post Office it was added on to the shop and is like that now. Finally at the end a public house called Nicky-Nack.

FERRYHILL AREA

● This unit contains descriptions of Ferryhill, the Dean and Chapter Colliery and a walk around Ferryhill, by D Wallace

When the Dean and Chapter Colliery was opened in 1904, coal mining was not a new industry to the area. Written evidence exists of a history of exploitation of the coal reserves dating back to the 14th century, when a coal mine was mentioned at the Induction of a Vicar of Merrington, a local village. In 1347 records show that Robert Todd and Hugh Smyth, both of Ferryhill, paid 36/- to the Abbey at Durham for local mining rights. In 1357 coal mines were leased for a period of 30 years to the Prior of Durham.

These early pits were known as "bell pits". They were simply holes hewn through the surface rock and into the coal seam. Using ladders to gain access, the miners worked the exposed coal face, leaving large, round shafts in the ground. As industrial demand for coal grew and technological advances created a more efficient mining industry, a much more extensive exploitation of Durham's great natural resource began. In 1902 the first shafts at Dean and Chapter Colliery, Ferryhill, were sunk the mine going into production two years later. The mine was to have a remarkable impact on the township, both physically and economically. In fact, the effects of the industry have out-lived the mine, which was to close in 1966.

The colliery lies on the eastern edge of the exposed part of the Durham Coalfield, the rich seams out-cropping at the surface. The 19th century village lies to the south-east, several hundred yards from the site of the old mine buildings. The existing population could not provide a sufficiently large work-force, and an influx of workers and their families from all four Home Counties caused a sudden housing and education problem. A new housing development, named Dean Bank and consisting of

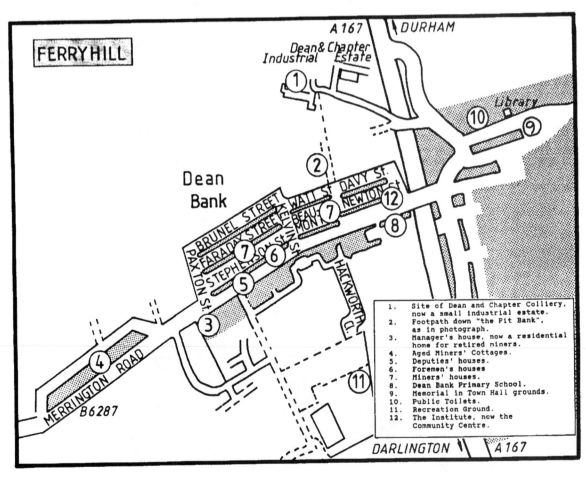

1. Site of Dean and Chapter Colliery, now a small industrial estate.
2. Footpath down "the Pit Bank", as in photograph.
3. Manager's house, now a residential home for retired miners.
4. Aged Miners' Cottages.
5. Deputies' houses.
6. Foremen's houses
7. Miners' houses.
8. Dean Bank Primary School.
9. Memorial in Town Hall grounds.
10. Public Toilets.
11. Recreation Ground.
12. The Institute, now the Community Centre.

solidly built and much acclaimed terraced housing, was begun in 1902. By 1907 it was complete. The design of the estate was extremely formal, and allocation of the houses conformed to a strict hierarchy. Those streets which were to house the ordinary miners, all named after great industrial inventors, were made up of small houses, each of which had a "knock-up slate" outside. This was a piece of slate on the wall beside the front door where the miner would write the time of his next shift so that he could be woken. Several of these slates are still in position. A single street of larger houses with a small front garden as well as a backyard was allocated to the shift foremen, and a row of six houses, much larger and each with a sizeable back garden and small front garden, housed the deputies. Set fittingly aside from the compact workers' development was the huge house used by the manager. This house, set in extensive grounds, is now a retirement home for ex-miners.

Also completed in 1907 was Dean Bank Council School, built to replace the suddenly inadequate school provision, and designed to educate 1,400 children at any one time. Road communications were improved to cope with the demands of the new industry. Another physical legacy from the miners is the town's

recreation ground - a large green area with good recreational facilities, originally financed by the mine workers to provide a recreation area for their families. There remains a small complex of bungalows built in 1931 to accommodate retired miners, still known as "the aged miners' homes".

Outside the Town Hall there stands a memorial, erected in 1906 by fellow mine workers, to a local hero, Mr. William Walton. An inscription on the stone memorial tells of Mr. Walton's bravery in sacrificing his own life to save those of two boys in Dean and Chapter Mine.

The centre of the miners' social organisation was the Miners' Institute, a two storey building which housed their library and offices where dues were to be paid, as well as rooms for social and professional meetings. The building is still in daily use as Ferryhill's Community Centre.

Very little remains of the old mine buildings, the pit-head gear having been dismantled soon after closure. A small industrial estate has now been built on the site, but the old footpath down the 'pit-bank' from Dean Bank to the Colliery is still used.

The huge spoil-heap, dangerously close to the main road, has now been levelled somewhat,

re-shaped and planted with grass and trees. It blends perfectly with the hilly landscape to provide pasture for sheep and a wooded back-drop to a nature reserve, itself located on the site of the old railway to East Howle, scene of another, now closed, colliery.

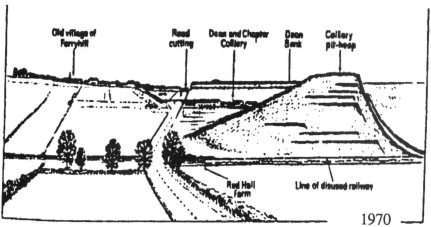

Ferryhill Village & the Dean and Chapter Colliery

By the time of the pit closure in 1966, when almost 600 men were employed there, the new community was firmly established. Although the town itself boasted only a little light industry, the neighbouring town of Spennymoor had a thriving industrial estate which absorbed many of the redundant mine-workers of Ferryhill. Thus the town survived the

closure of the pit. It continues to expand, and, although few of its workers are employed in Durham's remaining coal mines, its mining history still influences its way of life.

Other local villages were not always as lucky. For many, pit closure meant the decline of the community as a whole. Local mines, all now closed, are;

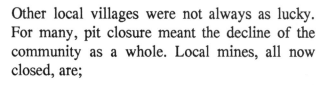

Mainsforth.................... 1904 - 1968

Metal Bridge.................. 1954 - 1978

East Howle.................... 1873 - 1905

Bishop Middleham.............. 1846 - 1876

Tursdale...................... 1859 - 1909

Windlestone................... 1877 - 1903

Diagrams taken from "North East England", by J. E. Waltham and W. D. Holmes, published by Cambridge University Press.

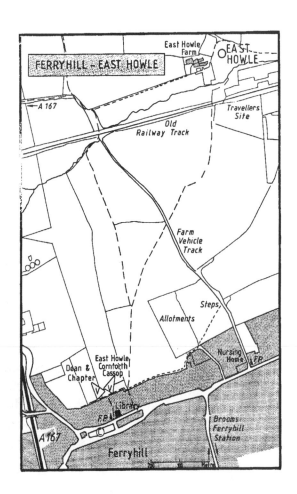

● This walk combines the efforts of Frank Burns, David Noble and the original Geography Curriculum Group 1972.

EAST HOWLE WALK

East Howle 1971 (looking East)

Walk to East Howle from Ferryhill (1.5 miles)

There is a large car park in Ferryhill town centre.

Take the footpath alongside the public library, through a gate and turn right along a path which goes behind gardens. The Dean and Chapter site can be seen to the left while East Howle Farm is to the right. Proceed to the fence with gate and you then have an alternative route.

1. Across the field by the footpath in a general NE direction or:

2. Keep going along the footpath at the rear of the gardens, past the allotments to where the path branches off left across a field to a set of brick steps leading down to a sunken lane.

If you take route 1. you cross the lane and follow the path to East Howle. If route 2. pick up route 1. downhill of the brick steps (300 metres). After crossing the former railway the footpath reaches the site of East Howle which can be studied by referring to the four plans. East Howle Farm is the one constant feature. The pit heaps lie North and East of the farm. East Howle was placed in category D in the 1951 county plan and the inadequate housing demolished in the 1960's and 70's. Return past the farm to rejoin the track to Ferryhill.

There are very extensive views from point A. The Dean and Chapter site, the line of the old railway, the Magnesian Limestone escarpment at Coxhoe and West Cornforth village where the Carlton Ironworks and Thrisleton Colliery were located. The footpaths are well defined but muddy in wet conditions.

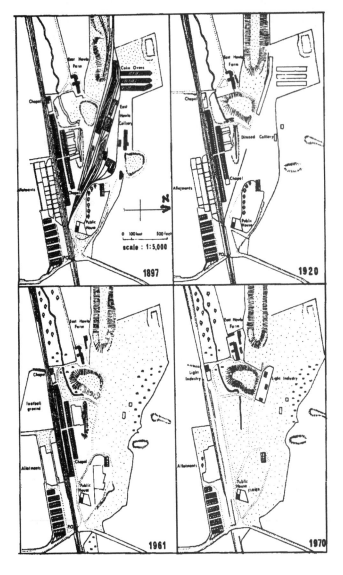

SACRISTON

Although Sacriston is not mentioned in the Boldon Book, the country manor of the Sacrists of Durham was a *Sacriston Heugh (Segrysteyn-hoe 1312:* Old French *Segrestein, Secrestein* from Latin *Sacristanus.* Old English hoh = a spur of land. The Sacriston's spur of land). There were two pits in Sacriston, Sacriston Colliery and Charlaw Colliery plus the Shield Row Drift. "Coal is known to have been worked in this village as far back as the eighteenth century. One of the managing directors, Colonel W C Blackett, owns a notice dated 1765 warning persons stealing coal that they were liable to be prosecuted.

Sinking of the Sacriston and Charlaw collieries began in 1833 and both were in production by 1839. There were two shafts at Charlaw one a furnace shaft to aid ventilation. The original workings were by bord and pillar. Charlaw pit was abandoned in 1884. Sacriston was worked firstly by Messrs Edward Richardson then by W H Bell and Co.

The seams worked at Sacriston were:-

Shield Row (High Main elsewhere) 1924-1941

Five Quarter (abandoned in 1884)

Main often named the Yard Seam (abandoned in 1881)

Low Main (2-3ft thick at 50fa. abandoned 1966)

Brass Thill (abandoned in 1965)

Hutton (2ft 6ins at 60fa. abandoned 1953)

Busty (4-5ft thick at 100fa. abandoned 1958)

1985 Pit Closed.

The Charlaw Colliery commenced working about the same time under Messrs. Richardson & Co. Coal from both pits was shipped at Sunderland and South Shields and was known in the market as "Acorn Close Wallsend". The agent's house is known, at Sacriston, as "Acorn Close" (Demolished 1942 approx.)

The output of Charlaw Colliery was estimated at about 500 tons per day when 300 men were

● Val McCourt from Sacriston Junior School was helped by Miss Bailey, P Bedingfield, Miss J Gill, Dr Standen, P Heron and D Hopper of NUM.

employed. The output at Sacriston Colliery was estimated at 1000 tons per day when the Colliery was in full working order, when 600 men were employed. The coke ovens were erected shortly afterwards in 1845. The coal was then shipped at Tyne Dock and was known as the West Leverson Wallsend.

1921 Census - population 8423 mainly colliery workmen.

The Colliery has its own farms, about 1100 acres in area, which supply food for the little pit ponies employed down the mines. The gas lime produced at the colliery is used on these farms as fertiliser. The chief crops are wheat, barley and oats.

The modern village of Sacriston grew up round the Colliery. About 1861, men were sent from Staffordshire to work at the Colliery. When they came, two long rows of houses were built for them and their families and called the Staffordshire Streets (demolished 1947). Various other streets have names to do with the Colliery.

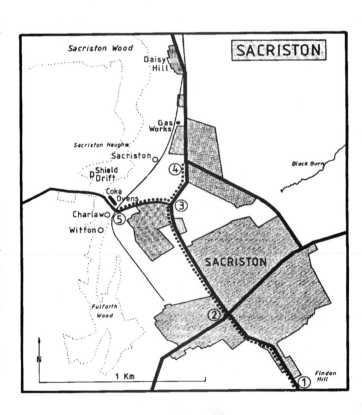

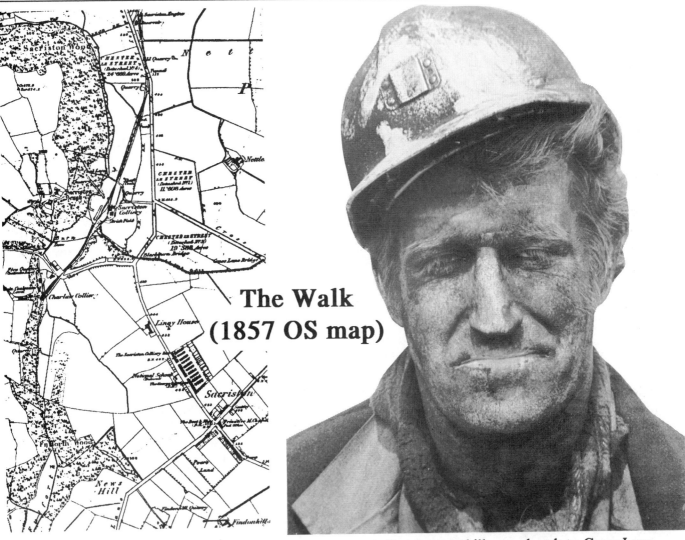

The Walk
(1857 OS map)

1. Brow of Findon Hill

Looking back towards Durham, Cathedral visible. Looking forwards, village displayed on hillside

Reservoir (hidden underground) LHS looking towards village

What changes can you see?

Look for commercial /industrial evidence

2. Walk down hill on RHS until you come to crossroads. Fyndoune Comprehensive School halfway down hill LHS.

At crossroads, winding wheel from pit displayed. Again note changes from map.

3. Cross over road (very busy) Look at shop types Look for evidence of industry

Continue to church of St Peter, Sacriston

(Phone Father Paul Murray, tel: 091-3711853 who will open church if required.

4. Continue up hill past church to Cross Lane

Sacriston Pit was on your left

What evidence can you see of its existence?

5. Return down hill past the double bend.

Cross over and go down Acorn Close Lane

The last remnants of Charlaw Colliery are visible here

6. Turn left opposite the site

It is possible from here to go up into wooded area but the public right of way ends in a dead end. If you go partway up the hillside, however, you can look down on the site.

There is space for the coach to wait off the road here.

Sacriston was the last deep mine to close in West Durham. Its band is still in existence.

Below ground, coal cutting machinery was used in the Hutton seam from 1904 and the Blackett conveyor system was pioneered at Sacriston. This was a coal moving system invented by Colonel Blackett, a mining engineer and was originally powered by a water powered engine. Longwall conveyor working began in 1936. In the Hutton seam, the pits at Nettlesworth and Sacriston worked in conjunction. This was in the 19th Century and would have simplified the ventilation system. Nettlesworth closed in 1894.

Sacriston was unusual in that they had a separate shaft for pumping water in addition to the two main shafts.

In the 1930's a system of work was employed where stone waste was drawn between 6pm and 3am. Stone was tipped and the tubs returned ready for production of coal and the drawing of coal from 3am to 6pm. Huge stone tips were produced both by mechanical production and through working of poorer quality seams.

On the surface the colliery had stables, a granary and a stackyard for pony food. There was a foundry near the site of Charlaw pit and in 1891 the new coke ovens were lit. There were three batteries of beehive ovens.

Coal was moved from the pit by rail. The wagons were hauled up the incline at Daisy Hill by a stationary steam engine and once they reached the summit ran under gravity to the sidings at Waldridge and Stella. Coal was moved from here to Tyne Dock, Monkwearmouth Dock and Hartlepool.

Coal from the Brass Thill and Hutton seams was sold locally for household use.

There is a major fault just North of the shafts NE to SW in direction which has a throw of 60 feet (20 metres). A second fault with a throw of 20 to 120 feet (6 to 40 metres) lies on the pit's western boundary.

Sacriston was the last pit in the area to use hand working methods. The high quality of the coking coal of the Victoria seam ensured that its extraction continued with men using pneumatic picks and hand filling. The Brockwell seam also had hand filling but had undercutting machinery installed. The coal had to be blasted down with explosives. In 1950 302 men produced 400 tons of coal per shift.

SEAHAM

● D Miller has contributed this material which will be of use to Seaham visitors who are not using the Seaham Harbour Coastal Centre.

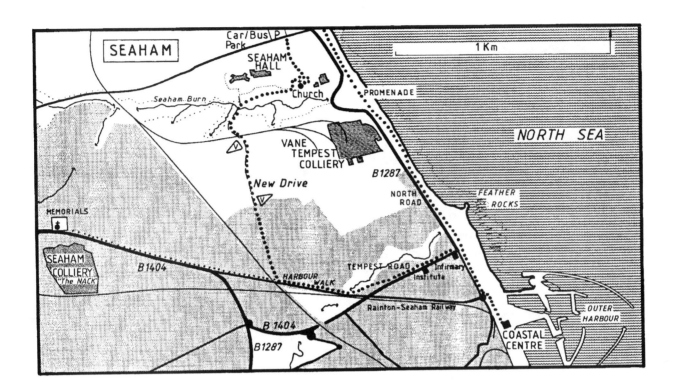

Park at Seaham Hall Car Park (northern edge of map).

Cross road at buildings (take care, especially watching vehicles from left).

Cross green to Church and Churchyard.

From Churchyard, return to green but follow track to left, passing in front of Seaham Hall.

Go down slope, cross bridge and rise to junction of tracks, then bear left.

Cross disused rail track. The first view point is at the entrance to the paying fields. From here can be seen Seaham Colliery and Christ Church. (those wishing to visit the memorials in Christ Church yard are recommended to use their transport).

Follow track passing cricket ground. Vane Tempest Colliery can be viewed by looking back.

Shortly after the beginning of the houses, Seaham Station is reached. Continue forward. crossing the triangular 'island'.

Harbour Walk offers no view of the harbour. Pass the Catholic Church, bear left into Tempest Road (traffic!)

Just after the garage The Literary Institute is opposite.

Continue to the cross roads. The terrace of houses on your left used to be known as Sebastopol Terrace. The grassed area opposite is the site of the Infirmary.

Time permitting, cross Tempest Road and then North Terrace to the grassy area on the cliff tops. (Bath Terrace is on your left).

Otherwise turn left into North Road. Cross at a safe place, to the broad pathway.

At the point where this narrows take the steep path to the promenade which you follow to its end.

Continue along the beach to the steps through the valley.

These steps bring you to the car park.

THE COASTAL WALKWAY

The coastline of East Durham extends eleven miles between Ryhope in the north to Crimdon in the south. The coastline is characterised by a number of wooded denes which extend several miles inland and extensive areas of crumbling sea cliffs. Although some beaches have been spoilt by the dumping of coal waste, fine golden sand beaches still exist, at Seaham in the north of the area and Crimdon in the south of the district. Public access to large sections of the coastline and a number of denes has been restricted for many years by the absence of footpaths and presence of port installations, industries and coal stocking on or adjacent to the cliff tops. Where footpaths do exist, however, there are fine views of coastal scenery, particularly at Blackhall Rocks where the path runs along high cliffs.

The problem of access to the coastline has been recognised over the past twenty years. Plans have been put forward to provide footpath access along the coast and into the denes, by maintaining and signposting the existing network and by creating new paths to establish a complete coastal footpath.

Durham County Council and Easington District Council have undertaken a joint programme of improving stretches of public rights-of-way adjacent to the coast or constructing new stretches of the Coastal Footpath, where none exists, using labour provided by the Manpower Services Commission. this has provided a network of interesting walks along stretches of the coast.

Dawdon Colliery Welfare Ground (4) is a good place to start walking along the next stretch of the Coastal Footpath. It is located at the focus of a number of footpaths and also provides parking space for cars. The first half mile of the walk is drab and uninspiring. The path heads in an easterly direction under the main coastal railway line and along an unmade track for 250 yards and then turns south for 500 yards as it passes a coal stocking area on the left and the storage area of Dawdon Colliery on the right (5). The Colliery has been in existence since the

● Extracted with kind permission from *East Durham Heritage Trails and Walkways* published by East Durham Community Arts and Easington District Council

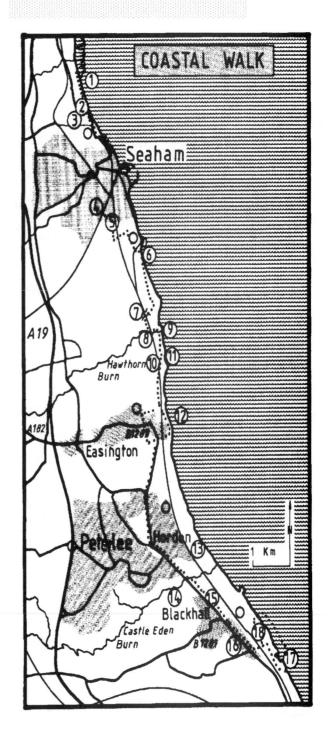

beginning of the Twentieth Century and now employs nearly 2,000 people and is one of the main sources of employment in Seaham. The path then passes through a low tunnel and under a bridge crossed by a mineral railway line leading into the Colliery. (Dawdon Colliery closed in 1991)

At this point, walkers get their first view of Noses Point on the Blast Beach (6). For over 80 years mine waste and slurry from collieries in the area have been dumped over the cliff at Noses Point and into the sea. This has resulted in the sea being pushed back over 200 metres and has created the Blast Beach, which is a man made "raised beach". Hopefully this scar on the landscape will be removed in the next few years when the tipping at Noses Point is transferred several hundred yards to the north at Bankside, enabling a reclamation scheme to be undertaken.

The footpath then diverges into two paths. The left fork - evocatively named "Nanny Goat's Path" - leads down to the Blast Beach but has suffered from erosion and has had to be closed. The Coastal Footpath ascends a flight of steps and then runs alongside the former mineral railway line and then the British Rail line, for

approximately one mile until it meets a bridge (7). At first the scenery is of an industrial nature, with coal stocking areas on the right hand side and views of the Blast Beach on the left. Gradually, it becomes more rural as Dawdon Colliery is left behind. The areas of the clifftops, which have not be cultivated for agricultural purposes, have been colonised by orchids and several other local plants such as moonwort and zigzag clover.

The footpath then crosses over the main coast railway line by a bridge and for the next one and a half miles to the Easington Conveyor is of a high quality dolomite construction. Immediately to the right is an informal car park used by walkers and fishermen, and Hawthorn Quarry which is still used for the extraction of magnesian limestone (8). The quarry is also unique in ecological terms in that it contains a variety of agal structures and yields a variety of fauna unknown at other outcrops. The footpath then crosses Hawthorn Dene (9) which is a local Nature Reserve and one of the most extensive and least disturbed areas of semi-natural woodland in East Durham. On the north side of the Dene the footpath passes through an area of magnesian limestone grassland and includes a variety of plants such as dyers greenweed, lesser

meadow rue and fragrant orchid. The path crosses the floor of the Dene using a bridge. Immediately to the east is the Hawthorn Railway Viaduct which towers some 30 ft. above the floor of the Dene. In recognition of its visual qualities it has been designated a Grade 2 listed building. On the south side of the Dene, the path ascends through an ash/elm woodland with yew occurring on steeper slopes to the west. The woodland ground flora is rich and dominated by plants such as ramsoms, dogs mercury, and sanicle. The path leaves the Dene and in a quarter of a mile passes two notable features. On the right is Beacon Hill (10) which is an outcrop of magnesian limestone towering some 100 ft. above sea level. Access to the hill can be gained by steps which cross the railway line and a footpath. The steps are, at the time of writing however, in a state of disrepair and extreme caution should be exercised when using them. On the left is Shippersea Bay (11) which is the location of the famous Easington Raised Beach, composed of a sequence of sand and gravels containing temperate marine shells resting on a rock platform 27 metres above the present sea level. The remainder of the walk to the Easington Conveyor is pleasant if not awe-inspiring. There are, however, good views of the Cleveland Hills to the south, whilst Easington Colliery looms large to the right. The

next feature on the walk is the British Coal Conveyor (12) which transports half a million tons of colliery waste from Easington Colliery into the sea, and is partly responsible for despoiling the six miles of coastline between Seaham and Horden.

The footpath passes underneath the Conveyor and in a quarter of a mile goes under the coastal railway line via a bridge. It then passes between the colliery yard and the Eastside allotments, under a further railway bridge and into the settlement of Easington Colliery.

No footpath exists adjacent to the two mile stretch of coastline between Easington Colliery and Castle Eden Dene Mouth. This is because a significant part of the land adjacent to the cliffs in this area has been used by British Coal as pit heaps or for coal stocking. Following the closure of Horden Colliery in February 1986, however, the County Council has purchased the area and is currently undertaking a reclamation scheme costing over £800,000. This will restore the area to agricultural land/woodland and also install a coastal footpath. A one mile walk south along the coast road brings you to the Colliery village of Horden (13)

During the inter-war years the village expanded westwards and southwards, new housing estates were developed and its population grew to a

peak of over 15,000 in 1951. In the post-war years, the village has undergone a transition and has lost population to its new neighbour Peterlee, which has expanded to the extent that the two settlements now form one built-up area. During this period most of the original housing was demolished and displaced inhabitants were rehoused in Peterlee leaving large areas of land vacant within the centre of the village, which have been reclaimed and remain as landscaped open spaces. The population has continued to decline to a current level of 8,500.

Following Nationalisation, the National Coal Board invested substantial sums of money in the modernisation of the colliery, which in its heyday employed in excess of 6,000 people.

"When I started there, there were 6,000 men employed at Horden Colliery. There was one manager, two undermanagers, then there was about five officials to each seam. Now there's two managers, there's not 2,000 men here now,

there's two managers, eleven undermanagers and officials. There's one boss for every two men now. Of course, now the pit has completely closed down."

With the prospect of considerable coal reserves being available under the North Sea its long term future seemed to be assured. In the mid 1980's, however, the Board discovered that off-shore reserves were not as good as first thought. This coupled with problems of faulting and flooding resulted in the decision to close the pit. The closure proposals were fought by the Unions and the County and District Councils who prepared a case which demonstrated that the social costs of closing the colliery (calculated in terms of redundancy payments, lost rates to the local authorities, low taxation to the exchequer and unemployment payments) exceeded the cost of keeping the pit open. The case was presented to an independent colliery review procedure, but rejected and the colliery duly closed in February 1987.

With the closure of the colliery the bond between the pit and the village has been broken. The source of employment, and prosperity has disappeared and the village has now become a dormitory settlement where residents have to seek employment in other places, such as Peterlee and miners have to commute to other collieries in the area. The local authorities have been left with the awesome task of removing the dereliction of the former colliery site and to their credit are succeeding. The County Council has transformed the former pit heaps on the east side of the railway line into agricultural land, woodland and open space. The District Council has developed the colliery site into an industrial estate and reclaimed the remainder to agricultural land, woodland and sports pitches. Only time will tell whether these initiatives will prove to be a 'phoenix' rising from the ashes of the former colliery.

After Horden, continue south along the road towards Blackhall Colliery. The road descends a steep bank. This is the valley of Castle Eden Dene a national nature reserve (14). Note the nine span brick railway bridge which before the road was built was the 'unofficial' and dangerous way of arriving at Blackhall (15).

"There were no roads into the village, one half was made from Hesleden and to get to Hartlepool you had to walk two miles to Hesleden Station. The fare to Hartlepool was 10d return, or go to Horden Station along the black path and under the viaduct, down 196 steps this side, 198 steps up Horden Way."

COASTAL FOOTPATH - BLACKHALL ROCKS NATURE RESERVE

Durham County Conservation Trust have described the sea cliff area around Blackhall and Blackhall Rocks as providing "interest for geologists, bird watchers and botanists, as well as fine seascapes for those who enjoy a coastal walk".

The coastal journey brings us to Blackhall, a typical colliery village. Although an Anglo-Saxon burial mound was discovered in 1916, on October 31, near the coastguard station, the village is essentially a product of the final phase of development of the Durham Coalfield as it reached out under the North Sea. The first coal was drawn in 1913 and electric winding gear could raise 18,000 tons a week although an early resident can remember that the method used to sink the shaft was the traditional one of the manual labour aided by steam winding gear.

"I can still remember seeing the sinkers working just a few yards down. Then later, I saw the wooden head gear erected for the North Pit. Steam was provided by six Lancashire boilers and a brick chimney stood 180 feet high.

Later, when electricity was installed, I saw the chimney pulled down in 1916 during the war".

"If a sinker was off work, they used to have what was called a "sinkers gathering". Every pit day a cap was put on a table and every sinker contributed a little to make sure the family had something going in, as there was no social security or dole money in those days, and sick pay was very small. Also the men were paid fortnightly and often there was no money left at the end of the fortnight."

It is hard to realise that this was not under hard-faced Victorian task masters but in the second decade of the Twentieth Century!

The earliest mineworkers fared a little better of course and solid brick streets were built; the names, however, were no more imaginative than First, Second, Third and so on. Officials lived elsewhere: in East Street, built by the private contractors, Peart and Proud.

"There wasn't a newspaper agent in the village. I had to meet the half past eight train at Horden, walk along the line and bring the papers back, and a cousin of mine that was stopping with us, she used to deliver them for me and then they built a shop, Curtis and Watt somebody called Barker had it, and one morning Harold Barker and I, we were going along the line and along the black path and we heard these bangs and it was foggy and misty, so we got on the line and ran to Horden Station and everyone was up on Horden Bridge and all we could see was the flashes of the German Warships firing onto Hartlepool, and I think we were the first ones to bring the news back what it was".

In addition to the poor communication pattern other amenities were limited to a few galvanised metal erections that comprised the school and the first church and church hall:

"The first tin school was built in 1911. I was at the opening and we were in one class at first until the population grew bigger; then we were put into classes, the first headmaster was Mr Ralph Goundry, the first colliery manager Mr Thornton, the first postmistress Miss Emily Hutson. It was hard work at school, Mr Goundry was a severe teacher, he knocked learning into you".

A new church eventually was purchased second hand for £300 from Stockton, and brought brick by brick to it's present site by a firm of Durham builders called Gradon and Son who charged £6000, a bargain even for the year 1930. The original tin shack of 1911 still stands (1987) as the R.A.F.A. Club. In the meantime, in 1923, roads had been built to link the community to the rest of the area. But little else that is new has been built and the pit head gear has now gone. Clearly then it is not the fabric of Blackhall that lays any claim for the attention of posterity but the community of people who looked to the pit for their livelihood. It is worth listening to the memories of one of these pitmen, Albert Allen, looking back on fifty years as a miner.

BLACKHALL COASTAL WALKWAY

Continue south along the coast road to Blackhall Rocks. At the Station Road/Mickle Hill Road crossroads (16) turn left, past Peroni's shop and pass under the railway viaduct. A further 200 metres brings you to the car park constructed by the County Council. Picnic tables are available.

This short walkway gives fine views of the East Durham coastline, north and south and will be of interest to geologists, bird watchers and botanists. The geologist interested in the magnesian limestone sea cliffs would also be interested to note that the present coastline coincidentally follows the line of an ancient coral barrier reef. The botanist will find examples of

arctic alpine plant life as well as numerous sea birds that inhabit this narrow strip of rough pasture.

The walk depends on the tide. If it is out a fine circular route is available by using the beach below the cliffs. Extreme caution must be exercised, firstly descending to the beach but also with the tide which has caught many unfortunate people in the past.

Walk to Fisherman's Point on the cliff edge, where the caves are directly below you, but please DO NOT VENTURE DOWN THE SLIPPERY TRACKS; they do not lead to the beach, and you will cause serious erosion. Turn southwards and survey the line of cliffs, pale yellow where freshly broken, and sloping above in the clay layer. Continue south, to descending steps called "Green Stairs" (17) which are in poor repair and not on Reserve land, to reach the beach.

Search the rock pools and you will find two brown seaweeds, bladder and toothed wrack, with limpets, whelks, shrimps and crabs sheltering amongst their fronds. Also present are sea anemones looking like pink flowers. Barnacles cover the exposed rocks, while mussels are also revealed at very low tide. Occasionally seals visit the beach, and whales and porpoises have been stranded here. If you visit after a storm look out for the green and red seaweed, and starfish from deeper water that are cast up by the waves.

If the tide is really low turn northwards and return via the caves and "Deadman's Steps" (18). The sea forms the caves by under-cutting the cliffs, thundering waves smashing into the cave mouths at high tide. Legends of smugglers are associated with one artificial cave which is said to have a connection with the Priest's hide at Hardwick Hall.

Once you have passed a point where you have a clear view northward you are safe from the rising tide, and can either enjoy the plants along the cliff edge or look for wading birds, such as oystercatchers, turnstones, redshanks and dunlin along the tideline.

The steps for the return journey are on the left past the single stack on the beach. (19)

HASWELL WALKWAY

● Extracted with kind permission from *East Durham Heritage Trails and Walkways* published by East Durham Community Arts and Easington District Council by Janet Hesletine, teacher at Haswell Primary School and pupils.

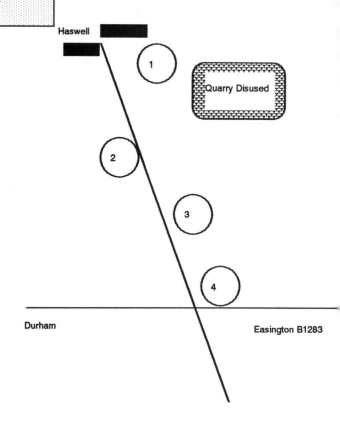

The Haswell to Hart Countryside Walkway runs for a distance of about nine miles from the village of Haswell, in the centre-west of the District, to Hart Station just outside Easington's boundary in County Cleveland. En route, the former railway line passes through the villages of Haswell, Shotton Colliery, Wellfield, Castle Eden and Hesleden. The path, which has an interesting history, is representative of the diverse range of urban, industrial and rural landscapes which comprise the heritage of the District.

George Stephenson the famous engineer who built 'The Rocket', designed the new railway, and its proposed branch lines from Thornley Crossings to Ludworth, Thornley and Cassop. On its opening day on 23rd November 1835, the track had only been completed as far north as Haswell and just one branch line, to Thornley had been provided. The line suffered a final death knell after Thornley Colliery closed in 1970. However, coal traffic on the line continued until 1980, when the final closure notice was approved, after 145 years use.

When walking the route, one can imagine the laboured pounding of heavy steam engines and the chatter of wagons which echoed along the line for over a hundred years. One can also sense what it must have been like to hear powerful diesel locomotives roar through the deep cuttings, before this important railway closed, having played a strategic role in the development of north-east England.

HASWELL TO SHOTTON

Access to the northern end of the walkway can be gained from Haswell Village by a short walk along either Chapel Lane or Hall Lane. The start of the walkway is marked by a stile and a number of signboards which regrettably have been vandalised (1). For the first 300 yards the walkway passes along an embankment and there are fine views of Mawsons Hill (2), rising some 530 feet above sea level to the east and the magnesian limestone plateau to the west. The walkway then passes into a cutting and where it meets the former branch line to Tuthill Quarry a small picnic area has been developed (3). The path then skirts a flooded area - created when the former railway tracks were lifted. This area has been colonised by wild life and contains a number of crested newts. The walkway remains in a cutting for a further mile. In that time it passes under Tuthill Bridge carrying the main Easington to Durham Road (4). On the edge of Shotton Colliery a footpath has been developed from the platform of the former station to a visitors' centre, housed in a caravan in the adjacent car park .

HASWELL

Haswell is one of the largest of the old townships of Easington parish; in the west the magnesian limestone rises to over 500 feet above sea level offering commanding views across County Durham towards the Pennines. Although it contains the long ribbon of settlement that makes up Haswell Village and the Haswell Plough and formerly used to include the mining settlement of South Hetton, when you stand on the windswept field at High Haswell you can imagine that you are in a remote corner of pre-industrial England. Indeed, here on its rounded hilltops there are remnants of settlements that predate even the famed Saxon churches at the mouths of the Tyne and the Wear.

At Pig Hill, over towards Easington Lane from High Haswell, the names conjure up images of a vanished landscape: Cherry Garth, High Fallowfield, Cockfield - with all those associated colours, pink and brown, and the gold of the ripening haycock - names that speak of a farming tradition, not of drab coalmines. On Pig Hill the long shadows of autumn reveal the remains of a medieval farmstead; and this stands on the earthworks of an earlier pre-Roman settlement. On the zig-zag road to Haswell Plough, your imagination can visualise that same road as a lane following its course round the long strips of open field in the days before the local Lords planted all the hedgerows.

HASWELL COLLIERY—THE SCENE OF THE LATE AWFUL EXPLOSION.

"There were no made up streets in those days, just rough sandstone. The road from Haswell to Haswell Plough was just a cart track. You couldn't get to Ludworth unless you went up what we called Hare Hill, over the fields. There was a toll gate and you had to pay a toll".

The great stone tower, over to the right, is the remains of the engine house of Haswell colliery defunct since 1895.

The original village of Haswell (Hessewelle) was sited at High Haswell. Hessewelle, an old English name, means 'Hazel Well' or 'Spring'.

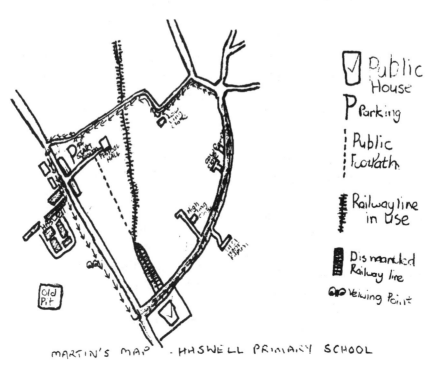

MARTIN'S MAP - HASWELL PRIMARY SCHOOL

V Public House
P Parking
⋮ Public Footath
⬛ Railway line in use
▮ Dismantled Railway line
👓 Veiwing Point

High Haswell gave its name to a local family and, in 1338, Talbot de Northallerton granted a rent charge out of the lands of Great Haswell to the Menville family who passed the estate on to a well known local family, the Claxtons. Many lords of the manor followed. The area was pleasantly rural until it was discovered that beneath the green fields lay a rich supply of coal, the lifeblood of the new, industrial age, Haswell Colliery, situated between the present day settlements of Haswell and Haswell Plough, was among the first to be sunk and had a comparatively short though eventful life. Sinking began in 1831 by the Haswell Coal Company and great technical difficulties were encountered and the project was abandoned. Further borings were tried in a field bought from the South Hetton Coal Company and these were successful.

The first shipment of coals took place on July 2nd 1835 and the first wagon to pass over the Durham and Sunderland Railway a year later took coals to Hendon on the river Wear. Eight years later came tragedy; 95 men were killed in a massive explosion. The inevitable inquest verdict "accidently and by misfortune killed by an explosion of fire damp ... no blame attributable to anyone" left the owners without moral or financial liability. Dependent wives and children were condemned to be hostages to fortune, relying upon the charity of their friends, neighbours and workmates. In the event the - for then - magnificent sum of £4,265 was raised as a relief fund.

The scale of the Haswell disaster of September

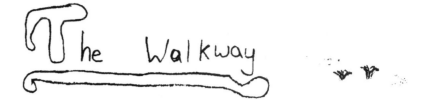

The Walkway

The walkway is a public footpath no horses or moter bikes are allowed in the walkway it goes from Haswell to Hart it used to be a railway line it opened in 1835 and closed in 1980. The walkway has a picnic area and two ponds with pond life in it The rail line is still vesed it takes coal to others places the people still work there and the get the coal from the quary which is not far from the railway line the quary has been there lots of years There is a road going stright up and if you go there you will end up at the farm. The farm was built by the monks there is a tunnel from the farm to the Cathedrel at Durham. There is a plant at the walkway called bacon and eggs

By Karen Lumley

1844 was immense. The disaster was far greater than the shareholders' funds could cope with. Five months of no coal production during a long miners' strike had seen to that and an appeal went out to the wider community. The richest of those appealed to, by far, was Lord Londonderry, and his overbearing paternalism was a byword in the County. His response seemed to lack compassion; he refused to donate. Some might say that Londonderry's lack of charity was only to be expected: he had just made it clear to the Seaham tradesmen that they should offer no credit to miners' families whatever the hardships they faced because of their striking menfolk. This disaster appeal was

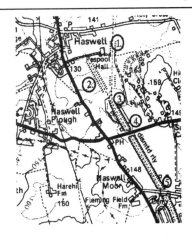

a different matter, however, his refusal was a matter of principle. Londonderry felt that the Haswell Coal Company should feel the same sense of obligation to its employees' families as any landed gentleman would for the least of his servants.

"A lad came out with his hands off. he had his hands on the rope and it went round the wheel and took his hands off by the wrists. Once when I was on night shift a man had committed suicide by jumping down the shaft, and there were parts of his body lying around. It was a very dangerous job down the mine, many a time you had to run when you heard the top cracking".

This lack of adequate provision for miners' dependents was eventually to lead to the miners' Association initiating its own welfare schemes. In 1896 the redundant colliery village at Haswell Moor was acquired by the Durham Miner's Association to provide Aged Miners' Homes; by this date, over half a century after the Haswell disaster appeal, a fair number of Coalowners made donations to the funding of the housing scheme.

"Oh! it's changed a lot, there used to be three or four shops in Haswell Plough, but we don't have any now to serve the two hundred houses. We have to rely on a travelling shop and of course, the prices are higher than in the main shops. There used to be a fish-shop, but now that has closed. I don't think I'll ever move from Haswell".

Today the village is essentially a dormitory settlement the majority of the people travelling outside the village to work.

THE HUNDRED MEN OF HASWELL

A poem written by George Weerth, and translated by Laura Lafargue, daughter of Karl Marx. Used for Propaganda, the poem was published in "THE COMMONWEALTH" in 1880.

The hundred men of Haswell,
  They all died in the same day;
  They all died in the same hour;
  They all went the self same way.
And When they were all buried,
  Came a hundred women, lo,
A hundred women of Haswell,
  It was a sight of woe!
  With all their children came they,
  With daughter and with son:
'Now, thou rich man of Haswell,
  Her wage to everyone!'
  By that rich man of Haswell
  Not long were they denied:
  A full week's wage he paid them
  For every man who died.
  And when the wage was given,
  His chest fast locked up he;
  The iron lock clicked sharply,
  The women wept bitterly.

WALKING IN MURTON AND SOUTH HETTON

● Using East Durham Heritage Trails and Walkways, Mrs A Henderson describes a circular walk in these two inland villages of East Durham and describes South Hetton in more detail

MURTON

Car parking is available about Murton Village war memorial. The walk begins outside the Murton Inn. Cross the busy road (B1285). Walk in a westerly direction past the garage until you see an obvious small roadway to your left. This is marked as a public footpath and is about 100m from the start of the walk (1).

The path crosses a five bar gate with a stile and is easy to follow. Continue along the rising path till it meets a much broader path which is used as a farm track (2). At this junction turn left and head up the hill. At the crest of the hill four collieries were visible. (3). To the North West Eppleton Colliery closed 1986; North East, Murton Colliery closed 1992; East, Hawthorn Colliery closed 1992; and South, South Hetton Colliery (demolished 1987). All these Collieries are within 3 miles walk demonstrating the extent of exploitation of the valuable coal seams lying 500 feet below you. This broad path/track is easy to follow, although it does dog leg 400 metres after the crest (4). At the dog leg take the broader path which leads off in a westerly (right) direction for about 800 metres till it

reaches a railway line (5). If you look around here you will see an old stile leading nowhere in particular and the remains of an old bridge. This bridge was known as *Dobson's Bridge* after the farmer who built it. The bridge was an important meeting place for both South Hetton and Murton folk. At one time a small plantation of trees also occupied this site and it was common for people from both villages to meet here and in the shelter of the plantation trees, gambling schools and bare knuckle fights were amongst other things which occurred.

The path now turns in a southerly direction. Keeping the railway cutting, then embankment on your right walk towards South Hetton past Murton Moor East Farm until the path crosses the railway line at South Hetton Junction 96. Caution must be exercised here as the railway line is still in use ferrying coal from hawthorn to the North Sea at Sunderland and Seaham. Carry on past the allotments and up to the Station Hotel (7). The car park behind the pub can also be used as an alternative starting point for this walk.

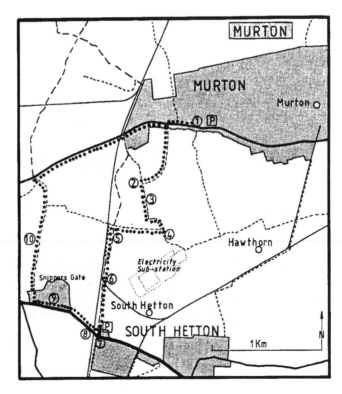

South Hetton has changed considerably in the last twenty years. The Category D philosophy of the 1950's and 60's saw the demolition of large chunks of the village. The land behind the station Hotel used to be the famous South Hetton Eight Rows which were demolished in the 50's. The Station is long gone now, so is the colliery agent's house; a fine Georgian style building that stood on the land which is now used for South Hetton Industrial Estate. The colliery gear is due for demolition (in September 1987) although the colliery buildings are being converted into new community association accommodation. South Hetton Colliery closed in 1982 one hundred and fifty two years after it was sunk - a proud mining history that will soon be commemorated by the erection of one of the pit gear wheels. From the Station Hotel notice the church of the Holy Trinity (8) built and paid for by the Burdon Family of Castle Eden. This church was the first building to be constructed in South Hetton, south of what is now Front Street. Stop and look inside the church where you will see one of the South Hetton Mining Lodge Banners.

Turn left at the Station Hotel and head down the bank in a westerly direction. Pass the shops; the open green spaces which now characterise the village are a result of the demolition of the Front Street houses in the 50's. You will eventually (300m) come to a row of houses still remaining on Front Street. This is known as Snippersgate (9). Prior to the sinking of the colliery a small cottage at 'Snippersgate' was the only building in this area. This is therefore the oldest part of the village. Carry on to the end of this row of houses then take right turn which will bring you to a stile and open fields. The path leads directly north for about one mile till it dissects the B1285 road. This path is regarded as the oldest (and longest) right of way in East Durham. it is called 'Salters Way' in several books it is described as Roman in origin; and may at one time have been the main trade route passing through Coastal Durham. West of Salters Lane path can be seen Easington Lane, Hetton le Hole and Eppleton (10). Once the road is reached (about 3 miles) turn right (east) and an easy path along the busy road for about one mile brings us back to the start of the walk at the Murton Inn. Time one and a half hours.

SOUTH HETTON

South Hetton Colliery was the first colliery to be opened in the Easington District. Prior to the sinking of the colliery, which was begun on 1st March 1831, the site of the present village was pleasant agricultural land with one or two farm buildings. Even during the sinking operation itself, housing provision was being made by Col. Bradyll's Hetton Coal Company for the men working on the coal shaft. Soon there was rapid housing development for the

miners themselves and, almost overnight it seemed, miners flooded in not only from the surrounding villages but also from different parts of the British Isles. Ask any of the older residents and you could receive an answer like this:

I was born in South Hetton in 1898. My father came from Berwick on Tweed. My mother came from Flint, North Wales. My father worked in the pit all his life.

It will be noted that both those parents had come from areas that had workable coal seams and quite often this pattern of miners moving from one mining area to another was to be repeated. Miners, however, had a reputation of working hard and playing hard and this coupled with a certain regional loyalty led to the vigorous new settlement gaining a name for itself as a centre of brawling:

Me grandad told me that there used to be hell on every weekend.

The resistance of the non-mining inhabitants of the older established settlements nearby was understandable in the circumstances and the traditional landowners, although willing to share

in the prosperity that coal would bring, were unwilling to release much land for the building of the colliery rows. The restrictions imposed by this lack of space produced quite noticeable patterns in the settlement lay out. Most of the houses lay either to the east or west of the mine shaft but even today there are few buildings to the south of the road from Snippersgate to Easington. Within this restricted space social divisions were obvious. There was the high side to the west, the Low Side to the east, and the Eight Rows in between, the latter being closest to the pit. All the social connotations of *High* and *Low*, together with the geographical significance of a *West End* were not lost on the residents of the miners' rows; the house of the agent for the Hetton Coal Company lay just to the west of the colliery in the large house, South Hetton Lodge.

South Hetton: it's a funny cross-eyed place. From end to end it's just about a mile in length and it is no width; and it is divided into three.

It was not long before the village grew large enough to have its chapel, an expression by the miners that they were not fettered by the bonds of traditional church, and as if to assert this message more clearly, the chapel was the first

...Those colliery houses, one room and an attic bedroom, that's all there was, and a big fireplace with a pot boiler and a round oven... with four big middens at the top of the street...

building to be erected on the south side of the road. On January 13th, 1863, the village became a separate parish from Easington and its main period of early growth was over.

Although the *raison d'etre* of the village by the end of the nineteenth century was coal mining it was an economy based on the marketability of the *Main* and *Hutton* seams - good domestic coal commanding high prices but vulnerable to competition from other British coal fields and to competition from electricity power and fuel oil. From quite an early date the coal owners sought to produce this coal at competitive rates.

They were hard days then, especially for the men who used to hew the coal down the pit. They used to work like slaves. As many as possible kept out of the pit because they didn't want to face the drudgery their father and grandfathers had. It was a dirty job and badly paid. Wages didn't start to rise and conditions didn't improve until after nationalisation.

One very obvious result of this cost controlling exercise was the quality of the housing stock. Very few new houses were added to the village between 1890 and 1910; the biggest injection of new houses was the council house boom in the 1920's and these emphasised the poor quality of the early colliery houses:

When the richest seams began to become exhausted (and remember that these are nearest to the surface at 140 and 180 fathoms) and the lower seams were becoming more and more costly to work, the neglect of the housing stock increased. Well before the Second world War the sub standard nature of the pit rows was recognised and in 1947 the local Council issued a demolition order on 279 of the houses in the historic settlement core. It more or less coincided with the beginning of the new town of Peterlee.

People were being encouraged to move to Peterlee; if you wanted a house, there were plenty in Peterlee. But people didn't want to go because it was taking people away from work and creating a lot of travelling as well as destroying the character of the village.

The end came finally for South Hetton Colliery at Easter 1983, almost exactly one hundred and fifty years after the first coal came out of the shaft. It seemed as if it were the end of an era. How much this mining tradition still means to the community is well brought out in the Heritage Trail; the pit gear has now gone but you will be intrigued to discover what use they have found for the site of the mine

19th CENTURY WINGATE

There are five colliery sites associated with the Wingate area.

- Wellfield Winning
- Wingate colliery
- Hutton Henry Colliery
- Station Town Pit
- South Wingate Colliery

● Extracts from two books by WA Moyes *WINGATE* published by Wingate Community Centre. 1962 and *MOSTLY MINING* published by Frank Graham 1969

A two - three mile linear walk through the straggling village enables a visit to all four sites to be made

WELLFIELD WINNING

In the 1830's the possibility that the Durham coalfield extended into this region was being realised, and alongside the development of the collieries was the extension of the new railways into the locality. As early as 1837 work on the first lines was being contracted out. It seems likely that sinking had begun at Wingate Grange and there were probably borings at Wellfield New Winning by then. By 1839, railway connections were made with Sunderland and Hartlepool and a branch connected with the main north-south line near Ferryhill. Wingate Grange had its own small line and sidings.

The sinking at Wellfield is said by some to have been originally for water - its present use - but the name New

Winning and expense of the undertaking would suggest that the original sinkers were more optimistic than this. However the Wellfield sinking produced no coal, and merely gave rise

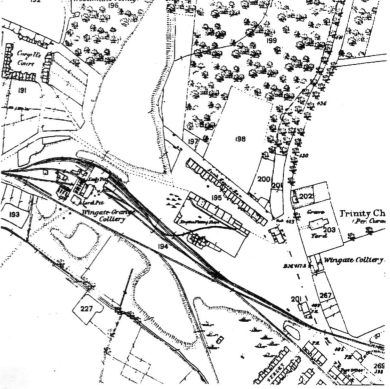

to a small settlement, consisting of two rows of cottages, High and Low Winning.

WINGATE GRANGE

Wingate Grange Lord and Lady pits had a capital investment of £60,000 and were sunk on either side of a small fault; coal was drawn from 1839 but not without difficulty. The water in the colliery exhibited corrosive properties not found elsewhere. At the rate of 1,800 gallons per

minute this caustic liquid was pumped to the surface badly corroding the metalwork of the pumps and boilers, blackening and making brittle the leather of the buckets. *Paints and varnishes of various kinds had been used to protect the iron work all of which proved ineffectual and it was at this stage that we had recourse to Faraday and other higher authorities* any suggestions were made *but much of the reasoning derived from experiment in the laboratory was falsified in the pit* where the factor of increased pressure had to be considered. The solution to the problem was of chemical interest only but before its application the colliery was hindered at considerable expense for seven or eight years.

August 3, 1839, is the date given for the reaching of the 5/4 seam at Wingate. The seam 3'10'' thick was of excellent coal, and lay at a depth of 66 fathoms. Two shafts were sunk to the Hutton seam and a boring was continued lower to prove the Harvey seam. The upcast shaft was called the Lord Shaft, and the downcast shaft was known as the Lady Shaft. They were named after the principal owners, Lord and Lady Howden (previously Sir John and Lady Cradock). The dual shaft sinking predated by more than four decades the Hartley Pit disaster which was instrumental in making the two shaft system compulsory by law. The date of the first coal drawn is December 1839.

Peter Lee described the primitive conditions in pit villages in the early years, and the circumstances described suggest that he may have been referring to Wingate.

In those days few of our villages had a good water supply. One of my earliest recollections is walking by the side of an elder sister who had to travel one mile to a well for water, and in after years, although still young, I found myself a carrier of water, with a girth and two pails for domestic use. There were very few homes with earth closets in those days but very large ash pits in the streets in which the refuse lay during the hot days of summer waiting for the farmers to come round in the autumn. There was also the open channel system and streets unmade. The material result was perpetual dust clouds in summer and great depths of mud in winter.

FRONT STREET, WINGATE. 2142.

Wingate Grange was soon the largest settlement in the immediate vicinity. To Sinker's Row and the early officials' houses known as Cargill's Court were added several monotonous rows of colliery workers' houses south-west of the crossing of the railway and the north-south road, and lying north-east of the stream. These were the four double rows Seymour, Pickering, Todd Streets and Humble Lane, a single row, Chapel Chare, two more double rows, Johnson's Square and Parkin's Palace, and then a short row of single storey houses known as Low Row. At right angles to these streets lay Front Row, which as the main road, featured the shops and public houses, the number and variety of which heralded the time when Wingate was to become the core of a larger settlement. North-east of the crossing Holy Trinity Church was built in 1841, and the Colliery School was established on an adjacent site, many years before educational provision was made compulsory by law. On the opposite side of the road were colliery buildings and two public houses. Some of the early building was of wood, but

Funeral Procession 1906.

most of limestone, rubble and mortar. They were nineteenth century dwellings of the meanest kind. Two such houses were joined to form a Wesleyan Methodist Chapel, and the Primitive Methodists built their commodious place of worship in Chapel Chare. Unmade roads and primitive sanitation were features of the settlement and water was carried from a spring along the road towards the Grange.

The Wingate and Station Town settlement is treated as one for the purpose of a brief county directory in 1894. By this time Reverend Simpson was Vicar of the enlarged parish, and there were six chapels well spread throughout the village. The Board Schools catered for about 600 children, while St. Mary's catered for another 134. Transfers between the two schools had been fairly frequent owing to a difference in the fees charged, but these were less frequent after September 1st, 1891, when education became free. There were occasions when Station Town children were not admitted to Wingate schools in view of capacity attendances by Wingate children, but the situation was eased when the Station Town school was built. Situated at the south end of Milbank Terrace, this school had Ebenezer Carr for its first headmaster. The Literary Institute had a library of 700 books, with recreation and reading rooms, as well as a large lecture hall.

A long strike occurred at Wingate in 1843 when the management introduced wire ropes for shaft haulage instead of the hemp ropes. Though it was pointed out that the men were 'foolishly prejudiced', much technical proof was required before the difficulties were resolved. The dispute took the form of an Assize trial at Durham, where despite evidence that strands of wire snapped from time to time and that in some collieries wire ropes had snapped, it was demonstrated beyond doubt that new wire rope would take a strain of up to 27 tons and the usual weight required was only three and a half tons.

HUTTON HENRY COLLIERY

Sinking for the Hutton Henry Colliery began in 1871 on the heathland to the east of Wingate Grange Colliery, and to the south-east of the

brickyards of R. Glass and G. & W. H. Carter. A ten foot diameter shaft, the Marley, was sunk to the Harvey seam in spite of the considerable engineering difficulties which were encountered and the setbacks which included some loss of life. The Perseverance (upcast) shaft, 14' in diameter was sunk to the Hutton seam in 1873, and the name bears testimony to the difficulties which had to be overcome. The Hutton seam at 115 fathoms was 3' thick, and the Harvey seam at 137 fathoms was 3'6''. The Busty seam 4'4'' was later proved at 141 fathoms. The first coals were drawn in 1876, and short stretches of railway were built to connect this colliery with the main lines to the west. The coal was of excellent quality, and a coke works was established, whose market was the rapidly developing industrial area of Teesside. Some 1,000 men and boys found employment on this site at its peak, and Wingate Grange was temporarily in second place as employer.

For some reason there were not many dwellings built near the colliery. At that time it was very common for rows of colliery streets to cluster near the pit head, but this did not happen here. Only one row, Heath View, was built on the site. The remainder were added to the geographical unit of Wingate Grange in the form of a rapid extension towards the south-east. By chance the boundary between Wingate and Hutton Henry townships ran along the beck, and so the development was in another parish and required another name. The station was the most southerly building of Wingate, and so the uninspiring name of Station Town was given to the new settlement.

Housing for the miners took the form of grid iron pattern colliery rows, typical of the period, built of brick in contrast to the early Wingate

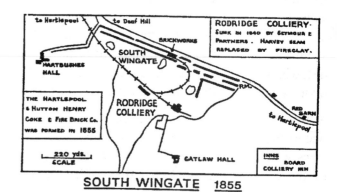

SOUTH WINGATE   1855

and South Wingate houses. The local brickyards flourished. The streets ran in a west-east direction, and are bounded on the east by the railway. The maximum number of houses were built in the smallest available area, and occupied the north-west corner of the estate of Frederick Acclom Milbank, whose name survives in two of the street names.

It may be wondered why the new colliery village did not have a separate site nearer the colliery. A number of factors would enter into such a decision - perhaps the difficulties of the land between the present site and the mine and coke works - perhaps.

The Hutton Henry Colliery did not fulfil its early promise. Faults began to occur frequently, causing a shortage of working places. Machinery was old fashioned and not too plentiful. The attention of successive managers and the profits of the company were diverted to attempt to open South Wingate Colliery, which was under the same ownership. All efforts were due to be frustrated, however, and the Hutton Henry Colliery closed in 1897 because of extensive flooding. The owners, the Hulam Coal Company, went into liquidation. They sold outto Horden Coal company, who never worked the colliery.

SOUTH WINGATE

The most southerly situated mine on the limestone plateau was Seymour and Company's Rodridge or Hartbushes Colliery at South Wingate. Well south of the dyke and adjacent to the red sandstone the shafts were sunk after at least one other expensive attempt in 1840. The seams were valuable. The wash out of the Harvey seam was not a total loss as its replacement by a four inch thick seam of fireclay gave rise to a profitable firebrick works. The short life of the colliery did not justify the cost of £20,000 for sinking and the £10,000 spent on machinery and railways for within two decades the mine was an encumbrance to its owners and a constant drain on their resources.

Miners and their families were not the only occupants of the settlement, but other occupations were poorly represented in lists of notables of the time. Others included the brick and tile manufacturer, E. Berkin, who lived at Rodridge Moor, two school masters, a blacksmith, a tailor, a boot and shoe maker and two grocers, one of whom sold draperies as a side line, while the other sold meat. There were two hostelries, the Colliery Inn and the Board Inn, as well as three beer shops. A Primitive Methodist chapel was situated to the south of the village.

This closely knit and independent community was prosperous for a very short time. In 1857 the amount of water accumulating in the mine was greater than could be conveniently dealt with by the pumping machinery then available. The colliery closed, and the brickworks were cut off from their source of raw materials. There was an immediate decline as miners and brickworkers sought work further north, and thereafter the reduction of numbers was a very gradual process.

William Coulson, the Master sinker, put down a bore hole on the Catley Hall estate, and found the Busty at 690'. Proving a good seam of coal made possible Rodridge or South Wingate colliery. This was the most south-easterly colliery of the Great Northern Coalfield. It was unusual in that the Harvey seam was washed out, being replaced by fireclay about 4' thick and containing small nodules of iron ore. The Rodridge firebricks works were based on this valuable seam of clay. A branch railway was built to join the lines at Wingate. coal shipments were received at Hartlepool and South Wingate became a flourishing village.

Hutton Henry Colliery, Upcast Shaft, 1898.

"He's had a bit of a mixed week. The pit his grandfather worked down isn't going to be reprieved — but he supports Norwich City."

How the Cartoonists Austin, Matt and McAllister saw coal's problems in early 1993

'It faints when the pit is about to be mothballed'

MINING FOLK REMEMBER

A series of personal contributions

CONTENTS

BEVIN BOYS

1943

Bevin Boys dig for victory

Ernest Bevin, Minister of Labour, announces that 1 in 10 conscripts will go down the mines

THE TIMES
FRIDAY DECEMBER 3 1943

Four years into the Second World War, it was realised that, from the outset, this country's manpower had been wrongly utilised. The *call-up* had been solely concerned with the needs of the Armed Forces, the requirements of essential industries neglected. Coal was the principal energy provider, supplying both electricity and fuel for strategic industries.

Britain employed almost one million men in the coal-mining industry, and produced almost 260 million tons of coal per year (1985 figures; 130,000 men producing 140 million tons).

As war-related industry reached a peak in 1943, it was realised that the military call-up had left the mining industry some 40,000 men short of its requirement. Under the *Emergency War-time Act*, 40,000 of the men who were destined for enlistment into the armed services were *called-up* into the mining industry and trained to work underground. These recruits were to take the name *Bevin Boys*, after the organiser of the whole operation Ernest Bevin, Minister of Labour.

● These two accounts of first hand experiences, one by Mr R.A.Wallace and the other by an anonymous contributor, tell us how the system worked and also about the drift mine at Waterhouses, the deep shaft colliery at Horden, and the East Hetton Colliery at Kelloe.

At the age of 19 I was employed as a teleprinter operator in Glasgow Head Post Office. Having passed my medical, I was daily expecting to be enlisted in the Royal Navy. My call-up papers duly arrived, but, instead of a Navy placing, I was ordered to report to the Training Centre at Annfield Plain, County Durham. I was also warned that any failure to comply could result in six months in prison, or a £100 fine, or both. I complied. After a training period of four weeks, I was assigned to Waterhouses Colliery, Co. Durham.

Approaching the hillside which housed the Colliery, there was little to see - a stable to house the ponies, a *check-cabin* and, most importantly, a layout of 2' gauge rail-track on which, I was to learn, sets of 40 -50 half-ton tubs were hauled into the pit empty, and out of it full of coal or stone. There was no shaft for access to the underground workings, instead, hardly discernable from a distance, were various tunnel openings, (drift mouths), let into the

hillside. Each was about 7' 6'' in diameter, with a rail track in the centre. The tunnel was lined with ring-type girders with horizontal timbers forced in between. There was no lighting, so, having left daylight behind, I found my self in complete, solid blackness. Every 20 yards was a refuge, man-sized, cut into the wall - an escape for any man walking along the tunnel when a set of tubs was on its way past. This was a life-saver, since the tubs filled the width of the tunnel and travelled very fast indeed.

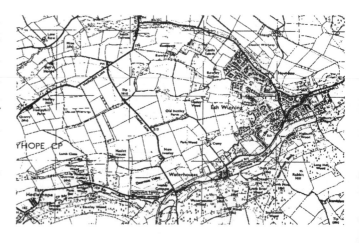

Waterhouses Colliery was known as a *wet pit*, suffering as it did from the natural water retention of the hill. It was, therefore non-gaseous, allowing the use of naked lights, including candles.

My clearest memory of that first introduction to the Colliery was the dampness, everything smelled dank, and the water was everywhere, in places even running down the walls and props and dripping from the roof.

Following the tunnel down, I reached the uppermost seam the thickness of which varied between 18'' and 30''.

The mine was operational twenty-four hours a day, two eight-hour shifts producing coal and a third removing stone from either the floor or the roof in order to provide the minimum working height of 3' 10''. The two coal producing shifts were known as the fore-shift and the back-shift, with the stone-removing shift operating during the night. Each shift overlapped the previous one in order to give the men time to travel *in-bye* and *out-bye*. Typical daily output was between two and eight tons per shift, depending upon the hardness of the coal.

Although 3'10'' was considered an acceptable working height, it was not sufficient for the main tunnel. This tunnel, which accessed to the surface, was a minimum of 9' wide and 7'6'' high, and so the secondary tunnels had to be gradually upgraded to this size. This was carried out in the stone shift by hewers chosen for their expertise and good work rate, using explosives.

The main, or *mother* tunnel had, naturally to be extremely durable, being the main highway for all of the workers and their output for perhaps ten years or more. In addition to props being placed every few feet, some of the stone removed was packed into the space left by the excavated coal in order to lend a little more support to the roof and walls.

As each seam was reached and the necessary opening constructed, a rail loop was formed in a specially widened part of the main tunnel. This formed an interchange for sets of tubs on their way in or out, and were the points to and from which ponies would haul the tubs. From here haulage was taken over by winding gear on the surface. This rope-haulage could pull 40 - 50 tubs to the surface at considerable speed along the main tunnel.

Coal was often removed using hand picks, but, during my time in Waterhouses, two electrically-driven coal cutting machines were in operation. Use of these much more powerful and efficient tools depended upon the geological conditions being suitable.

As a newcomer, I found a world quite unknown to most of us, in which men toiled to produce vast quantities of coal, often under difficult conditions. I had, in my ignorance, condemned miners as unskilled labourers. Instead, I found them to be, often, highly skilled men, regarded as inferior by the majority, and grossly exploited and underpaid.

RECOLLECTIONS OF A BEVIN BOY

We met on King's Cross Station on Monday, January 24th 1944. There could have been 300 of us altogether. Another boy from my home town in Surrey travelled up to King's Cross with me, but we parted there as he was going to Morrison Old Pit at Stanley to do his training and I was destined for West Hartlepool, to train at nearby Horden Colliery. When our train arrived at York, those of us who were going to West Hartlepool were transferred to another train which travelled via Eaglescliffe to our destination. We arrived an hour and a half late and, after being sorted out at the local labour exchange, we were taken to our lodgings and given instructions about buses and trains we were to catch to get to Horden the next morning.

My landlady had a full dinner waiting for me at half past five, for which I arrived at seven o'clock - it was a good start! I was at this lodging for the length of my training, which was four weeks.

Our training consisted of: -

half a day down the pit.

half a day P.T.

a full day in the classroom

half a day P.T.

half a day sawing wood in pit yard

a full day in the classroom

So we did half a day down the pit out of four days!

I trained for compressed air direct haulage, which was a single drum hauler to pull empty tubs up an incline and to lower them on to another track. While I was using this machine one day I thought I was stopping the hauler by winding off the air, but, by mistake, I was opening the valve and giving it more power. When I saw the tubs getting near the drum I noticed a mell hammer out of gear, thus stopping the drum.

The next time we went down the pit we were taught to work with ponies. After my training I was sent to Kelloe to work. Kelloe was all-electric and, I was told, had no ponies after 1937.

My first two weeks at East Hetton Colliery, Kelloe, were spent at bank, or above ground, sorting stone from coal on the belts, and getting used to fore-shift, starting at 3.50 am, and back-shift, starting at 1.50 am. There was a bait time half way through each shift. After two weeks I was told I was in fore-shift, down the Hutton Seam and working for an overman named Alf West. I was supplied at Horden with my first pit helmet and my first pair of pit boots, but the overalls which I was given at Horden were taken back. At the lamp cabin I

was supplied with a number and a large hand lamp and a small disc, or token, with my number on it. I would go to the lamp cabin window and shout out my number. I would then receive my lamp and token, then take my token to the token cabin and then go on the bank to the Hutton Shaft. At bank, the banksman would load the cage with men, give the winding engine man a three bell signal to let him know he was riding men and signal him to lower the cage to the shaft bottom.

While this was going on at bank, the on-setter at the shaft bottom was also signalling the same messages to the winding man to say he was sending men up to bank. Let it be said it was like riding on a bumpy lift.

The district I was sent to work in was a wet district called Coxhoe, after the village under which it went. My main job was coupling full tubs together as they came out from under the loader, making up sets of 42 which were sent out by main and tail hauler to the shaft bottom, to be taken to bank in the cage, two tubs in the top deck and two in the bottom. When coal was being taken to bank it was called drawing, so the cages were either drawing coal or riding men. I worked in this district for about two or three months, until the summer holidays, then I got a warrant from the labour exchange, which was at a place called Wingate. Bevin Boys had to pay seven shillings and sixpence, which is thirty seven and a halfpence in today's money, for a return ticket to wherever we lived. I lived about twenty miles south west of London. We got three of these warrants a year. After the summer holiday I returned to find our old face and district had been stopped. I didn't ask why. I found myself sent down the other shaft, called the Harvey Shaft. The first shaft I went down was the Hutton Shaft, this was the down-cast shaft, or the air shaft to ventilate the pit. The Harvey Shaft was the up-cast shaft, which brought the bad air out of the pit. The job I had at the Harvey Shaft bottom was to couple emptytubs, or chum, together in sets of 42 to go in-bye from the shaft landing, to a district near the coal face where, at another landing, would be a loader end where these tubs were filled and sent out-bye to the shaft for the whole of the shift.

After about six months of this work I was put on what they called trapping. At the top of an upcast shaft landing is a set of ventilated doors, one large enough to allow the sets of tubs to go through, and a small one for the men to go through on their way in or out-bye. The trapper had to make sure that these doors were kept closed as much as possible, and he also had to change the set ends from full to chum as quickly as possible, then send the chum set in-bye, closing the doors as soon as he could. I did this job for the rest of my time as a Bevin Boy.

Bevin Boys were taken into the pits to allow local miners of eighteen years or over to go on to piece work when their time came, and the Bevin Boys usually stayed on datal work, the lowest jobs on the pay scale.

BLACKHALL COLLIERY

● By John Winter of Eden Hall Primary School Peterlee, this account tells us of the coastal colliery Sunk and Closed during this century. Information supplied by John Welsh.

Before the colliery began to tip waste into the sea, the beach was a stretch of golden sand: now it is covered with a thick layer of colliery waste.

Prior to the sinking of the colliery, Blackhall was an agricultural site. There were three farms - Blue House Farm, Mickle Hill Farm and Tweddle Blackhall Farm.

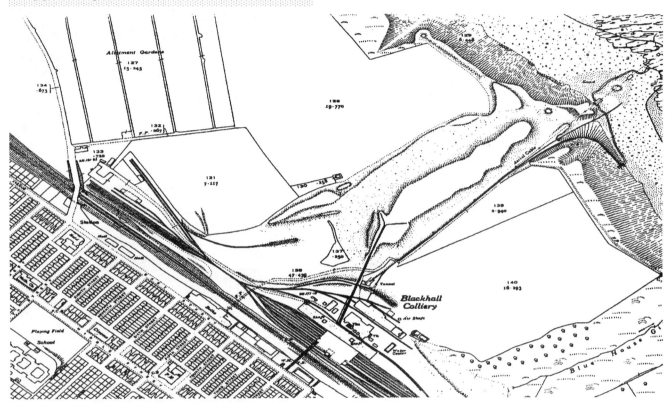

In 1908 the sidings were laid in preparation for the sinking of the mine at Blackhall by the Horden Coal Company. In 1900 this company, under its chairman Mr Hugh Bell, had bought the Castle Eden colliery (situated at Hesleden and which had closed in 1893 because of flooding), Shotton Colliery which had closed in 1874 due to a general depression in the trade, together with a twenty-eight square miles royalty which stretched from Shotton to the coast.

Shotton colliery was re-opened in 1904 to provide coal and materials for the sinking of the Horden and Blackhall collieries on either side of Castle Eden Dene. Hesleden (the site of Castle Eden colliery) had a good stock of brick houses which were used after 1910 to accommodate some of the new work force at Blackhall.

The first shaft to be sunk at Blackhall was called the *Staple* and its purpose was to provide water for the new village (there being no other fresh water supply available), rather than to raise coal. The water was found to be very salty and could only be used for washing and cleaning. Water for drinking had to be carried from a spring just below the Blue House Farm cottages.

The sinking of the main shaft for the mining of coal began in 1909 and the first coals were drawn in 1913. The difficult nature of the strata created great problems. The thick cover of permian limestone was underlaid by a porous, friable sand containing large volumes of water, the depth of the sand being about sixteen metres. To overcome the problem this section of the strata was frozen when it was reached by the sinkers.

Water ingress was to be a perennial problem for the colliery and was a major factor in its eventual closure. In 1923 water from the old workings of the Castle Eden colliery broke into the Blackhall Colliery workings. To contain the water, pumping engines were employed at the shaft continuously. The Castle Eden shaft was kept open and pumping engines were employed there too.

The shaft was sunk to a depth of between four hundred and forty and four hundred and seventy metres and passed through, at different levels, the Three-Quarter, Five Quarter, Main, Low Main and Hutton seams.

The colliery between the Wars employed over two thousand men and produced about two thousand tons a day. The village had a population of approximately six thousand. This was a difficult period, however, for the mining families of Blackhall and for the coalmining community in general. In 1921 the colliery owners reacted to the fall in demand for coal by making drastic wage cuts. The miners went on strike but returned after three months on the owners' terms.

A similar pattern of events resulted in the 1926 strike with, once again, the miners returning to work on the owners' terms - an increase in the hours worked and a reduction in wages of one shilling per shift.

At Blackhall, during both of these strikes, soup kitchens were set up to feed the children in the Granary building which housed the boys' school. Miners and their wives co-operated with the teachers in preparing and serving meals to the children. One witness remembers:

"We got a bowl of soup, or a bit of stew; a cup of cocoa and a slice of bread. My sister and I went. We didn't go at first, but if we went it meant a little bit extra for the rest of the family."

The miners were given vouchers by the union to buy flour, sugar, eggs and butter for their families. These were signed for and when the men returned to work the vouchers were expected to be paid for. Records show that not all of the miners at Blackhall actually paid for the vouchers they had used.

To keep the home fires burning and their time usefully occupied, the men went down to the beach and picked coal from the tip and the seashore, frequently using this as an excuse to gamble at *pitch and toss.*

From 1927 until re-armament in 1936 the coal trade was in the doldrums, with excess capacity and low demand. The fall of France in 1940 brought a collapse in the export market for coal. As the bulk of Blackhall's coal was exported, the pit was put on short time working. The men worked only one week in three.

The more perceptive and ambitious young men of the village moved their families to look for greater security, better working conditions and more congenial surroundings in the Midlands, mainly Coventry and Nuneaton, finding work in the pits and factories there. Some men went to work in the shipyards at Hartlepool. Later in the War, however, when the demand for coal grew, many of them came back to the colliery.

The village was heavily dependent on the pit for employment. It was estimated that approximately ninety per cent of the insured men were employed at the pit. There was no real alternative employment in the area to mining and its associated industries.

Short time working and poor wages at the pit produced a climate of poverty in the village, and in the area generally, which effected other jobs in the building and distributive trades. Jobs in the service industries were few. The spending capacity of the community, after meeting basic requirements, was very limited.

The only bright spot on the horizon was the knowledge that Blackhall's reserves of good, easily accessible coal and short communications by both rail and road, resulting in cheaper transport and maintenance costs, gave it a small but significant advantage over the older collieries in the region.

At Blackhall, as in other pits, the importance attached to the job a miner did was reflected in his wages. The *hewer* was the best paid, followed by the *putter* and then the *driver* who was the least well paid of the three. The nearer to the face a miner worked the better he was paid. The wages also reflected the physical

demands of the job and the skills required. The natural progression was for the *driver* to become the *putter* and for the *putter* to become the *hewer*.

From the landing to the shaft bottom, the tubs were hauled by an endless rope haulage system. This involved boys being employed both at the shaft and at the landing to put the tubs into sets and to attach them to (or detach them from) the haulage rope.

Other boys were employed as *trappers* to look after the opening and closing of the canvas ventilation doors that prevented the ingress of foul air into the working areas. One old Blackhall miner recalls a frightening experience as a fifteen year old *trapper*.

' *I was there for three days, eight hours each day, in the dark. This was because one of the putters took my lamp off me because his lamp had gone out.* ''

One retired Blackhall miner remembers taking home his first pay:

''It was nine shillings and four pence. My mother gave me eighteen pence back for my pocket money. I bought her a twopenny bar of chocolate and she was over the moon''. (c. 1926)

Putters and *hewers* often worked in seams no more than a metre high with only about four centimetres clearance between the tubs and the roof supports. A retired miner who worked as a *putter* in the First South-East district recalls:

''It was hard work. We had to keep our backs low. If we didn't we scraped them on the roof or the supports and got nasty cuts which we used to call *buttons*.''

Mining in all its aspects was hard and exhausting work. One former *putter* recalls:

''After night shift we would reach home after eleven o'clock. I've seen me and my brother strip off and count each other for the ''buttons'' (bruises) on our backs. We used to be that tired. We used to get our suppers first. My mother would have the big pan boiling on the hob. She used to put the cold water in the bath and tell us ''Now there's the soap and flannel. Get washed and get to bed''. Many's the time she would come down the next morning at half past eight to get the bairns off to school and we were still lying there ... black. The fire was out and the

water in the pan was cold. She had to start all over afresh. We got many a good rollicking over that.'' (c.1930)

This incident demonstrates how beneficial to the Blackhall miner and his family was the opening of the pithead baths in 1934. For the miner himself, it meant that he could have a hot shower immediately on reaching the surface. He could get rid of his pit dirt without inhibition or restriction, leave his pit clothes in his baths' locker and get changed into clean clothes.

It must have been even more welcome to the mother or wife of the miner. No more filling and emptying the tin bath. No more pans of boiling water standing permanently on the hob. No more dirty pit clothes just flung on to the kitchen floor, having to be picked up and *dadded* against the yard wall to get rid of the coal dust. No more the need to have the kitchen or living room serve as a bathroom and the rest of the family having to scatter while the pitman bathed. This routine might be performed two or three times a day.

The nature and environment of mining meant that at Blackhall, as at every other colliery, there was always the risk of accidents happening, either through roof falls or as the result of incidents involving tubs on the haulage and pony roads. One witness recollects such an accident on the coal face in the Fifth North District. It involved a miner filling on the face:

"A plank had been set up on a prop that we called *middle timber*. The weight of the roof was resting on this. The plank at each end where there was no support started to bend downwards. The man was shovelling coal under one of these unsupported ends when suddenly a stone slid down the plank catching him on the forearm, breaking it and cutting it badly with the bone protruding through it. The accident happened about a mile and a half in-bye. The man walked out-bye with his arm held up and out in a most awkward position. He refused to get on a stretcher. He was taken to Hartlepool Hospital. I think the colliery paid a contribution to the hospital and so many beds were made available to the colliery.''

The accident occurred after the coast road was opened in 1924. Before that the ambulance would have had to go up to Castle Eden, on to the A19, on to Elwick and then from Elwick along old cart tracks to Hartlepool. The journey would have taken much longer and would have been much more uncomfortable.

MURTON

Mr. Lowes was born at Silver Street, Cornwall Estate, Murton, in 1890. His father was a miner at the colliery in Murton. His grandmother was the first woman born in Murton. The people lived in wooden huts in those days. Her father helped to sink the colliery. He was a *'sinker'*. As a child Mr. Lowes attended the colliery school (now demolished) from the age of five until he finished at thirteen years of age.

His childhood was comfortable compared with that of many. In those days families were large and lots of children went to school without shoes or stockings. Mr. Lowes' father had a Sunday paper business selling *Sunday Chronicles, Lloyd's News, Empires and Dispatch.* They sold magazines like *Companion* and *Police News.* His parents also kept pigs. He remembered his father filling a pig, then throwing hot water over it and scraping the hairs off its body with can or tin lids. The pork would be sold to neighbours.

He left school one Friday aged thirteen and started work at the pit the following Monday for 10d old money (4p) working ten hours a day.

Mr. Lowes' first job was as a trapper boy, opening a big wooden door on the engine plain (roadway) to let the sets of tubs run through. He would close it again (for ventilation). Describing his early mining career he said, "Then I went on driving for two years after that job. There were about five lads on driving in the south-east drift, with big ponies in the main coal seam pulling the tubs of coal on to the kip (an incline) and the landing (station). Then I went on to wayside putting, score price putting and after that coal-hewing."

As a coal hewer his wage was about 32 shillings (£1.60) a week but he had 8 shillings (40p) rent to pay.

He was in his early twenties when the 1914/1918 war broke out. Mr. Lowes joined the 15th Durhams (D.L.I.) but returned to the pit after the war.

This unit by Mrs B Henderson of Murton Jubilee Junior School includes:

● The memories of Mr J Lowes, born 1890, who talked to Mr J Porter of Easington District Council.

● The memories of Mr Elliot who visited the school and talked to the children.

● A description of the McNally memorial

The hardest work he did down the pit was hewing coal with an old hand pick and shaft. "It was hard coal and if you didn't get the coal you got no pay (on piece work)". One got 6d (old money) for filling ten cwt of coal. Mr.

Lowes recalled how Durham Big Meeting was a major event and how some miners contributed a small some of money weekly which was paid out on the day of the gala. The money which amounted to 5/- was paid out on the racecourse at Durham. If you didn't attend you got no money.

One of the changes Mr. Lowes welcomed was the building of the pithead baths in 1939. Prior to this miners had to bath at home in a tin bath in front of the fire using pans of hot water. Another advantage was that miners could now get changed for work at the pithead baths using the lockers provided. It dispensed with the inconvenience of having dirty pit clothes in the house.

Mr. Lowes recalled how the Big Club (Victoria Club) bought a charabanc (motor car) for its members' use. On weekends it would take the members out on trips to different seaside resorts.

Hawthorn sands or Dalton-le-Dale dene were popular places for many people in Murton. Mr. Lowes described how he had a kettle and pan which he used to hide in the cliff side. These he would cover over with bracken and sand and he would dig them out each time his family went there. They would spend hours gathering winkles off the rocks.

Mr. Lowes said, "The road to Hawthorn from Murton was black with people going back and forth from the dene and the beach. Some used the road but others used the bridle path ''.

Families had their own fires made with coal washed up on the seashore. People would dance and sing along to records played on gramophones. It was a wonderful atmosphere.

In the 1930's Murton had a successful football team in the North Eastern League which attracted a popular following. It was reputed that players could get a good job at the pit if they played for the team. Sport played an important part in community life. Besides football other sporting interests included cricket, handball, quoits and the traditional interest of pit villagers in pigeon racing and whippets.

Mr Elliot

Murton Ladies Football Team - 1926

Mr. Elliott, a former miner, was born in Murton in 1924 the son of a miner. His father was originally from Carlisle and had been in the army.

The first school Mr. Elliott attended was the County Infants' School at the age of five. When he went to the Senior School his favourite subject was Geography.

He was fourteen years old when he started work in 1938 at the pit and worked there for forty-four years. He retired early at the age of fifty-eight. His first job was at the surface on the screens picking stone out of the coal. He started work at 5 am until 1.30 pm. On Saturdays he worked from 5 am to noon. His wage was ten shillings and sixpence old money (52p) a week.

His first job underground was carrying wooden sprags or dregs to put in the wheels of the tubs. This steadied the tubs or slowed them down as was required. He did not enjoy working in the pit but it was the only work available at that time.

On his first day underground another boy took

him to his place of work at the shaft bottom.

Of the conditions underground Mr. Elliott said he was never lonely nor frightened as there was always other people working nearby.

There were electric lights underground but none once you left the shaft bottom. He drank water out of a tin bottle and ate jam sandwiches for his 'bait'. Sometimes he had bread and butter with a sprinkling of sugar. The hardest work he did was filling coal with a shovel into a tub. Each tub held 10 cwt. of coal. He was paid by the number of tubs filled this was called 'piece' work.. He was paid by the score (20 tubs plus one extra - the extra tub was filled with concessionary coal, for miners, retired miners and miner's widows).

The shifts worked were:

   3.30 am,   10.00 am,   3.30 pm,   10.00 pm

Each lasted seven and a half hours. One had to be sixteen years old before you could work overtime or earlier than 5 am.

His first holiday with pay was in 1938 for three days. He stayed with relatives.

He was underground in 1942 when there was an explosion at the pit and thirteen men were killed.

Mr. Elliott preferred his last job at the pit. He was a linesman with the Surveyors' Department.

His retirement is spent. watching cricket, walking and going on holidays. Instead of working in the pit Mr. Elliott would have liked to have joined the army.

Murton War Memorial Park

SERGEANT W. McNALLY

In the memorial park beside the cenotaph a memorial to Sergeant W. McNally was built in 1977. Murton is proud of Mr. W. McNally who was awarded a Victoria Cross in the great war 1914/1918.

"While serving with the Green Howards in Italy on October 27th 1918, he and his company were seriously hampered by machine gun fire in an advance across the River Piave. Disregarding personal safety, he rushed the machine gun post, killed the gunners and captured the gun. Two days later with his company again under heavy fire he crept to the rear of the enemy's position, again captured a machine-gun post and later repelled a heavy counter attack''.

His Military Medal was won aiding a wounded officer, a bar was added for rescuing men of a platoon wounded or buried by shellfire. There were great celebrations the day he arrived homes from the war. The pit was closed down for the day and he was met at the railway station by the colliery manager. The local colliery band accompanied a procession through the village.

Sergeant W. McNally lived until 1976 dying at the age of eighty-three.

VILLAGE LIFE IN PAGE BANK

There's a village in Durham by the Wear,

Stands out in my memory each year,

Of strange things that happened so full of mirth,

The name of Page Bank, the home of my birth.

So wrote Edward Raisbeck many years ago of the village in which he was born and raised. He remembers it with great fondness, a feeling shared by many.

' *There's a place at Page Bank on the top of the hill. It's a field an' it wes Paradise te me when ah wes a kid''.* Paradise it certainly seemed to be, but then early life always seemed to be so for a child in those days. But what of the adults? Mining life is hard and Page Bank had known tragedy, and the economy of the village never hung by more than a strong thread, but life went on.

The Watchers Field, mentioned above, was where "they used to have the Shows --- the Flower Shows, and the Vegetable Shows, and parade the Pit ponies aroun, an' have the Race Meetin's. It was also the Picnic field. In those far off days, "the summers were lovely hot days, and the winters very cold. The snow seemed to last for a lot longer than it does today, and it was a different kind of snow. The days were happy, good days, the people in the village were kind, considerate, sincere folks, always ready to help in times of trouble."

From the Watchers Field, manned 24 hours a day by retired or injured miners, there to watch for signs of trouble, the village lay before the watching eyes --- East Terrace, Railway Terrace, Long Row, Old Row, Chapel Row, School Row .... all dominated by the Sega Heap and its attendant Pit Heaps, and the Brick Works, punctuated by the noise of Daddy Elwell's Fan Engine competing with Jackie Mason's Triple Compound, and both envious of the ability of Bob Hodgson's engine to blow smoke-rings!

From the School, where the Boys learned Geology and Mining, and the Girls Embroidery and Housework, the 'Black Hand Gang' and

● A collection by John Nelson and the children of King Street Junior School, Spennymoor.

Bill Lyn talks

others would race up the Sega Heap to sledge down on Pit shovels, (girls as well) even having front doors opened to let them slide into the houses. In Winter too, some would persuade Neddy Hodgson to make some skates, and away they'd go while the ice stayed for ever.

The older youths and the men would often go to the four railway carriages on one of the heaps and converted into a Rifle Range, sometimes joined by some of the more daring boys. There was a full range of sports played ---

Soccer, Cricket, and even Rugby if the teacher said so! On dark Winter nights, the streets would echo to the shouts of 'White Horse Kick!', or 'Jack Shine the Maggie', and then what larks trying to find the lantern among the Brick Flats! In the summer, privileged lads were allowed to join in Cricket matches led by Mr Cockburn and Wilf Riley, the 'Larwood' of Page Bank.

Precious memories have to include the landing in 1922 of an aeroplane in the Watchers Field, ensuring its mention in every Airfield manual for years to come. A quick fill-up from a Willington Garage, and away again --- the only casualty being PC Cole's bike, 'accidentally' trodden on when he'd left it in the grass!

The ladies of Page Bank, apart from keeping their families together, were, many of them, famous for their prowess at Quilt-Making. Where are they now, these precious souvenirs?

Giants strode the streets of Page Bank --- Daddy Elwell, Charlie Mason, PC Cole, Johnny Sutherland, and Alf Atkinson, the Horse keeper, setting the Pony Express away round the Pits to collect the mail, and even collecting Jackie Waugh when he fell off'. The horses too, loom larger than life --- Duke and Drummer come to mind, and 'Anty' Arbuckle's horse, Brisk.

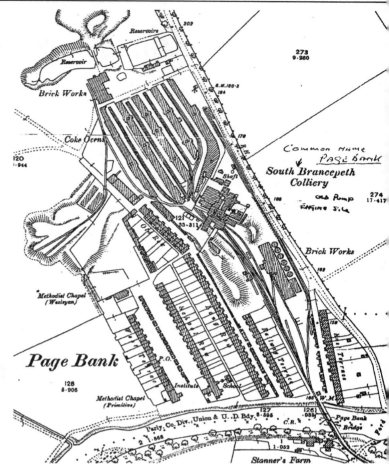

Times were hard quite often, but the dignity of life was always preserved. In those days, if you didn't have something, you either made it. worked for it, or did without. No one went short of food. Many grew vegetables in their gardens, or the New Allotments. If you needed meat you kept Pigs, or else "yer Mam sent yer to have a word with Joe Reynolds, the local 'Meat Supplier'. For sixpence, he'll see yer right for a Rabbit for the Sunday Pot!

Page Bank was flooded on the nigh of November 5th, 1967, but it effectively died when the Pit closed in 1932. Bureaucratic blindness refused to let it rise from its ashes. But has it died? Not while there are two memories to rub together it hasn't!

Dear John,

Received your letter of April 3rd, well lad, to me your project of recording on tape events, people, and places, of Spennymoor and surrounding area surely is reet worthwhile, I touch me cap ti thee lad! When I was a pupil at Rosa Street school we were taught to acknowledge our teachers in that way, if it was a lady teacher we raised our caps, and woe betide us if we didn't do so!

You are friendly wi my ard pal "Bill Lynn", eh? well that means you are a friend o mine also so you've no need to ask my forgiveness for the use of my nick name – by the way John, if its of interest ti thee I usually refer to my ard pal Bill as W/O/P/B, "WILL O PAGE BANK", for he was bred r born there!

Our family moved to Page Bank from Spennymoor just soon after the 1926 strike was ended, I was 10 years old, after closure of the colliery in DECEMBER 1930, we, our family, moved to Yorkshire in the MARCH of 1932 and my Father r I started work at UPTON colliery under the same management that closed-down our colliery of Page Bank - "DORMAN LONG r CO."

Yes friend John, I still treasure the many memories I have of that dear old village r villagers by the banks of the river WEAR - they never fade ──

● A letter from G R James, who now lives in South Yorkshire to John Nelson in response to an appeal for oral history of Page Bank

No, after all these years r as each one passes somehow my memories of P/BANK and all those grand folk living there at that time become more beautiful and very precious to me.

Seeing as how over the past few years I have recorded a tape or two for my pal W/O/P/B (recitations of poetry r monologues) for both Bill r I are a wee-bit pixilated on poetry!) 'twill be my pleasure to help you with some of my anecdotes on tape, there's no need for you to send me any blank tape seeing that I have some spare 60 MIN ones on hand.

Don't become despondent John if it takes 4 or 5 weeks for me to fulfill the recorded tape I've promised just you know this lad that I will do the best I can, with the hope that the eventual tape will meet with your approval.

I am yours sincerely
G. R. Jones.

P.S. Wen the sees Bill next, shak his hand r gi' him a big kiss fre me. HE, HE, HE!

A MINER'S DAY

● The personal reminiscences of Chris Edward retired Overman from Belmont. After training and working in Bowburn he transferred in 1966 to Dawdon Colliery - A pit with a long future

I qualified as deputy and then overman in 1974.

In 1980 Dawdon was a high technology coastal colliery with still high future prospects. The colliery employed 2,000 men - 300 miners in each shift working underground.

Daily Routine

Living 10 miles away from the colliery I chose to travel with the colliery transport at a weekly cost of £1. The journey was slow due to the route needed to pick up miners in outlying districts, but it was to car driving for most of us were too tired to drive at the end of a shift and what is more we were able to chat with mates - usually local and national sporting events from darts to rugby being topics of conversation.

High Speed Trolley Locomotive

I worked 4 shifts in rotation.:-

First shift 5a.m. - 12.15p.m.

Back shift 10.45a.m. - 6p.m.

Night shift 5p.m. - 12.15a.m.

All night shift 10.45p.m. - 6.00a.m.

As the work was composite, shift changes made no difference to the nature of work undertaken, unlike in the early days at Bowburn when each shift was designated for specific work - cutting - filling - drawing (lifting the belts into position)

On arrival at the pit head first stop was the locker rooms where we changed into our work clothing and greased our boots. Once ready it was time for a last cigarette before entering the pit, then into the lamp room where we picked up our tokens, lamps and self-rescuers.

At the pit head we were searched for matches and cigarettes. Descent into the pit some 1600 ft. was via the man riding shaft in a double deck cage holding 64 men, controlled by the banksman on the surface and the onsetter underground. Materials required underground were also carried in the manshaft. The coal shaft was used as its name suggests for carrying coal but we used it in emergencies for man riding. To reach the face we travelled by train from the shaft to the inbye station then walked an average of two miles to the face.

As overman I met the men at a meeting station where the men were deployed to various districts and machines. My responsibilities were overseeing the production and supplying on average 3 or 4 deputies' districts.

In each district a deputy was in charge of several machine workers, 2 supply men, men on transfer points (The points where two belts meet and where coal spillage was lifted back on to the belt) an electrician and a fitter. The districts were either for coal production or development.

My shift was spent walking around the districts ensuring supplies were available for efficient working. The deputies themselves were responsible for the safety and welfare of the miners. (Testing for gas with flame lamps, checking roof supports and machinery etc.) Being a modern mine coal cutting was by a shearer, a large circular cutting disc capable of taking 10 feet advance of coal (each face being on average 250 yards long) per shift, coal being automatically filled onto the conveyor belt.

Work was continuous throughout the shift, cutting coal, advancing the roof supports - the men taking only 20 minutes break for sandwiches in the gates away from the face. Absenteeism was sometimes higher on Mondays particularly in the early or first shift but shorthanded situation wasn't a grouse as the men benefitted in their wage packets as a result of bonuses.

The miner's (N.U.M.) strike of '84/'85 soured what had been very good relationships between miners and officials. Effects were still felt more than a year after the strike, morale was lowered and it seemed the pre-strike atmosphere and respect for officials had disappeared. Prospects for the future of the colliery suffered also from the problematic seam fault, too expensive apparently in the end to overcome.

I controlled the districts with the aid of telephones. I was kept informed of the state of the districts, breakdown in machinery etc. I made notes and any necessary action was taken. I maintained contact with surface by phone relaying information as necessary.

At the end of each shift the gear head man would shout the welcome words "End of shift." The outward journey was the reverse of the inward - back to cage and up to surface.

The machines in each shift were expected to work 260 minutes leaving about 90 minutes each way for travelling underground.

Back on surface we were searched for stolen items - brass, wood etc. We then returned to the lamp room where we put our lamps to be recharged for the next shift. The miners immediately went for showers while officials handed in shift reports at the control room. The reports from four successive shifts giving a general picture over 24hrs, which determined requirements for the next day's work.

MY FIRST DAY AT WORK

● Information provided about his grandfather by Keith Watson a pupil of Cassop Primary School.

This is a transcript of the letter above.

My first payslip at the age of 14 years old, working on the screens picking stones from coal. Four and a half shifts of 8 hours 20 minutes duration. The 20 minutes allowed for *Bait Time*.

The 7 shillings and 5 pence (7/5), (today approx 37 and a half pence) was the basic wage for a 14 year old boy on the screens. That works out to just over 1/7 per shift.

Off takes were Doctors 5d., Band 1d., Aged Miners Homes 1d., Welfare 1d., Nursing Assoc. 1d.

The other note was for (piece work) picking small stones from the coal and putting them into boxes. Boxes 18 inches x 12 inches by 12 inches deep, paid for at 1 penny for 12 boxes, hence 373 boxes = 2/7.

Take home pay 9/5 = approx 49 pence.

Form of Pay Note agreed to, Nov. 5th, 1909.

Nº 52

THE WEARDALE STEEL, COAL & COKE CO., LTD.

WHEATLEY HILL COLLIERY. Pay ending August 2, 1930.

Name *R. Watson*   No. of Shifts 4½

	£	s.	d.	£	s.	d.
Earnings at Tonnage or Score Prices		4	6			
Earnings at Yard Work						
Consideration		2	11			
Sundries						
Percentage Additions ... %				1	5	
House Rent Allowance						
TOTAL						
OFF-TAKES:—Laid Out						
Set Out						
Fire Coals						
Glass						
Explosives						
Water						
Cash Advanced						
Lost Tokens						
Nat. Insurance						
Unemployment Ins.						
Electric Light						
Housing Scheme						
Smith						
P. R. Fund						
Dr. Ryan		5				
Dr. Cooper						
Dr. Russell						
Dr. Jack						
Dr. Todd						
Band						
R. C. Church		1				
Hospital						
Checkweigh F.		1				
A. M. Homes						
Welfare Fund						
Nursing Assoc.		1				
Credit						
Death Fund						
Relief						
Fines					9	
BALANCE ... ... £					6	8

Any man questioning the accuracy of the number of shifts must not occasion inconvenience by doing so at the Pay Office, but must take some suitable opportunity for enquiry.

Any Workman (not bound by agreement) wishing to quit the service of Weardale Steel, Coal and Coke Co. (Limited), must give FOURTEEN DAYS' Notice in Writing. Any Workman who leaves the Company's service without first giving Fourteen Days' Notice on a separate Sheet will forfeit all wages which may be due to him, and render himself liable to be prosecuted. Workmen (also not bound) may demand an equal notice from this Company or its Agents, unless they have been guilty of misconduct.

UNDERGROUND WORKERS

Before 1842, children under the age of 10 were found working under ground in coal mines. The working conditions of the miners was hard and difficult and the men and boys were little more than slaves to their masters.

TRAPPERS

Young boys would start work underground as trappers. It is assumed that the Evenwood boys would have been employed in either the Evenwood or Norwood Colliery. An account in Thomas Burt's autobiography, of the working life of the trapper boy read as follows:

"The clatter, the bustle and confusion, the darkness relieved only by glimmering flickering lamps, the men and boys flitting hither and thither, resembling grim shadows rather than human figures - all this seemed a fantastic dream, novel and bewildering. To direct the air currents of the mines, doors were placed at certain points, and it was my business to tend one of these, to open and shut it when the putters pass through on their way to the workings and on their return journey to the flat or station. The trappers hours were normally 12, really about 13 a day; his pay was tenpence a day, and he was expected to remain at his post the whole time in total darkness."

● Evenwood Primary School describe workers down pits in the mid-nineteenth century. Mine drawings from Methuen 'Coal Mines and Miners' Tomalin

ROLLEY DRIVERS

At about thirteen or fourteen years of age, the pit boys would be entrusted with the duties of rolley drivers; the first phase of raising the coal to the surface from the coal face. Most collieries used wheeled wagons running on light rails or wooden boards sometimes wooden sledges were used. These wagons were hauled by the youths from the face to the haulage road. There, the coal would be transferred into larger tubs, hauled by the small pit pony and driven by the putter.

PUTTERS

The hand putters job involved manhandling tubs of coal to the flat or station before they were placed on rolleys and removed to the shaft bottom by horse. This work required a great deal of strength and stamina and was reserved for active and powerful young men who could sustain excessively hard work over long hours, shifting tubs of coal weighing up to a quarter of a ton.

PONY PUTTERS

Ponies generally not much more than one metre high were introduced into the mines of Durham in about 1840. With the increased output of coal and the need to reduce costs the use of the pony became widespread. The work of the pony putter was supposed to be easy work compared to that of the hand putter, this may be so since the pony did the heaviest part of the pulling.

However, the danger was constant if the props of timber set along the roadway were too close to the tramways then, if the tub was heavily laden, there was every chance of an accident. possibly causing a roof fall. The putter for the most part "Rode on the Limbers" crouching so as to occupy as little space as possible. If they did not crouch there was a chance that they might crack their heads or shoulders on the roof which could cause serious injury or even in extreme cases death. There

was also the risk of being jammed between the timbers and the tub which could also cause many injuries.

HEWERS

These were the men employed to dig the coal. A skilled hewer had to have the ability to interpret sounds and smells of danger and to adopt safe working procedures as a matter of habit. The hewer was paid by the ton and his earnings depended on his own efforts and partly upon luck as some working places were better than others.

THE LIFE OF A MINER'S WIFE

● Christine Kirkwood talks of the difficult and labourious lot of the women of the coalfield

There is no denying that the life for a miner in the Durham Coalfield in the early part of this century was gruelling but his wife's day revolved around the men in the family and was arduous in a different way. Often her day began an hour or so before that of her husband in preparing breakfast, maintaining the fire, boiling water for cooking and washing and preparing the bait for the day.

Her day was a round of "routines" and was made more difficult if there was more than one man in the family to look after. If the pit worked a multiple shift system, whereby the men were coming and going, sleeping and eating all the day because of the demands of the pit, it was a wife's job to be available whenever the men prepared or returned from a shift. Some days she would rise before dawn to prepare breakfast and bait for those members of the family starting the four o'clock shift. If there was time she might catch an hour's sleep before going through the same routine for another son or husband whose shift began at six o'clock. It was also possible that as one member of the family departed for work another may be returning from the night shift. He would require breakfast and a bath before going to bed.

Few colliery houses had bathrooms and bathing took place in a tin bath in front of the fire. Boiling water for the bath had to be prepared well in advance of the men returning from work as it took some considerable time for the water to boil on the range. Although as new equipment became available some houses did have a boiler installed but for many the old routine of boiling water persisted in many households well into the 1940's.

Doing the laundry was often an all day task and traditionally took place on Monday, never on a Sunday, which was usually set aside for church. In some households the water for washing had to be collected from a stand pipe at the end of the street - she would make this journey several times. Preparations began with clothes being boiled to ensure they were particularly clean.

Usually they were boiled in a pan for twenty minutes or so before being removed, with a stick, and rinsed. They were then "blued" to improve the brightness, starched to make them crisp and finally dried.

There were no biological washing powders or easy care synthetic fibres, so she had to use a good deal of "elbow grease" to ensure that the clothes were really clean. As you can imagine the men's working clothes would be particularly difficult to clean for they would be covered in coal dust and grime.

Although in the 1940's electric washing tubs were available, the money to purchase such items was often beyond the purse of many households. These new machines did no more than agitate the clothes which, whilst removing the drudgery of scrubbing, still had to be rinsed by hand and then wrung between two rollers which squeezed out the excess water. However, it was many years before the traditional mangle was replaced by a machine which both washed and dried the clothes.

If washday was fine, then the clothes could be hung out in the yard or lane. Row upon row of washing fluttered in the breeze, proclaiming to the world that the day was Monday.

The washing could not be left to another day for

Wringing and Possing c1910

Hanging out the washing

Swilling the channel near the
communal tap

The old bake oven

each day of the week was set aside for different tasks, so come rain or shine the washing had to be done. Therefore, in poor weather, the clothes were usually dried in front of the fire or the range, which was often the focal point of the house. This entailed hanging the laundry over wooden clothes horses and as a result the house became very hot and humid. Such days were often labelled "the devil's birthday".

It was a very strenuous day for once the clothes were dry they then had to be ironed. For many wives the flat iron was still popular despite the more labour saving versions being on the market. Many of the older wives preferred the flat iron and refused to change. Preparing to iron involved heating several flat irons on the fire to ensure that when one began to cool another was available. Once heated she had to remove the iron from the fire using a cloth to protect her hands from the heat. They then had to be wiped clean for they were often covered in soot. Many of the clothes were made from natural materials such as, cotton, which was particularly difficult to iron once dried. It was on washday that she also had to repair damaged clothes for new clothes were rarely purchased. Clothes were handed down from one generation to another, so had to last! The day often ended around midnight, only for the wife to rise again between 3/4 o'clock.

Families were often large and as mother finished looking after the needs of the working men there were often young children to cater for. They too needed breakfast and prepared for a day at school. Mother had little time to rest for the daily round of chores was just beginning.

Every day was a baking day. A great deal of bread was eaten, so the wife often baked daily and sometimes twice a day. This was done early on a morning before the men returned from their shift and the children from school. There were no school meals so the children returned each lunchtime or took sandwiches if the school was too far away.

Shopping was made easier with the introduction of the Co-operative Society and the following is a typical shopping list for one week:

2 stone flour
2lbs butter
1lb cheshire cheese
1lb margarine
4lbs sugar
1lb bacon
1lb currants
1lb towel soap
1 tin Nestle's milk
1 stone potatoes
2 doz match boxes
2lbs candles
2 tins boot polish
2 doz eggs
1/4lb tea
1lb rice
2 oz tobacco

The original cost of the items would have been 16/7d (in today's money 83p). This was about one third of a man's wages.

The women of colliery villages had an intense pride about their houses. Everything was kept neat and tidy, even to the point of only using some rooms for special occasions. They would scrub steps, wash the front lane and clean the backyard. Inside the house was cleaned everyday - the steel fender and brasses had to be polished,

ovens cleaned and, because the cutlery was often made from steel rather than stainless steel, they had to be cleaned on a knife board. At times the younger members of the family were given jobs to do to help their mother.

The responsibilities of the colliery wife were quite clear - she looked after every respect of the home and its occupants, looked after the wages and kept strict accounts. Her days were long and strenuous, and, as a result, she aged much more quickly than her present-day counterpart.

THORNLEY COLLIERY - A PERSONAL VIEW

From my sister's dining room I could see the wasteland spreading across the far hillside, the dark bruises of coal and slag hiding the workshops and offices of Thornley colliery, and throwing into relief the faded red and white of the houses.

Sunk in 1835, the colliery had its first trouble eight years later when 68 miners withdrew their labour. The dispute was about the stone content in tubs, and the men were charged with breaking their bond. They were sick of the bond, and were beginning to realise that their subjective conditions were not decreed by heaven.

Thornley was one of the cornerstones of the Durham Miners' Association, and the Lodge Banner decorated the platform on the first Gala. Mr A Cairns was for a short time, secretary of the young Association and another Thornley man, Mr John Jackson was a committee member in those days when miners were "after their reets".

Every time I look at the wasteland, I am taken back for a decade or more to the time when my father used to put on his pit clothes pick up his bait tin and made the long walk to the pit - through the cut by the vegetable plots and pigeon crees, past the girls' school over the eternal winter fields to the pit heaps, glowering, low browed in daylight but transformed by darkness into insubstantial shapes which played around the engine house where the old wheels grinned into the night. It was a soulless grin, born of the blackness of hell, and generations of pitmen have gone up and down in cages like beasts shuffling to and from some cavernous zoo.

There are three roads into the village. The mournful road from Ludworth creeps by the cemetery as if afraid of breaking the sleep of gravestones, pallid in the long grass. It climbs by the new Welfare Hall where miners pay their union, listen to the sonorous click of snooker balls and pass the easy hour in tobacco and talk.

● *The Colliery can never be the same* says Bill Dowding in these memories of his childhood days

It stops at the broken white line, deferring to the road from Wheatley Hill which twists from the grimed scarlet of the Catholic school over the bog of the gassy gutter, to stumble across a mis-shapen bridge by the banner front of the one-time Salvation Army Citadel and the old Hippodrome, where I used to go to the gaff. This road is credited to Peter Lee.

The pit and its trappings and flung lines curb the expanse of colliery housing on one side of the High Street but the village pushes away across the fields to Ludworth as if pursued. In the wings of the dwellings stand the worshipful pair of Methodist Churches, Rose Street and Bow Street, and I have happy memories of the singing hours spent in Guild and Endeavour meetings.

The focal point of the High Street for the youngsters at least, was Baldasera's Ice Cream parlour, where the hot tongue cooled in sweet whiteness and the feet drummed to the hurried blare of the juke box. Outside was the roaring of the long street, the black pit and the gassy gutter. Inside was sweetness and light.

The gutter was a geographical sore point. As a Wheatley Hillite I regarded it as being nearer to Thornley, and a walk down Thornley road when it was in smell was a shake of the head, a blowing of the nose and a quick passing.

The terraced houses of the lower half of the village were red faced, squat from much living and being lived in and they threw out their miscellany of kids, whippets and pinnied womenfolk for every passerby. The coal clay surface under the pit line oozed over the sleepers on wet days and crossing the line was a perilous business, as the tanky was always fussing up and down like an old pot bubbling and boiling for a cup of tea.

Living conditions in the 30's

The lines driven through the red ash hills to the neighbouring colliery were polished to a slipper sheen by the turning wheels of truculent little engines and clanking waggons. They were busy, busy days with not a thought of redundancy.

The only yawning part of the pit was the gates. They gawped at the old clock which had been idling in the Market Square since 1937, and right in front of the Police Station, at that. I had never seen anybody wind the clock but it kept pretty good time, and I often set my watch by it when sitting in the red United or the brown and yellow G and B waiting for the bus to resume the journey to Durham.

The miners would come with their peculiar gait, some of them with leggings binding their carves into the stiffkneed rejection, the bait tins tucked in the crook of the arm, the heavy boots thumping out a stoical acceptance of the

measure of their owners - solid, loyal, decent - as they beat upon the pavements, into the lamp cabin, the cage and in-bye for another shift at the coal.

From the pit, up the sprawling bank to the Roman Catholic Church, lay the prefabs, squatting pale blue away from the grey road. Behind them wormed the Hilly-howly and the hedgerows to Thornley Hall farm and the Trimdon road. Further up were the houses privileged with gardens, and the Half-way House where the first delegate meeting was held before the founding of the D.M.A. Before the inn was the dog track, and after it the long, dipping road to Signing Bank and the valleyed Cathedral of Durham.

Thornley Colliery, as I remember it. Now the wheels will stop, and the men will no longer blacken themselves in this local Calcutta, and the village - will it be categorised or given a new lease of life as it peers uncertainly into the seventies?

PETER LEE

● This brief biography of the life of Peter Lee is taken from *WINGATE* by W A Moyes published by The Wingate and District Community Association

Tom Lee brought his wife and family from Lancashire into County Durham about 1860. A hewer of great strength, he found no difficulty in gaining employment, and worked at Wingate until a disagreement with William Armstrong prompted him to move on to Cassop. As a result, the children rarely received any schooling, and by the time Peter Lee was 10 years old, he had had no formal education. In this illiterate state he became a pony driver, working ten hours a day at Littletown Colliery. By the time he was twenty one he had worked at fifteen different collieries, and this included periods of work at Wingate Grange. It was on one of these occasions that he realised his lack of education and the futility of the roughness of a miner's life.

The first step in his life of service was to become better educated, and he did this by attending night classes in Wingate and by travelling abroad. Peter Lee was in the United States for a year in 1886, and during his stay he managed to save sufficient money to return, which was more than most of his companions did. It was to Wingate he returned, and within three months was elected delegate to the Miner's Council. This brought him into contact with the well known leaders of the time. The strike of 1892 led to his appointment as checkweighman, but his activities did not endear him to the management, for there was no colliery house for him when he married Alice Thompson of Thornley. Unavoidably his public life gained him enemies among the men as well, and on more than one occasion fist fighting was resorted to with painful results for all concerned. Opposition and his wandering inclinations led him away from Wingate in 1896 to travel to South Africa.

On his return he found employment in Thornley, and then in the west of the county before being brought to Wheatley Hill with the invitation to become checkweighman. He quickly became Chairman of the Parish Council, the Rural District Council and the Co-Operative Society, and in addition became a local preacher.

It was in 1909 that Peter Lee became a County Councillor, and he represented an area which included Wingate. In 1919 the first Labour Council elected him as chairman. Born in Duffheap Row, Trimdon in 1864, he was now the civic leader of the County at the age of 55.

This post he combined with that of miners' agent, and he moved into Durham, the geographical centre of the area under his control.

His period of high county office coincided with many improvements, and not the least of these was his work for the Durham County Water Board, of which he was Chairman for sixteen years. The strikes of the twenties engaged all of his energy and application; in 1930 he was elected General Secretary of the Durham Miners' Association, and three years later, President of the Miners' Federation of Great Britain. In 1934 he was chairman of the International Miners' Conference in France, and this honour must surely be the summit of a miner's aspirations.

Peter Lee died on July 16th, 1935, and is buried at Wheatley Hill. His name lives on in the New Town which bears his name.

Plate 26. Opening of Wellfield A. J. Dawson Grammar School 1930.
Photograph loaned by the Headmaster.
Copyright reserved by the Northern Echo.
Left to right Ald. Bloomfield, Ald. Robson, Mr. Ingram, Mr. Crossland,
Mr. W. N. Smith, Mr. Wilkinson and Peter Lee.

Redhills, DMA Headquarters

LORD LONDONDERRY'S HARBOUR

● This unit by Don Miller outlines the development of Seaham Harbour

Lord Londonderry's predecessor at Seaham Hall, Sir Ralph Milbanke, had investigated the possibility of building a harbour at Seaham. Plans had been drawn up by William Chapman, an eminent local engineer. Milbanke did not proceed with the plan. Instead he sold his estates to Charles Stewart, later Lord Londonderry. Was Stewart's interest in the estates due to the potential for building a harbour?

Chapman's estimated cost for the harbour was £6060, later amended to £7000 and, in addition, £6000 for a protective pier. Against these costs had to be set the anticipated savings on the transport of coal from the pits in central Durham to the collier brigs. Using the River Wear costs were 3/3d (16p) per ton. Estimated costs using Seaham were 1/3d (6p) a considerable saving!

Lord Londonderry had some difficulty in finding supporters for the scheme which was described as *visionary and absurd*. He eventually decided to go ahead without support, going close to bankruptcy in the process.

Work commenced on 13th September 1828. Seeking much-needed publicity, Lord Londonderry arranged for the laying of a foundation stone on 28th November attended by 7000 people. Where did they come from? How did they get here? Apart from workmen's huts the only settlements within a mile were farms. In fact Lord Londonderry's seven year old son laid the foundation stone for the town's first house as part of the ceremony.

Phase one of the construction involved the North Dock. Today this area is freely accessibly to the general public. It is used exclusively by the fishing fleet.

Stone used in the building, obtained from a quarry at Penshaw, was brought in by horse and cart and, later, by three-men keel boats from the river Wear. Evidence remains of the coal-loading spouts. The entrance to the dock incorporated a rise and fall gate, opened at high tide.

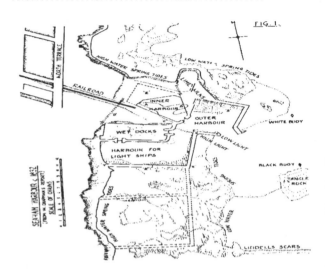

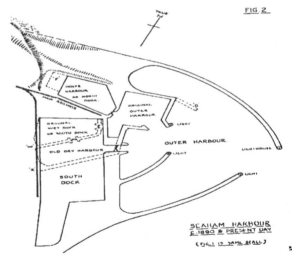

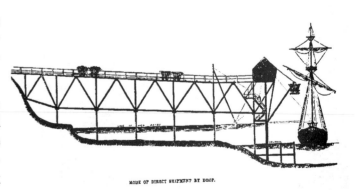

The first cargo of coal was shipped on 25 July 1831 in the Lord Seaham, a collier brig holding 300 tons.

Building the South Dock was undertaken at the same time, but was a more ambitious project. It is only possible to gain an impression of its structure from maps, engravings and old photographs. Major structural changes took place in 1905 when the present lock gates were built. This was to accommodate the larger steamships which had almost totally replaced the sailing ships which had first used the port. To make the harbour safer for the larger ships the outer piers were also added.

Further extension in the 1930s brought the harbour to its present state, although the concrete staiths from which the coal was loaded have now been demolished because of changes in cargoes and handling procedures. Some indication of the size of these can be experienced by looking at the remains, set into the cliffs on the west wall and clearly visible from Seaham Harbour Coastal Centre.

At the beginning of 1992, with coalmining almost at an end, what of the future of Seaham Harbour?

Visitors to Seaham Harbour Coastal Centre have the opportunity to investigate the past and present features of the harbour and the process of handling cargoes.

THE 1926 STRIKE
A PERSONAL EXPERIENCE

● This description of events at the time of the 1926 strike is from *OF MINING LIFE AND AAL ITS WAYS* by Ned Cowans

When the "great strike" came in 1926, I was chairman of Bewicke Main Lodge, having been elected in 1925. The Pelaw Main Collieries Federation Board had formed a "Council of Action" to deal with urgent matters affecting its members. The first job we accomplished was the establishment of soup kitchens in each area. The headquarters were at the Co-operation Hall, Birtley, and the Birtley Co-op Society were the bankers and were most helpful in allowing credit. Bread and meat were sent from here to the kitchens. At Bewicke Main the foreover-man's wash house was used to make the soup and as a distribution centre for rations to each family. There was a collecting committee and business people contributed food. Food was sent to old and sick people who could not collect it themselves.

It was reported to the Council of Action that lorry loads of coal were being transported through Birtley at night. We decided to arrange for pickets to prevent this. I was chosen as one of the leaders. We intercepted various lorries but none contained coal. We did have a laugh however when we stopped a car whose driver informed us that he was carrying ladies' underwear.

Next we stopped two large covered lorries. Out jumped Birtley Police Sergeant shouting, "Do you call this peaceful picketing putting obstacles on the road?" We knew nothing of this, and told him so. Then up went the covers on the lorries and out jumped forty policemen with drawn batons. There was a tremendous commotion. I had three stitches in my chin, and a dislocated shoulder. So much for peaceful picketing! We learnt later that another picket from the Betty pit had been putting obstacles on the road, and this had caused the police action. Next morning I was visited by the doctor and

the police. The doctor examined me, and I gave his report to the police. At a special court at Chester-le-Street, I was bound over for six months to keep the peace.

We had a meeting of the Local Miners' Federation where it was reported that the Birtley Co-operative Store, would allow vouchers to the value of £3 per member provided the lodge officials would sign as a guarantee to have this money deducted from the wages once the strike was settled. This was greatly appreciated and accepted by all lodges.

It was arranged that the General Secretary of the Miners' Federation of Great Britain, Mr. A. J. Cook should speak at Shadon's Hill. All lodges were invited to attend with bands and banners. I helped to carry him shoulder high on to the hill. He was a wonderful orator. His slogan was, "Not a penny off the pay, not a minute on the day". Thousands listened to him.

Mr. A J Cook

The strike, meanwhile, was not going too well for the miners. Breakaways were reported at many pits, two of these in the Birtley area. At a meeting at the Travellers Rest, Sheriff Hill, it was decided that we would visit the men concerned. Jim Esther, the Urpeth Miner's Delegate and I were given the Deckham area to cover. The first person we visited was one of Jim's relatives. The first thing I noticed on entering the house was a gun above the mantelpiece. Persuasion had no effect on this man. Eventually, he jumped up, reached for the gun, and told us to leave. We left!

At our next meeting there was very little progress to report, because in most cases the blacklegs would not open their doors to hear our pickets speak. We then decided to contact these breakaways as they left the pit. The police were taken unawares the first day we picketed at Ouston E pit. As the men left the pit, and entered the covered wagons which were to take them home, stones were showered on them from the nearby stone heap. They literally ran for their lives over the fields to Ouston, Pelton and Perkinsville. Others ran into the fireholes in the pit and then on to their homes at Pelton.

During the next week a special meeting of Delegates was held at Red Hills, Durham to discuss the members who had started, those still holding out and the prospects of continuing the strike. The reports were not good, and it seemed apparent that the end was not far away. Shortly afterwards instructions were sent out to the Lodges to meet their Colliery Managers to settle terms for resumption of work. We presented ourselves, two from each Lodge at the Mining Offices at Birtley. The agent of Pelaw Main Collieries however refused to meet any Federation Board. He said he would meet each lodge separately. We retired to discuss the situation. Whilst we were talking he came out and told us which pits were starting the following day, and that the men had to sign on immediately. The Federation Board officials could represent only their own collieries.

The representatives from the largest lodge Ouston E pit, went in first. Ben Oliver came out, and informed us that there was nothing to discuss; the settlement was already typed out for each pit.

1 All below ground workmen to work eight hours except for deputies and coal hewers who would work seven and a half hours.
2. A reduction in the percentage on basic wage of 21%
3. A reduction in the subsistence wage from seven shillings and six and a halfpence to six shillings and eight and a halfpence per shift.
4. All piece prices reduced.

At last it was our turn. We were reminded that Bewicke Main had only a short life. The cost of getting it into full production was hardly worthwhile. If there was any trouble it would be closed. I reminded him of a Federation agreement that workmen of Pelaw Main Collieries had priority over others. He said that he could employ whom he liked. Our argument continued about who should be selected first and he said, "You won't be one to be employed, because it is shifters we want to make a road into the face, and you are a coal hewer". "Fair enough" said I: "We won't always have our hand in the dog's mouth". We left.

One good agreement we obtained was for rent to be charged for those living in colliery houses, unable to obtain work at the pit. Rents would be allotted according to the size of the house. No evictions would take place. That night we had a Lodge Meeting. It was one of the fullest and roughest meetings we had ever held. Feelings ran very high when it was reported that some "blue eyed boys" had already signed on that day and were then at work in the pit. It was insisted upon that the meeting be adjourned whilst we all marched over to the pit for a show-down. I would not agree to this and reminded the meeting what those who were shouting for action now, were the very first to run away in a police baton charge, leaving just a few of us to stand our ground. This eased the tension a little.

Next morning we went to the Colliery Office. The undermanager told us that if our names were not on the sheet in the window he could not meet us. My name was not on the list.

THE MINER'S STRIKE 1984-85
ONE FAMILY'S EXPERIENCE

● An anonymous contribution

At the start of the strike there was a lot of confusion. The Coal Board's decision to close Cortonwood Pit in South Yorkshire was the spark which set the strike off, but there was not a mass meeting at my pit, where we made our decision to join in. When I went to work that night I was surprised to find the pit road full of pickets. I didn't recognise any of the pickets, they must have been from other areas, so I turned back. I reported to my union representatives; they said the strike was on, and we would meet to talk things over tomorrow. That's how it began. It took a long time for me to

It all began at Cortonwood

realise that the situation was hopeless and that we wouldn't win. It was like Liverpool v Hartlepool; Government v Miners. We had a young baby, and an older child and we were apprehensive about how long it would last. I did think about going back to work when things got tough but I'm glad that I didn't. Both our fathers had worked at the pit and they and other members of our family gave us tremendous support. I don't think I could have stayed out without their help.

We had a meeting in the Welfare Hall every day and we soon got to take no notice of the TV reports of what McGregor said or what Government Ministers stated. I gave my full support to the strike and went picketing to Fishburn, Philadelphia works and Redcar Steel works. I didn't go to Orgreave though and I'm glad I didn't after what happened there. I can honestly say that I had nothing to do with violence or hurling abuse at people. I didn't think that was right.

I saw things happen that should not have happened. My mam was very worried when she

knew I was going picketing because of what she saw on TV. She would not believe what I told her about some of the behaviour. Of course, not all police behaved badly as not all pickets did either. I was at Easington when they bussed in the man Wilkinson there were terrible scenes, the strength of feelings involved were not appreciated by those outside the industry.

When we were on picket duty we got £2 a day in county, £4 if we went to other areas. That is all the cash we got from the Union, but the Government assumed that we were getting £16 a week strike pay and cut our social security payments. We had a soup kitchen in the Welfare hall where the whole family could go for a hot meal each day. We got food parcels from Russia and French miners sent lots of presents for the bairns at Christmas. We had a great party that Christmas 1984. We made a great effort to see that the children had a good time. The union had money donated by people from all over the country and at the 1985 Gala there were quite a lot of support groups in the procession. I had to sell our car, camera and the video went back. I would take my lad down to the old mineral line where we could pick up coal. I went on my bike and pushed it back up with a sack of coal on the crossbar and him on the carry seat. I also went out logging, anything to burn in the grate was welcome. When I was picketing at Fishburn the security men told us we could have the coke which fell onto the road from the lorries. It seemed a bit dodgy to me but we brought a few sacks back home. There were some prosecutions for stealing coal off the pit stockpile and lots of court cases, some for violence. Some men lost their jobs! they were out of order with what they did, but I don't think they should have lost their job, its punishing a man twice for the same offence. I said we were lucky having such support from our parents and family. Single miners were the worst off, they had no social security and had to rely on handouts. Non miners often said "stick it out lads" but gave no other support to us. All talk ... no action!

When the strike ended we all formed up in the road and marched back behind our banner. All together, no matter what shift we were starting on. As we started off, a whole shift of men came out, I felt angry that they had gone back and got pay when we were out. Some had gone back before Christmas, BBCs we called them Back Before Christmas, they got a cash bonus for that. But some had only gone back a week before the strike ended.

Conditions in the pit were very bad. There was lots of water and machines were jammed into the face. One face was lost completely. I told my wife "expect me next week" as I did not know how long we would have to work to get things right.

This area stuck together pretty well throughout but there was some trouble at Murton and Seaham over VDM members. There were poor bonus payments at work too and I could see the writing on the wall and asked for redundancy. I got it two years later and now work out of the industry.

I am proud that I stuck it out to the bitter end. We got badges, those of us who stayed out. My mate said "look this cost us £14000". You know, Arthur Scargill was proved right over pit closures. But he seriously over-estimated the help we would get from the railwaymen, steelworkers and other unions. Money, yes, but practical support, no.

You know it wasn't all deadly serious we did have a few humorous moments.

My mate had short back and sides and one day we were at Redcar picketing when we were followed by three fellows, they thought he was an undercover policeman, he had some explaining to do, we had to call the Durham NUM man over to clear things up. We had a laugh over it afterwards. The same over an incident at Fishburn. As I have told you we had picked up coke from the road and we had it in sacks in the car. We were in the car parked up when a mini bus full of police arrived. My mate was really scared, it was his car you see, but they were all tired out and just stayed dozing in the van.

Arthur Scargill NUM President

DURHAM MINERS GALA -the Big Meeting

● Extract from "The Banner Book" by W.A.Moyes (published 1974 by Frank Graham)

Through the old city streets there flows a tide
Of men and women marching side by side,
Love and happiness shining in their eyes
Whilst overhead their own Lodge banner flies.
                    Anon

Suddenly we can hear the drums
Banging down the street;
And the brassy roaring of the bands,
And the rustle of marching feet,
And, with steadfast hands to hold them high
The silken banners go swaying by.
Mary Wilson's Selected Poems, (Hutchinson & Co.)

Aa divvnent knaa what it is. Ye come here and get pushed about and squeezed in the crowds and yet aa wadn't miss it for worlds. So spoke a miner who had come to Durham to get his 'reets'. *We dinnat knaa what they are* he said, *but we've come to get them.*

Many writers of prose and poetry, well known or anonymous, talented or with more limited powers of expression, have been inspired by the Big Meeting but Prof. E. Allen says "There is too much for one writer to discern and express, from the first snatch of the music of a band as it enters the city early in the morning, to 'Gresford', to the political speeches, to the dancing in the streets, to the throng of folk as they pack the narrow streets, to the uninhibited drinking that starts early and goes on late, to the service in the Cathedral and the crepe upon the banners of those lodges which have suffered fatal accidents since the last Gala, to the final scenes of the late evening. It is a canvas: a full canvas: a medieval canvas - a Breughel in modern dress; yet it is more than a canvas, for there is noise, laughter, music and talk."

Inspiration can be of many sorts. The great occasion and the sight of the huge crowd, sub-divided into groups with local loyalties but united in the main purpose, has been a favourite subject for speakers. Hugh Dalton has no doubt about this as a political training ground and he urged aspiring politicians to come and see the Gala in order to draw inspiration (his word) from the miners and their banners. James Callaghan claimed in 1963 that the greatest occasion and greatest privilege that could be offered to any Labour M.P. was to come to Durham and see the scene as the bands and banners and members of the Lodges go by. Michael Foot echoed the sentiments 'I don't believe there is any more wonderful sight than to see the bands playing and the banners blowing through the city of Durham. The banners of the Durham Miners' Gala are history on tapestry - a history of which everyone in the Labour movement is proud.'

The morn is wor Big Meetin' day,
The grandest day of all.
The Banner lifts at 8 o'clock
Ootside the Miners' Hall.
Wor lass and bairns'll all be there
And Granny in her shaal.
We'll march through Durham's coggly streets
To music from wor Band,
Wi' croods in front and croods ahint
And croods on eether hand.
And on wor backs'll be the bairns,
The bonniest in the land.
The speakin' starts at 12 o'clock;
We'll hear Clem Attlee's pattor,
He'll talk aboot the Government
Or some such vital mattor.
And if he disn't please us, why
We'll hoy him in the wattor.
And when the speechifyin's done,
And all the Nobs have went,
We'll find a seat and hev wor bait,
In the aad Esh Winnin' Tent,
Then join the folks aroond the Shows
That's all on pleasure bent.
Back in the toon we'll tak a drink
And flirt wi' all the lasses,
And spare a word for all we meet,
All kinds, all creeds, all classes.
But canny on, me bonny lads,
And divven't smash the glasses!
And as the darkness comes to end
This best of all good neets,
We'll climb the hill and leave behind
The friendly, homely streets,
And though we're tired and footsore, why
At least we've had wor reets!

Sam Watson was fond of saying of the Gala that there was nothing like it in the world. Speaking of the gathering of 300,000 people in 1952 he said "No regimentation, no Police Officers with guns, no harsh commands - just the best disorganised organisation that can be seen anywhere." Sid Chaplin made the same point when he said "There are no marshals, nor are any needed." But the truth of the matter is that there is control and it is mainly by means of the banners. In exactly the same way as Richard Fynes described the Black Fell Meeting of 1832 'The meeting then broke up, the men formed under their respective banners and left the place of meeting in a most peaceable manner' so the banners are used as markers. The sound of the band and the sight of the banner are signals in the whole chain of action throughout the day.

It has been said that no great literary account has ever been written about the Durham Miners' Gala. Novels which involve the Big Meeting don't really count and it seems that other writers have concentrated on one or other aspect of the Day. Very few detailed essays appear in print though there are several writers of mining subjects who have included the subject in their larger work. Anthony Greenwood wrote a succinct account (about 1,600 words) of the Big Meeting in 1959. Because the motive was political, the emphasis is on workers' rights, workers' freedom, the fight against exploitation, the heroes of 'our Movement' and 'the greatness of a Movement which hundreds of thousands of humbler men and women struggled and suffered to create'.

"One by one the Lodges march in from the banks of the coaly Tyne, from the mouth of the Wear, from the villages crouching under slag heaps - they stream into the city: men and women of fierce pride and dignity of bearing, able to doff the helmet of danger and the fear of the pit for one day of rich embroidery." writes Bill Dowding and one wonders whether a purely political gathering would gain such a following. The organiser of any political meeting would count himself fortunate if this were so.

The sequence of the day's events is continued by Sid Chaplin: "The narrow streets from Framwellgate to Elvet fill with people. One by one representatives of every colliery in the county pass in procession. Each Lodge - or branch - marches under its own banner, and is 'played in' by its own band. The banners are great squares of silk depicting scenes from the miners' struggle, or bearing portraits of their leaders. From some flutters a length of crepe - a sign that one man who marched last year has fallen in action underground. As works of art these banners may be negligible, but their combined effect is hypnotic.

The procession is not organised. There are no marshals, nor are any needed. Even during the ugly days of strike and depression the note of good humour was never lost. The banners are carried over the twelfth-century bridges to the race-course where a great picnic takes place around the platforms."

According to Peter White, the author of 'Portrait of County Durham' (Hale 1967) the best way to see Gala Day is to take part in it by joining one of the Lodge parties soon after breakfast as it unfurls its banner, marshals the band and marches to the city."The drum strikes up, the wind billows the banner, and the gaily-dressed teenagers dance before it, arm in arm, chanting the name of the pit......"

"One by one, the banners are set up round the huge field, and the bandsmen's abandoned instruments heaped beneath them and left in the care of old blue-scarred pitmen." "At the racecourse, the reception committee has provided far more than the refreshment tent, the lost children's hut, and the temporary toilet facilities. Dozens of roundabouts and side shows.... balloons dance on strings above itinerant hawkers.... Riverside stalls offer everything from toffee apples to tomatoes "Television cameras film leaders of Government or Opposition.... Five thousand or more, the crowd listens, as the fairground Ferris Wheel goes round and round and the distant midgets on the cathedral tower look down on this swarming ant hill..."

"The political speakers preach to the converted and use the occasion to stamp out their philosophy without harassment and heckling of a less biased audience. The list of speakers over the century reads like a left wing role of honour, a chronicle of the Labour Movement. Thomas Burt, Alexander Mac-Donald, Charles Bradlaugh, Joseph Arch, Ben Pickard, J. Havelock Wilson, Tom Mann, J. Keir Hardie and George Lansbury. Then Ramsay MacDonald, Ellen Wilkinson, Ernest Bevin, A.J.Cook. In the late forties, Attlee, Bevan, Dalton, Morrison, Shawcross, Cripps and more recently, Harold Wilson, Michael Foot Anthony Wedgewood Benn and Neil Kinnock."

"The political platform, through the modern media of communication, is a way of speaking to the nation and it is often used with skill for this purpose."

Families sit on the grass all over the course eating the home made fare prepared by the women of the household and watching out for old friends who have moved to other collieries but who are certain to return to the racecourse for the Big Meeting. But the emphasis is not solely on feasting unless it includes that of the Spirit. As Jack Lawson eloquently says of the crowd on the racecourse "Wherever they are, Whatever they are doing, the gala spirit manifests itself. It is the day of the year and old Durham is theirs. They have marched through the city once a year. Their fathers have done it before them. From boyhood and girlhood they had heard this day spoken of in the home as though it was a sacred day - withall a day of rejoicing - and this city is their Mecca."

The Unity is fostered when the mighty of the land and the common folk unite in listening to the playing of Gresford. Gresford is the miners' special hymn written in 1936 by Robert Saint, a Hebburn miner, commemorating the disaster at the pit of that name in North Wales. The chosen bands strike up the tune. The late John McCutcheon tells the story "An incredible quiet possesses and enfolds the vast multitude like a mantle of silence. Hushed for a time are the other familiar sounds of the gala gathering..... Odd details catch the eye during the great silence - the cameramen freeze with a pose of inaction; a bath of multi-coloured balloons, no longer earthbound, soar upwards until but a speck in the faraway blue; a row of tall poplars in full foliage stand sentinal in the College grounds across the river.

At the end of the racecourse meeting many people move towards the Cathedral. Since 1897 the religious service there has been one of the main attractions for those whose mood has been shaped by the solemn playing of the massed bands. Lodges with bands and banners have been selected to march up Owengate onto Palace Green and into that magnificent building.

The Cathedral is packed full. "This audience listens now with its heart. Time, epochs and economics are forgotten for they seek what the soul of man has sought in all ages and all lands and always will seek - that which satisfies the spirit."

Jack Lawson's stirring description continues: "I looked on the faces of the men and women around me, seeing the eager light in their eyes and the features softened by the influence of the place. I thought of their work, their courage, their love of home and the patient sacrifice with which they were building up organisations for the winning of economic freedom; I thought of all the way this people had come - and victory over the grim things of our life seemed certain."

Bill Dowding expounds. "The bands have gone, the last banner waving a nostalgic farewell some hours ago. The streets are empty, only the pubs and the shows have custom and clamour. Paper blows across the racecourse and frisks over empty bottles where their contents were guzzled. Some have tasted the day to the full in the only way they know how and they lie on the pavement, or sit, head in hands, the great experience aching through what consciousness they have. A boy kicks at an empty can. The grey city prepares for the darkness and for sleep."

THE DURHAM MINERS' ASSOCIATION

Milestones from NUM records

1869 November 20th First meeting in Market Hotel, Durham

1870 December 3rd First A.G.M. Durham Miners' Association

1871 August 12th First Annual Gala at Wharton Park

1872 February 17th Abolition of the yearly bond

1876 June 3rd Opening of Miners' Hall in North Road Durham

1885 November W. Crawford (mid Durham) and J. Wilson (Houghton-le-Spring) first members of Parliament from D.M.A.

1897 First Cathedral Service for Gala Day

1899 June 1st Aged Miners' Homes opened Haswell Moor

1908 Durham joined the Miners' Federation

1909 February 16th West Stanley disaster 168 lives lost

1911 Coal Mines Regulation Act

1912 Minimum Wage Act passed in Parliament following a strike End of fortnightly pay - weekly pay begins

1915 Opening of new Miners' Hall at Redhills

1917 War wage granted

1919 Coal Commission commenced (Lord Sankey) Peter Lee elected agent D.M.A.

1920 June 18th Houses Rent and Fire Coal Agreement Rent = 10d per shift (4p) Coal Allowance 12 - 15 tons per family for year

1921 March Wage for age agreement for boys both underground and on surface April 1st Great Lock Out following the ending of the Wartime control over mines

1924 Subsistance wage for low paid day wage men fixed at 7 shillings and sixpence per shift (37p)

1926 National Stoppage May - November (lockout) miners have to accept (i) reduction in wages (ii) increase in hours

1927 First pit head baths opened at Boldon

1930 July Seven and a half hour shift in Coal Mines Act

1935 June 16th Death of Peter Lee

1936 July 1st Election of Sam Watson as agent

1938 April 19th Holidays with pay agreement

1939 War

1943 December Government direct youth into coal mining, Bevin Boys

1945 Formation of National Union of Mineworkers

1946 Payment for statutory holidays (Bank Holidays)

1947 Coal industry nationalised

1951 May Easington Colliery disaster 83 lives lost

1951 Miners head industrial workers earnings league

1952 Mineworkers' pension scheme inaugurated

1958 Sick pay scheme

1960 With increasing numbers of pit closures N.U.M. ask for (i) redundancy pay (ii) alternative industries in mining areas (iii) cuts in open cast works (iv) co-ordinated fuel policy

1961 Opening Sam Watson Rest Home for Miners' Wives at Richmond.

1962 Inter Coalfield Transfer Scheme. Miners leave contracting Durham Coalfield for Yorkshire and Nottinghamshire where pits need workers

1968 Redundancy payments scheme begins

1970 Minimum wage demand £21 pw underground, £20 surface workers, Coal imports begin after lapse of 12 years

1972 Jan. - Feb. National miners' strike January 8th - February 28th September Plan for coal

1973 November Overtime ban begins Government call "State of Emergency" December Power cuts Three day week working throughout Britain

1974 February 9th Strike begins February 28th General election results in defeat of Edward Heath March 6th Agreement reached on new pay and conditions package. March 10th Strike ends

1974 November Dawdon gets world's first tunnelling machine at a cost of £1/2 million

1975 April Earnings related pension scheme starts October First North Sea Oil pumped to Teesside

1976 August Coal Board offers most of its houses for sale to tenants

1977 Early retirement scheme begins

1981 Britain produces cheapest deep mined coal in Europe

1983 July 16th Centenary Gala

1984 March 14th Strike against pit closures begins

1985 March 5th Strike ends

1986 Horden Colliery closes

1991 Dawdon and Murton Collieries close.

1993 Vane Tempest closed. The three remaining pits mothballed. These are the last pits in Co.Durham

NORTHUMBERLAND & DURHAM MINERS'
ESTABLISHED JUNE 7 1862

PERMANENT RELIEF FUND

BENEVOLENCE UNITED WITH PRUDENCE IN THE RELIEF OF DISTRESS.

This is to Certify that *Christopher Bell*

South Hetton is enrolled a Member of the above Fund

Witness our hand this the *Eleventh* day of *July* 186

Instructions for claiming Compensation for Accidents.

1.—Should any member receive any accident, however slight, while following his employment, he ought to report the same to the first official he meets before leaving the mine. Should no official be found, the accident must be reported as soon as he arrives at bank.

2.—If a person is of work one week on account of an accident, he shall be paid one week's smart money. If off work one week, but less than two, he shall be paid one week's smart money, the odd days over the week shall he paid for as compensation. If off work two clear weeks, his compensation shall be paid from the day of accident.

3.—Compensation is now paid for the following diseases: Beat-hand, Beat-knee, Beat-elbow, Straining of the wrist joint and tendon sheaths, Compressed air illness or its sequel, Glanders, from handling carcases of animal suffering from glanders, Nystagmus, which is irregular or twitching movement of eyeballs, Miner's Worm Ankylostomiasis,.

Anyone suffering from any of the diseases must apply to the Certifying Surgeon for the district, who is appointed by the Government, and who at present is Dr. Oliver Connor.

NOTE.—Under Rule 45 members must pay 4d. per fortnight to insure themselves for the Death Benefits if otherwise exempt under Rule 44.

Big Pay.
DURHAM MINERS'
ASSOCIATION
AND
BENEFIT SOCIETY.

East Hetton Lodge.

Mr. ....

No. ....

Contributions taken at Davy Lamp every Friday from 2-30 till 3-30, and from 5 till 8 p.m., at Quarrington Hill.

Any member allowing his contributions, levies, and fines to run eight weeks in arrears shall have no claim on the funds, and will be suspended from all benefits until all arrears are paid; and for the period of one month after such arrears have been paid.

MATTHEW TATE. Finan. al Secretary,
20, Council Board, Davy Lamp, Kelloe.

The Secretary will not be accountable for any money unless paid at the desk.

Veitch and Sons, Ltd., Printers, &c., Durham.

DON'T GO DOWN THE MINE DAD

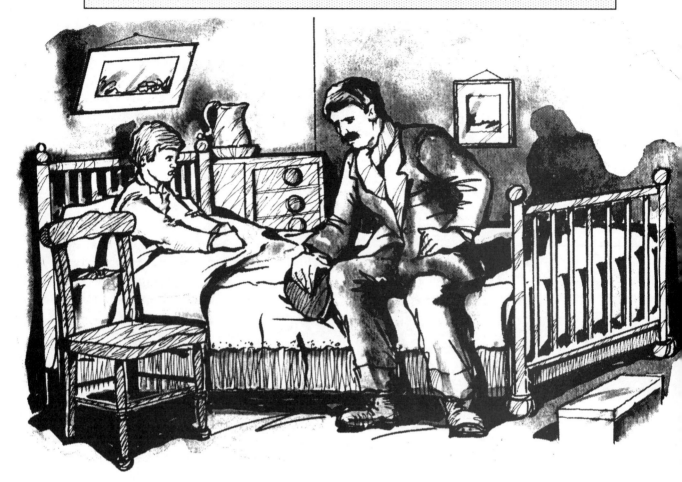

1.
A miner was leaving his home for his work,
When he heard his little child scream;
He went to his bedside, his little white face,
"Oh, Daddy, I've had such a dream:
I dreamt that I saw the pit all afire,
And men struggled hard for their lives;
The scene it then changed, and the top of the mine
Was surrounded by sweethearts and wives."

CHORUS

"Don't go down the mine, Dad,
Dreams very often come true;
Daddy, you know it would break my heart
If anything happened to you;
Just go and tell my dream to your mates,
And as true as the stars that shine,
Something is going to happen today.
Dear Daddy, don't go down the mine!"

2.
The miner, a man with a heart good and kind,
Sat by the side of his son:
He said: "It's my living, I can't stay away,
For duty, my lad, must be done."
The little one look'd up, and sadly he said:
"Oh, please stay today with me , Dad!"
But as the brave miner went forth to his work,
He heard his little lad cry!

CHORUS

3.
Whilst waiting his turn with his mates to descend
He could not banish his fears;
He return'd home again to his wife and his child,
These words seem'd to ring through his ears,
And ere the day ended, the pit was on fire,
When a score of brave men lost their lives;
He thanked God above for the dream his child had,
As once more the little one cried -

CHORUS

● Information on the Trimdon Grange and Fishburn disasters collected by Enid Williams and C Gibson. Seaham explosion from *Troubled Seams* by J McCutcheon.

SOME DISASTERS AND THEIR MEMORIALS

The Trimdon Grange Disaster is still remembered by both young and old in the Trimdon area and throughout the County of Durham.

The explosion took place at Trimdon Grange Mine on Thursday, 16th February, 1882. 93 men and boys went down the mine on the morning of that sunny and unseasonally warm February day. At 2.30 p.m. an ominous sound was heard, rather like the sound of a boiler exploding. As people looked towards the mouth of the pit, smoke and ashes were seen rising from the Harvey shaft. The news spread quickly and people hurried to the mine. Offerings of help came in from all around, from miners, engineers and surgeons. Men volunteered to enter the mine to assess the extent of the damage and to bring out the survivors, if there were any.

Of the 93 who had gone down that morning only 26 were brought out alive. Nine of these were saved by one Jacob Soulsby senior, a miner for many years, who through presence of mind kept them out of danger. Sadly, Mr. Soulsby's son, also named Jacob died. He was 27 years old.

The last survivor was brought up shortly after 9 o'clock on the evening of the 16th and it was felt that those left could not possibly have survived the very destructive explosion.

Work continued day and night to bring out the dead, the last body being recovered early on the following Monday morning. It is thought that all the dead died within minutes of the explosion and that they could not have suffered for long. One man, John Errington, was found with a boy on each arm and another laid across him. He had clearly been trying to save them, and had, himself, perished.

Many of the victims were only boys. Out of 68 who perished as a result of the explosion, 31 were under 21 years of age. Of this 31, eight were only 13 years old.

One of the survivors, Peter Brown, was horrifically burnt and, after great suffering, died of his injuries on the following Tuesday, 21st February.

Those who died did not only come from Trimdon but from the neighbouring villages of Kelloe, Cassop-cum-Quarrington and Shadforth. where they are buried.

The effect of the explosion was not just confined to Trimdon Grange mine but was felt further afield because the deadly gas had forced its way into the nearby Kelloe Pit through a connecting passage and miners there had to flee for their lives. Six men died in the Kelloe Pit. Some of them, including the Manager, Mr H C Schier, died while trying to open a way through to the Trimdon Grange Mine. Mr Schier, aged 23, was buried at Croxdale.

Immediately after the explosion the following poem was written by pitman/poet Thomas Armstrong.

THE TRIMDON GRANGE EXPLOSION

Words by Thomas Armstrong, pitman-poet, written in 1882, immediately after the explosion. Performed by Bob Fox at the Trimdons Festival, September 17th 1988. This poem has been set to music and is performed regularly in Folk Clubs.

This version is substantially the same as that noted by A.L. Lloyd in 1951.Originally set to the tune of Go and Leave Me If You Wish It. (The Cottage By the Sea).

Oh, let's not think of tomorrow lest we disappointed be.
Our joys may turn to sorrow as we all may daily see.
Today we're strong and healthy, but tomorrow comes a change,
As we may see from the explosion that's occurred at Trimdon Grange.
Men and boys set out that morning for to earn their daily bread,
Not thinking that by evening they'd be numbered with the dead.
Let's think of Mrs. Burnett, once had sons but now has none -
By the Trimdon Grange explosion, Joseph, George and James have gone.
February left behind it what will never be forgot;
Weeping widows, helpless children may be found in many a cot.
They ask if father's left them, and the mother hangs her head,
With a weeping widow's feelings, tells the child its father's dead.
God protect the lonely widow and raise up each drooping head;
Be a father to the orphans, do not let them cry for bread.
Death will pay us all a visit. They have only gone before,
And we'll meet the Trimdon victims where explosions are no more.

Mrs. Burnett's sons, Joseph 23, George 19 and James 17, who are immortalised in the poem, are buried in Trimdon Village cemetery where there is a very impressive memorial to the dead. The cemetery is situated at the east end of the village. The memorial has recently been restored with the names and ages of those buried there carved on new stones as the old stones were badly eroded.

In Trimdon Grange there is a memorial to all 74 who died. This was made from one of the actual pit top wheels kept when the pit top workings were dismantled following its closure in 1968.

Two further memorials exist in Trimdon Grange. These are situated in St. Alban's Church and are to commemorate those who died for their Country during the First and Second World Wars.

FISHBURN

Fishburn pit was sunk in 1912, opening in 1913. Unlike Trimdon Grange mine there were no official disasters at Fishburn but nevertheless tragedies continually occurred. The first fatal accident at Fishburn happened on 27th November 1921 to J.G. Westgarth, a hewer, aged 24. The last one occurred on 30th April 1971 involving B. Barnes, a power loader, aged 45.

In all, 57 men and boys, ages ranging from 15 to 64, died in the mine, each and every one leaving loved ones to mourn their loss.

The mine itself was not without its troubles. Flooding forced its closure in 1919 and it did not re-open until 1922. The pit flooded again on 10th December 1968. Even with the use of modern equipment it still took 3 weeks to clear.

The mine finally closed in 1973 to the relief of most people in the village.

In the close-knit communities existing because of the mines each fatal accident affected the whole village. There were few households which did not have at least one member working down the mine. News of such a death spread rapidly through the village. Whispers of "Someone has been killed in the mine" must have brought feelings of dread to every wife, mother, sister and daughter. What thoughts went through the minds of everyone can only be imagined. Fear for loved ones, hope, relief that this time it was someone else, despair, compassion for those closely affected. These must surely have been some of them.

One such incident occurred on 21st March 1949. Mrs. Ivy Hicklin, a young woman at the time, was a frequent visitor to the house of Mr and Mrs Nuttall. Mrs Hicklin heard a rumour in the village that Mr Nutall had been killed in the mine. Fearing the worst and not wanting to believe what she had heard she ran all the way to the Nutall house and was faced with the terrible truth. Mr Nutall was dead. She still recalls the horror and distress of that day.

Men were also affected. Mr Draycott remembers that day with sadness. Mr Nuttall had been well-liked by young and old in Fishburn. He was always friendly and pleasant. He always had sweets to give to children he met. No worries here about taking sweets from strangers. Over the years Mr Draycott has lost several friends and workmates to pit accidents.

There was no "memorial" for the 57 men and boys killed in Fishburn except in the minds of the survivors of the mine until the publication of "Further Fishburn Folklore" where, inside the front and back covers, there is a list, giving the dates of the accidents, the names and ages of the victims, and the jobs they were employed to do. This list covers all who died during the 60 years the mine was open. Every coal mine in the country must have a similar list.

There is one official memorial in Fishburn. This is in the church and commemorates the 8 men who died during the Second World War.

There is an ongoing exhibition of war memorabilia in the Fishburn Working Mens' Club.

Hero of the coalface

WILLIAM Younger, who has died aged 83, was the last of four County Durham miners venerated for their heroism in the Louisa colliery disaster of 1947. Risking explosions and gas so poisonous that a canary lowered to test levels died within a minute, they entirely disregarded their own safety and were all awarded the Edward Medal, a civilian equivalent of the Victoria Cross.

Younger was also the last surviving winner of the EM, which was withdrawn in 1971 when holders were given the option of exchanging it with the better-known George Cross. Younger took the opportunity, and gave his Edward Medal to the Beamish industrial museum, where accounts of disasters like the Louisa tragedy still quieten fresh generations.

The old section of the pit, at South Moor near Stanley, exploded on August 22, 1947, coal dust and firedamp (a volatile mixture of methane, nitrogen and carbon dioxide) igniting and wrecking the seam's main working face. Nineteen of the 24 miners in the narrow roadway were killed instantly, and procedure would have encouraged the rapid return to the surface of all others, with further explosions probable.

Instead, Younger made carefully for the shattered face, easing his way past derailed coaltubs and buckled props with two fellow-deputies, Harry Robinson and Joseph Shanley. Gently and slowly, taking care to avoid the least movement which could trigger an explosion, they moved the five injured survivors to a drift where they had found a slight current of tolerable air.

The operation, joined by an overman John Hutchinson, who came down from the pithead, took nearly two hours and two of the injured men later died in hospital. But the other three survived and their rescuers' citation referred to "circumstances and conditions which would have tested the courage and fortitude of the bravest and strongest".

The episode caught the public's imagination, with its elements of courage, back-breaking work and comradeship — traditionally associated with miners and partly responsible for the wave of national feeling over pit closures last autumn. Typically, Younger put up with all the fuss good-humouredly, before going back underground and retiring only in 1969. His safety work as a deputy paralleled long voluntary service in the St John Ambulance Brigade, which awarded him its long service medal with two bars.

Like Harry Robinson, who died in 1970 after a quiet retirement, Younger lived modestly in County Durham, although he was delighted to receive the Queen's Silver Jubilee medal in 1977.

The man who left elementary school at the age of 12 would have been tickled to know that his obituary appeared in national newspapers alongside those of the Chief Justice of Nigeria and Brian Inglis.

Martin Wainwright

William Younger, GC, born South Moor, Co. Durham, March 24, 1909; died Consett, Co. Durham, February 6, 1993.

The Guardian published this article in early 1993.

THE LOW PIT. SEAHAM (NOS. 1 & 2 PIT SHAFTS)

SEAHAM

A series of explosions occurring in the early years of mining at Seaham Colliery, culminating in one of the most serious explosions in terms of loss or life.

12 August 1845 Sinking commenced at Seaton Colliery, known as the High Pit.

13 April 1849 Sinking commenced at Seaham Colliery, known as the Low Pit and about 150 metres away.

1852

Explosion No. 1

Explosion No. 2

Explosion No. 3: 6 lives lost, youngest 10 years

1864   Explosion No. 4: 2 lives lost.

1864, November Amalgamation of High and Low Pits to form Seaham Colliery, known as the "Nicky-Nack", or just the "Nack"

1871   Explosion No. 5: 26 lives lost, youngest 13 years

1872   Explosion No. 6

1880   Explosion No. 7: 164 lives lost; youngest 14 years

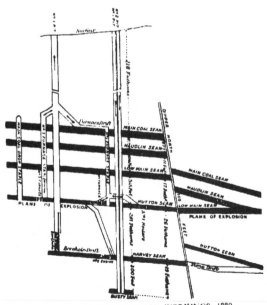

SECTION
Shewing the position of the
SHAFTS SEAMS FAULTS DRIFTS &c
AT
SEAHAM COLLIERY
SEPT 8TH 1880.

PLAN OF SEAHAM COLLIERY WORKINGS. 1880
From "Explosions in Coal Mines" by W. N. & J. B. Atkinson, 1886.
PHOTO BY J. C. CURRY, SEAHAM

Enquiries into Causes of Explosions

Explosion No. 3: Igniting of fire damp by the flame of a candle used to provide light for the miners.

Explosion No. 5: Probably a shot-firing, to loosen coal, but not confirmed by the inquest.

Explosion No. 7: The inquest was inconclusive. There were two conflicting theories:

1. Gas released by a fall of stone, and ignited by flame from a safety lamp.

2. Shot-firing

Whatever the cause of this explosion, 164 men and boys lost their lives.

Background Information

1. The explosion occurred at 2.20 am on Wednesday 8th September.

2. The explosion was on the eve of Seaham's Annual Flower Show, held at Seaham Hall and an important event in the social calendar.

3. One of the survivors of the 1871 explosion, whose son was killed then, died in the 1880 disaster.

4. Only five men survived, one of whom was experiencing being underground during an explosion for the fifth time!

5. Two lucky people: One miner slept in, missing his shift. Another miner who went underground, was unwell and left the pit, arriving "at bank" (on the surface) just two minutes before the explosion.

Underground not everyone died instantaneously. Some of those trapped left messages.

A miner who was able to communicate with rescuers, and who could have been saved died because he insisted on staying to comfort an injured lad.

Found chalked on a plank were the words:

"We have been praying to God" and "The Lord has been with us. We are all ready for heaven".

This message was scratched on to the surface of a metal water bottle:

Dear Margaret

There was 40 of us altogether at 7 am. Some was singing hymns but my thoughts was on my little Michael that him and I would meet in heaven at the same time. Oh Dear wife, God save you and the children, and pray for me ... Dear wife, Farewell. My last thoughts are about you and the children. Be sure and learn the children to pray for me. Oh what an awful position we are in!''

"Little Michael" died the same day.

This one of many explosions and other accidents in which miners have died. Their lasting memorials are in many places. Those who died in the two major disasters at Seaham are commemorated in a Garden of Remembrance in Christ Church churchyard, just across the road from the Nicky-Nack. All miners killed in Durham pits are remembered in the Miners' Memorial on the south side of the nave in Durham Cathedral.

The victims of the Easington and Eppleton Colliery explosions 1951. From Mostly Mining, Original i
NUM Headquarters Redhills

The disaster at the Burns Pit in 1909, the greatest recorded calamity on the Durham
Coalfield, cost West Stanley 168 lives.

PIT TALK

A mine of information

CONTENTS

MINING TERMS

● These mining terms were collated by D Rendle, Headteacher at Edmondsley Junior School, from *Practical Coal Mining for Miners* by M D Virtue & Co.

Abutment. An area of unworked coal or of consolidated waste bounding a working area.

Adit. A more or less horizontal entrance to a mine.

Afterdamp. Carbon Monoxide.

Andre. A direction of coal face roughly half-way between the main (bord) and secondary (end) cleavages; "on the cross".

Arrow. A thin metal peg, used by surveyors.

Back ripping. Ripping other than that near the coal face.

Back-bye. Any kind of operation in a mine not immediately concerned with production or transport; literally work behind the face; repairs to roads.

Back-shift. The afternoon or night shift; any shift which does not fill coal or is not the main coal-production shift.

Back-stay. Cow.

Back work. Back-bye.

Backing deal. Planks placed behind roof and side supports of roads or behind temporary lining rings in sinking shafts to prevent pieces of loose rock and coal falling away.

Baff week. Miners were paid fortnightly, this was the week without a pay day.

Balk. A beam, baulk, bar of timber.

Bank. The colliery surface near the shaft and at the level from which the cages are loaded and unloaded.

Banksman. The person in charge of the shaft and cage or skip at the surface of the colliery.

Bar. A strap or beam used to support the roof between two props or other supports.

Baulk. A beam of wood.

Beam. A bar or straight girder used to support a span of roof between two support props or walls.

Big Landing. An underground junction point where full tubs were coupled into 'sets'.

Binder. A wood or metal guide on a haulage road bend or curve.

Blackdamp. A gas which puts flame-lamps out; choke damp; stythe.

Bodger. Lever, tommy-bar, poker.

Booster. A machine helping another machine.

Bord. The main cleavage or cleat in coal seams.

Bordway. A road at right angles to the main cleat. A road with solid coal sides.

Bord-and-pillar. One of the pillar methods of working.

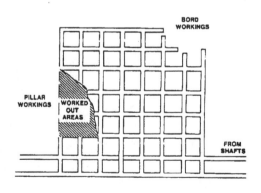

Plan view of bord and pillar workings

Bowk. Bucket; kibble; hoppit used in sinking.

Box. Tub; waggon; tram; corve; hutch.

Brace. To strengthen with a strap.

Brasses. Iron pyrites

Brattice. A ventilation partition.

Brattice-cloth. Cloth used for brattices or doors.

Brow. Hill or bank.

Bucket. Hoppit - see Bowk.

Buddy. Mate, 'Marra', partner.

Builder. Packer; a stone suitable for a pack wall.

Bump. A noise caused by a break in the roof underground. The actual movement due to the break. A sudden floor uplift due to a break in the floor.

Buttock. A corner formed by two coal faces more or less at right angles.

Buttons. Scars on miner's back, caused by catching on roof.

Byework, Bywork. Back work; datalwork; day work; day-wagework.

Byeworker. Byworker. Dataller; repairer; day-wage repair worker.

Camber. A beam or girder bent like a bow.

Canch. Stone removed from the roof and floor of the roads to make them tub height.

Cap. Lid, a piece of wood placed at the top of a prop. The coloured flame in a safety lamp.

Car. A mine wagon.

Cavilling. Drawing lots for working areas.

Cave. To allow the roof to fall.

Check. Token, tally, motty.

Checkweighman. Union official, checked the weight of each tub as it came out of the mine.

Chock. A roof support made of interlaced horizontal pieces; a stack, cog.

Chokedamp. Blackdamp.

Chum. Empty tub.

Clack. Automatic valve.

Clam. A clip; a haulage clip; an appliance for attaching mine cars to a rope.

Cleat, Cleavage. The Plane more or less at right angles to the roof and floor of a seam along which the coal tends to easily split. The main cleavage is called the 'bord' or 'face', secondary cleavage planes are called ENDS.

Clevis. A shackle for coupling and uncoupling the links in chains in haulage winding etc.

Clip. Clam.

Cockering. Herring-bone supports.

Collier. An experienced coal-getter.

Corve. Tub, tram, mine wagon.

Cow. A drag or trailer fixed at the back of a haulage train (or set) as a safety device when going uphill.

Cramp. Rail bender, Jim Crow.

Creep. The gradual lifting of floor or carving of roof and sides caused by a flowing action in the rock.

Cropping. Coal-cutting beyond and above the normal cutting plane.

Cross. Andre

Cross-cut. A road connecting two other more important roads.

Crush. Crumbling of pillars, or of side due to roof pressures.

Crut. A cross-measure tunnel or drift.

Curb. Binder. Also a shaft support ring for walling or tubbing.

Cut. The space in a coal face from which coal has been cut.

Cut-through. Thirling, slit, a short connecting road.

Cutting. Holing by hand or machine.

Cuttings. Small pieces of coal and coal dust left after cutting.

Cycle. The sequence of operations during a shift.

Dataller. Day wage worker.

Deadwork. Any kind of miner's work other than actual coal getting and transport.

Debris. Loose rock and coal after a fall or explosion.

Deep, Deep side. The side which is dipping away and downhill.

Deepcast. Deep, shaft mine.

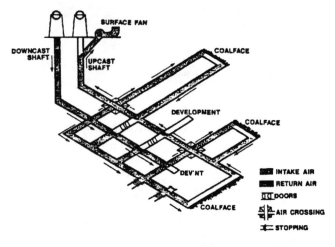

Mine ventilation system

Deputy. Deputy Overman. The statutory underground official in charge of safety in a district or unit. Inspects the workings before and during the shift.

Derrick. A three (or more) legged framework for supporting drill rods and tackle in deep boring; a temporary three-legged headframe, or headgear, for a shaft.

Devil. Drag; backstay; trailer.

Dint. To rip the floor.

Dip. To slope downhill.

Dip side. The side dipping downhill away from

the point of reference.

Dirt. Stone; shale; anything solid other than coal and wood.

Dog. A kind of nail with the top bent at right angles instead of having a head.

Downcast. The shaft through which air enters the mine.

Draw. To wind or to transport by hand; to put; to tram.

Drawer. Removes supports from the coal face.

Drift. A road driven in solid ground; a road in solid ground, but not in coal; a mine entrance or road inclined from the surface.

Drifting. Tunnelling; cutting.

Dross. Rock, shale etc. in cut coal.

Dyke. A sheet of igneous rock crossing the strata at right angles to the bedding plane.

Easer. A shot bored at an angle about half-way

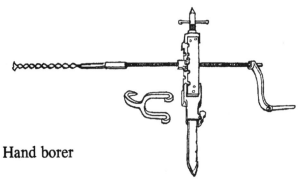

Hand borer

between that of the sumping shot and perpendicular to the face of the drivage in drifting.

Empty. An empty car, truck, tub, box or wagon.

End. The secondary cleavage at right angles to the bord or face cleat.

Ending. A road driven at right angles to the end cleat.

Endless Rope. A type of road haulage used in Durham pits.

Face. The actual coal wall where the coal is being got; the wall of operations in front of any drivage. The main cleavage, bord cleat.

Fandrift. The enclosed air-tight passage, road or gallery from the mine to the fan.

Fast. Having a solid side more or less at right angles to the working face.

Fast Jenkins. Cutting into and through a pillar or roof support.

Fast side. The end of the coal face where there is a solid face more or less at right angles.

Filler. One who fills.

Firedamp. Inflammable gas.

Fireman. Deputy.

Flat. An area behind the face where the tubs were collected, in 2's and 3's, before being hauled to the Big Landing.

Flatsheet. A square iron or steel plate used for turning mine tubs.

Fleetwheel, Fleeting Wheel. Surge wheel.

Fluke. A devise for automatic re-railing of tubs or cars; ramp, re-railer.

Foot-ridding. Dinting.

Fore-overman. Senior overman on a shift.

Fore-set. Temporary forward support; a middle prop under a bar.

Fulls. Full boxes, cars, tubs, wagons or trams.

Gallery. Underground road.

Ganister. Hard siliceous sandstone.

Gas. Firedamp.

Gate. Road

Gin. An old fashioned form of hoisting engine.

Goaf (Goaves). Waste; rock debris; gob.

Grit. Sharp-edged, coarse grained sandstone.

Guide. Rope or rigid conductors to guide the cages and skips in the shaft.

Gummer. A person or machine that cleans the cut behind the coal-cutting machine.

Gummings. Cleaned up by the Gummer.

Hanger-on. Onsetter.

Header. Brick or stone laid with the narrow end towards the face of a wall.

Headgear. The head frame of a mine shaft.

Heading. A road in the solid strata but also in the seam; a road in solid coal.

Headsticks, Headtree, Heapstead. Headgear; head frame. The Heapstead may also include all the raised structures and machinery around the shaft used for loading and unloading cages.

Heatings. Spontaneous combustion.

Herring-bone. Cockering.

Hewer. Collier, coal-winner.

Hogger. Air line, for pneumatic tools.

Holing. Cutting.

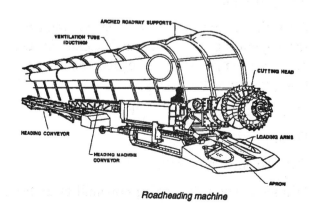

Roadheading machine

Hooker-on. Onsetter.

Hoppit. Bowk; bucket; kibble (singing bucket).

Hurdle. A brattice with a space left at the top.

Ignite. To set fire to.

Ignition. An outburst of fire or an explosion.

Inset. The entrance to underground roads from the shaft.

Jib-in. To start a cut by swinging the jib of the coal-cutter (while the chain is cutting) from the front of the face to the full cutting position.

Jig. A kind of shaker conveyor.

Jim Crow. Rail bender.

Jump. Hurdle sheet.

Kanch, Kench. Canch; ripping.

Keeker. Bank Inspector, examined loaded tubs for excessive amounts of stone amongst the coal.

Keps. Catches to hold the cage, usually at the surface.

Kerf. The cut in mechanical coal cutting.

Kibble. Hoppit, small open-ended tub.

Kick-ups. Automatic tipplers or holding frames, to discharge contents of tubs into screens.

Kirvings. Gummings, cuttings.

Kist. Deputy's desk.

Knobber. Miner who straightens by hand before a coal-cutting machine can start work.

Lash, Lash-on. To attach a chain to a haulage rope by wrapping or lapping the end of the chain round the rope, the other end of the chain is attached to a mine wagon.

Leg. Prop; support.

Lining. Road or shaft supports.

Long Wall. A method of mining in which 2 parallel roadways are driven forward. The coal face, often several hundred metres long, lies at right angles between them. All the coal is extracted from the face, which then moves forward. Debris and waste is packed behind the face and the roof collapsed.

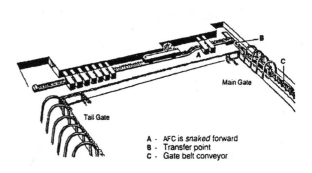

A - AFC is *snaked* forward
B - Transfer point
C - Gate belt conveyor

Layout of modern longwall face

Load. Full mine wagon.

Lower side. Dip side.

Main and Tail. A form of rope haulage.

Manchester Gate. A block-shaped device used to stop cars, wagons or tubs or to hold them against a gradient.

Marry. To combine; couple; attach.

Match. Part of a detonator.

Move-up. Extension; move forward.

Muck. Stone; dirt; debris.

Mucking. Loading or moving stone, dirt or debris.

Mussel bed. A band of rock containing or mainly composed of mussel-like shell fossils.

Nether Strata. The roof and rock strata immediately above the coal seam.

Nick. Cutting the coal from the face of the long face in longwall mining.

Occluded. When gas or water is contained in pores in the rock.

O.M.S. Output per man-shift.

Onsetter. The person in charge of winding operations underground. From his Inset he gives signals to the Banksman.

Opencast. Surface coal mine or coal quarry. Worked by Sunshine Miners.

Optimum. The best results.

Orifice. A ventilation hole in a very thin plate.

Overcast. A ventilation air-crossing.

Overlooker, Overman. A mine official, between a deputy and undermanager.

Pack. A form of permanent roof support in mines consisting of mine debris surrounded by vertical stone walls, all tightly packed to the roof.

Packer. A miner who builds packs or a piece of stone suitable for a pack-wall.

Pan. The coal-carrying trough of a conveyor or the framework of a belt or chain conveyor.

Panman, Panner. A mine engineer who dismantles or builds conveyors.

Pass-by. The double-track part of any single-track system of transport.

Picket. A surveying pole.

Pile. A spiked or sharp edged wooden plank, beam or metal pipe or girder which is as a support.

Pit bank, Pit brow, Pit head, Pit hill. Heapstead.

Plough. A coal-face machine which wedges off the coal from the face and ploughs it on to a conveyor.

Post. Wooden or stone prop.

Puffler. A man in charge of others who is paid for the whole job and himself pays those under him.

Pull. To wind; to hoist.

Put. To haul, often by hand.

Putter. Someone who hauls by hand.

Ram. To push.

Rammer. Miner who pushes over face conveyor.

Rank or Renk. A set distance for which a putter would be paid for pushing a tub. Distances over the set rank would pay extra.

Rap. Signal; knock.

Rib. Buttock

Ripping. Brushing. Normally enlarging a road by taking down the roof, but also extending to the sides and floor as well.

Rise. A road inclined uphill.

Road. Any mine passage or tunnel.

Rob. To get coal from pillars of coal. To get coal from where it should not normally be got.

Roll. Washout; partial washout. A downward irregularlity in the roof causing a thinning of a seam of coal.

Room and Pillar. An early method of mining used throughout the Durham Coalfield. Driving headings in the coal seam, leaving pillars of coal to support the roof. Superseded by the Longwall method of mining.

Runner. Bearer or carrier girder, beam or bar.

Score. 20 or 21 tubs.

Self-act. Gravity haulage.

Set. Train of tubs, taken from the Flat to the Landing to be made into a score.

Shaft. The vertical entrance-way to a deepcast mine. Usually circular in shape but may be rectangular if a shallow mine.

Slew. To turn round.

Slickensides. The smooth walls of a fault.

Slip. A joint or pronounced cleavage plane.

Slit. A connecting road.

Slusher. A mechanical drag-shovel loader.

Solid. Unmined, ungot.

Splay. Arch whose straight limbs instead of being vertical are spread (splayed) outwards.

Spline. A groove or rib on a shaft or inside a wheel or pulley which allows axial sliding but not rotation.

Split. A ventilation branch or to drive a road through a pillar.

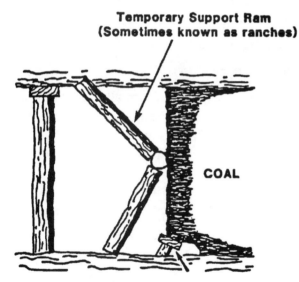

Wooden supports and sprags

Sprag. A relatively short prop either set slantwise from the vertical or set under holed or cut coal; a nog.

Stall. A working place at the coal face; usually associated with narrow workings.

Stell. Sprag. Stem. Ram.

Step. Fault; a small fault; a small fault in a stepped series of faults.

Stinkdamp. Hydrogen sulphide.

Stone-dust. Limestone used to make coal dust incombustible.

Stoop-and-room. Room-and-pillar.

Stow. To gob; to fill the waste; to put debris into the waste.

Strap. A bar; a beam; a coal-face bar.

Strike. The direction of the level line on the floor of a seam. To withdraw supports.

Strip. To fill prepared coal from a coal face. To complete the filling of prepared coal from the face.

Strut. A prop; any structural member or support under compression.

Sump. Water storage reservoir for the suction end of a pump. To drill diagonally.

Sumper. A shot-hole drilled diagonally.

Superincumbent strata. Strata above the nether strata.

Surge. To move sideways; to fleet.

Surge wheel. A wheel or pulley which drives an endless rope.

Swilley. A depression in a mine road from which the road rises both ways.

Tab. Token, check, tally.

Take. The area of coal allotted to a mine or project.

Tally. Tab.

Thirling. A connecting road; slit; cross-cut; through-cut.

Token. **Tally**. Used to check on the number of men in the mine, in case of accident. A different set of tokens were used to mark individual coal tubs, checking on the output of each worker.

Tram. Wagon; car; tub; corve.

Trapper. A young boy who opened and closed doors on a main airway.

Traverser. A mechanical device for moving a mine car bodily sideways from one rail track to another one running parallel.

Trimmer. A shot-hole bored slightly outwards to trim the drivage to the shape required.

Trouble. Fault.

Tub. Mine wagon.

Tubbing. Iron or steel segments to support the shaft sides against water under pressure.

Turn. Bend; branch; junction; points and crossings. A Shift.

Undercast. Air-crossing where the intake is bridged over the return.

Upcast. The return (ventilation) shaft.

Virgin. Unworked; untouched; areas where there has been no coal mining.

Waggon, Wagon. Any vehicle for carrying coal or debris.

Wailor. Young boy employed to pick shale and waste from the coal on the Picking Belts after being sorted and screened (size graded).

Waste. (1) Loosely applied to that area from which coal has been worked. (2) The unpacked and unsupported area behind the working face.

Water hammer. Sharp, hammer-like blow delivered by water being suddenly stopped when in motion.

Way. Road, channel, gate gallery.

Weight, Weighting. Roof movement, especially when it can be seen or heard.

Whitedamp. Carbon monoxide; a gas associated with white fumes.

Wind. Compressed air.

Windy Pick. Pneumatic drill.

Withdraw. To draw off; to take out supports.

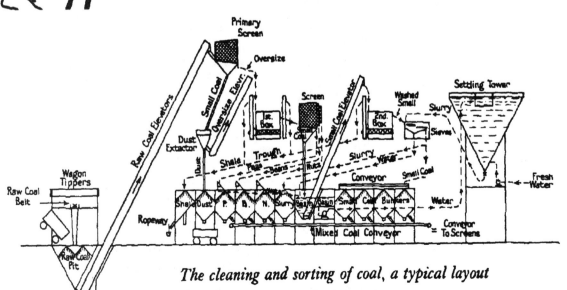

The cleaning and sorting of coal, a typical layout

● Peter Andrew looks at the formation of coal over the centuries

BLACK GOLD

The story of coal starts about 250 million years ago. Much of the land was covered by swamps and forests.

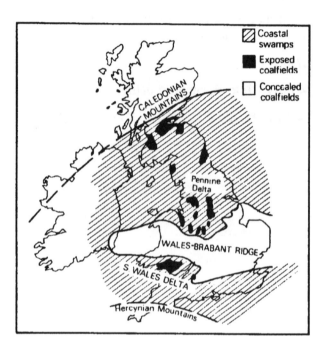

The plants were very different from those of today. Some trees had soft trunks, hollow stems or were like giant ferns.

The weather was hot and damp. When the trees died they began rotting away and new ones grew quickly in their place. Dead plant material piled up in a thick layer of peat. When the bottom of the swamp sank, rivers brought in sediments. The layer of dead plant and animal materials were buried and squashed and gradually turned into varieties of coal.

A layer of coal is called a seam. Coal seams are found in sedimentary rocks.

As the sediments accumulated, they provided a suitable surface for more plants to grow. The process of trees dying and rotting was repeated, and the swamp area once again subsided and more sediments were brought in.

This cycle was repeated many times and this is why coal seams are separated from one another by sandstones and shales. Coal bands represent periods during which subsidence was slight; the thickness of the bands indicates the amount of time during which the plants had time to grow before they were submerged by either fresh or sea water. If the submergence was by fresh water, the sediments contain plant materials or fresh water mussels. If the submergence was by sea water then there are marine fossils.

Some of the fossils which are found in the coals, sandstones and shales are forms which no longer exist on earth, but some of them are very like plants and animals which still exist on the earth today.

Some of the more common plant fossils found in coal are shown below.

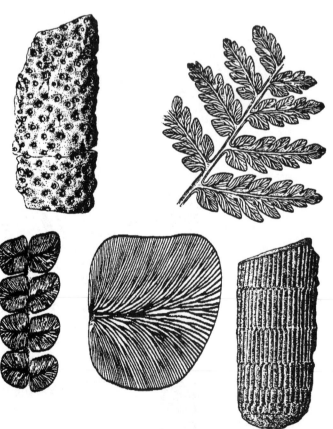

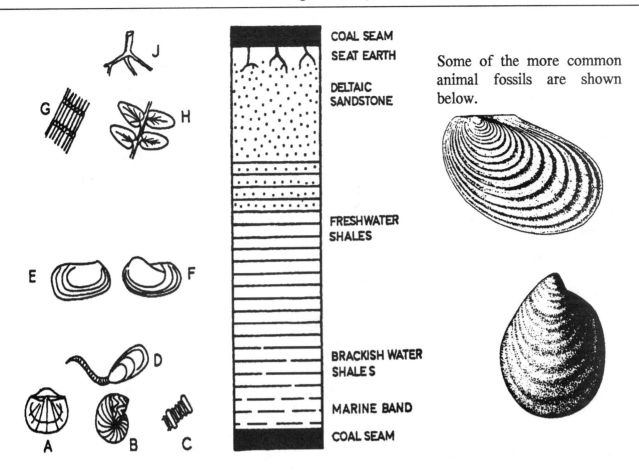

Some of the more common animal fossils are shown below.

Typical fossils of the several units are: Marine Band: A *Productus*; B Goniatite; C Crinoid ossicles: Brackish water shales: D *Lingula*. Freshwater shales (lamellibranchs): E *Carbonicola*; F *Anthraconauta*. Deltaic Sandstone: G Stems of *Calamites*; H Leaves of *Neuropteris*. Seat Earth: J Stigmarian roots

The Coal Swamp

Until quite recently man was dependent almost exclusively on wood for fuel. Man started to become independent of this source of fuel around about 2000 years ago in China. The Romans in Britain exploited the coal measures and by 1269 the monks of Tynemouth were shipping coals from the Tyne.

The British Iron Industry had flourished in the major forest regions in the Weald of Surrey, Sussex and the Forest of Dean. By the middle of the 18th. century, just as the English woodlands were reaching exhaustion, Abraham Darby found he could use coal as a source of carbon and developed an iron smelting works at Coalbrookdale. This signalled the move of the Iron Industries to the coal areas. Since 1800 the principal sources of Britain's industrial energy have been the fossil fuels and until the 20th. century, coal has provided the greatest proportion.

HOW THE CARBONIFEROUS ROCKS WERE MADE.

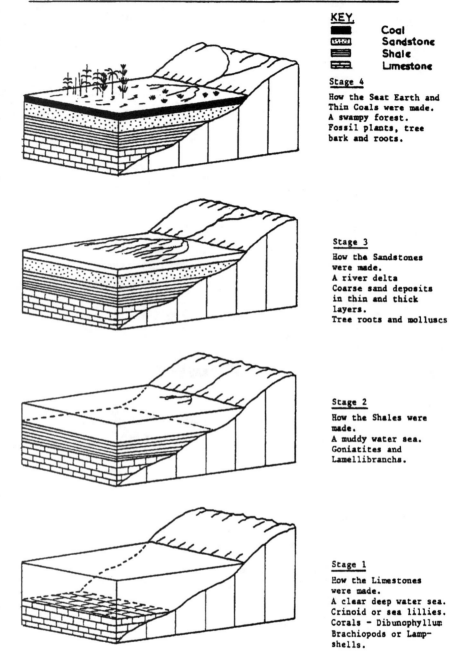

KEY.

Coal
Sandstone
Shale
Limestone

Stage 4
How the Seat Earth and Thin Coals were made.
A swampy forest.
Fossil plants, tree bark and roots.

Stage 3
How the Sandstones were made.
A river delta
Coarse sand deposits in thin and thick layers.
Tree roots and molluscs

Stage 2
How the Shales were made.
A muddy water sea.
Goniatites and Lamellibranchs.

Stage 1
How the Limestones were made.
A clear deep water sea.
Crinoid or sea lillies.
Corals - Dibunophyllum
Brachiopods or Lampshells.

Coal is however a non-renewable resource and although there are adequate supplies, alternative energy supplies will be needed in the future.

THE COAL MEASURES

● A summary of the coal measures, part of the Carboniferous series of Durham, has been produced by Frank Burns and illustrated by David Noble

Coal in County Durham occurs in many seams of varying thickness and quality, interspaced with sandstones and shales (as shown in the diagram). The whole series of rocks in the Carboniferous series is over 700m thick in the county. Not all the coal seams are workable but those which are number 21 and are given names of which:-

● Busty

● Brockwell

● Maudlin

● Hutton

are the most important. These names can sometimes be confusing as some seams have different names in the West and East of the County. For example, the Low Main of West and Mid Durham becomes the Maudlin of the East.

In the West is the exposed coalfield where the coal seams outcrop on the surface or are covered by sand, clay or gravel (known as drift).

It was this area of the Western coalfield and the river valleys of the Derwent, Wear and Gaunless, where coal was first worked. The coal was close to the surface and relatively easy to obtain. In the Eastern area mining developed later, not only because of the depth of the seams, but the shaft sinkers had to overcome enormous quantities of water as they penetrated the Magnesian Limestone.

Coal seams can vary considerably in thickness and quality, even over a small area, and the diagrams show the break of the seams caused by faults. The seams can dip and rise at quite steep angles and it is these variations which cause the mine serious problems and are often responsible for a pit closing.

Traditionally, many of the West Durham seams contained coal which was soft and bright and was particularly useful to produce coke for iron and steel works. Gas was produced with the coke and before the discovery of Natural Gas under the North Sea in the 1960's, all gas for household and industrial use was produced from coal.

Harder coal was used for fires in factories ships boilers, locomotives and burning in open fires in the home. Eighty years ago this is where most of our coal was used and millions of tons were exported from the Tyne, Wear and Tees to other countries.

Today most of the County's coal production is burned in electricity power stations with some for household use, only a fraction of that used in the past. As a consequence of the change of fuels, difficulties in mining, exhaustion of seams and changes in economic conditions, the mining industry of County Durham has declined from 150,000 miners producing 50 million tons of coal in 1913 to 6,000 miners producing 8 million tons in 1991.

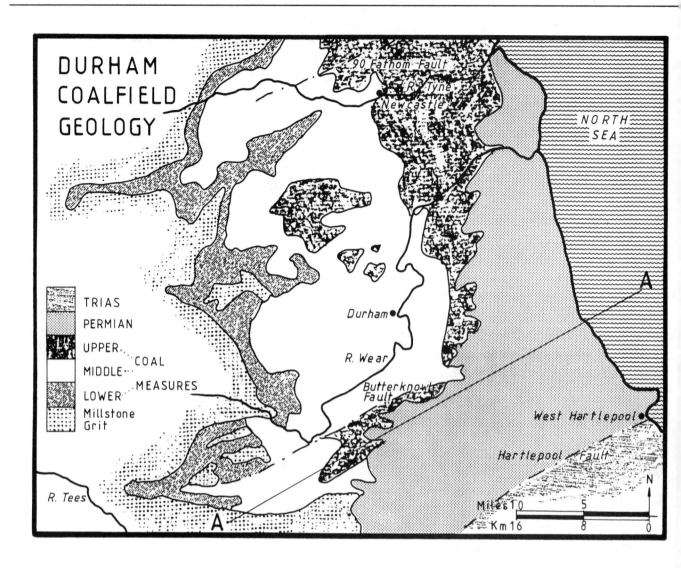

DURHAM
COALFIELD
GEOLOGY

90 Fathom Fault
R. Tyne
Newcastle

NORTH
SEA

TRIAS
PERMIAN
UPPER
MIDDLE ⎫ COAL
LOWER ⎭ MEASURES
Millstone Grit

Durham

R. Wear

Butterknowle
Fault

West Hartlepool

Hartlepool Fault

R. Tees

A

A

Miles 10   5
Km 16   8   0

N

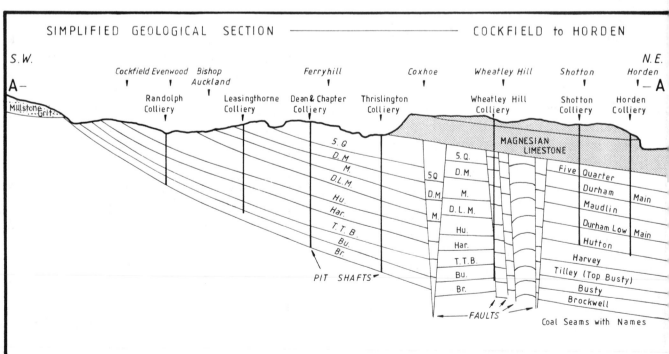

SIMPLIFIED GEOLOGICAL SECTION ——————— COCKFIELD to HORDEN

S.W.   N.E.
A–   Horden
                                                                          –A

Cockfield Evenwood Bishop   Ferryhill   Coxhoe   Wheatley Hill   Shotton
                    Auckland

        Randolph   Leasingthorne Dean & Chapter Thrislington Wheatley Hill   Shotton   Horden
        Colliery   Colliery   Colliery   Colliery   Colliery   Colliery   Colliery

Millstone
Grit

MAGNESIAN
LIMESTONE

S.Q.
D.M.
M.
D.L.M.
Hu.
Har.
T.T.B.
Bu.
Br.

S.Q.
D.M.
M.
D.L.M.
Hu.
Har.
T.T.B.
Bu.
Br.

5Q
D.M
M.

Five Quarter
Durham   Main
Maudlin
Durham Low   Main
Hutton
Harvey
Tilley (Top Busty)
Busty
Brockwell

PIT SHAFTS

—FAULTS

Coal Seams with Names

DURHAM COAL SEAMS

THICKNESS OF COAL MEASURES		NAMES *WEST DURHAM*	THICKNESS OF SEAMS		
feet 0	metres		feet'-inches"	metres	
200	65	CLOSING HILL COAL	1' 2"	0·36	UPPER COAL MEASURES
400	125	HEBBURN FELL	3'	1·0	
600	190				
800	260	FIVE QUARTER	1'8" – 5'	0·5 – 1·5	
1000	320	THREE QUARTER	1'6" – 3'4"	0·5 – 1·0	
		SHIELD ROW = FIVE QUARTER	3' – 8'	1·0 – 2·5	
1200	395	BRASS THILL	1' – 2'7"	0·3 – 0·8	MIDDLE COAL MEASURES *MOST PRODUCTIVE*
		FIVE QUARTER	1'6" – 6'6"	0·5 – 1·0	
		MAIN COAL = *BRASS THILL*	2' – 7'	0·6 – 2·2	
		MAUDLIN	1' – 9'	0·3 – 1·5	
1400	460	LOW MAIN	1'6" – 5'	0·5 – 1·5	
		BRASS THILL= *LOW MAIN*	4 – 5	0·1 – 1·5	
		HUTTON = MAIN COAL	2' – 6'6"	0·6 – 2·0	
		RULER	1'10"– 2'2"	0·5 – 0·6	
1600	520	HARVEY = *TOWNLEY*	1'3" – 6	0·3 – 2·0	
		TILLEY = TOP BUSTY	2" – 5'8"	0·05 – 1·8	
		BUSTY=BROCKWELL= *BALLARAT*	5' – 10'	1·6 – 3·0	
1800	585	THREE QUARTER	1' – 3'6"	0·3 – 3·0	
		BROCKWELL	10" – 8'	0·3 – 2·5	
2000	650	VICTORIA	1' – 2'5"	0·3 – 0·8	LOWER COAL MEASURES
		MARSHALL GREEN	1'6"	0·5	
2200	700				

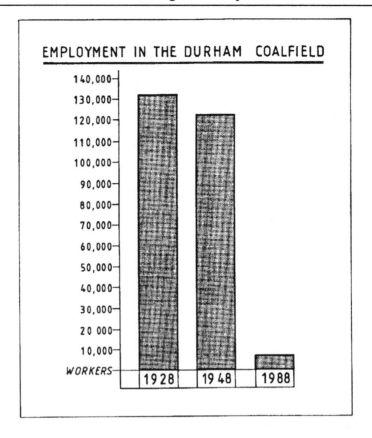

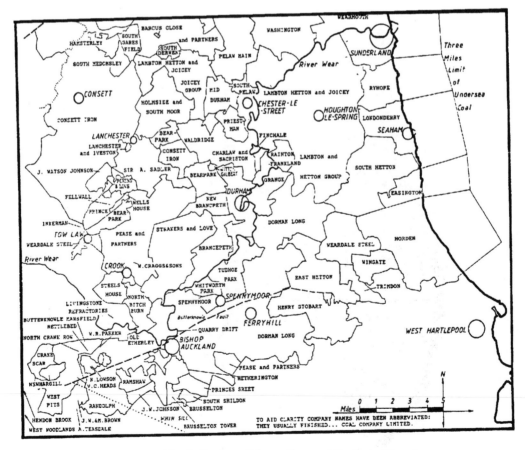

Coal Ownership prior to Nationalisation

Uses of Coal

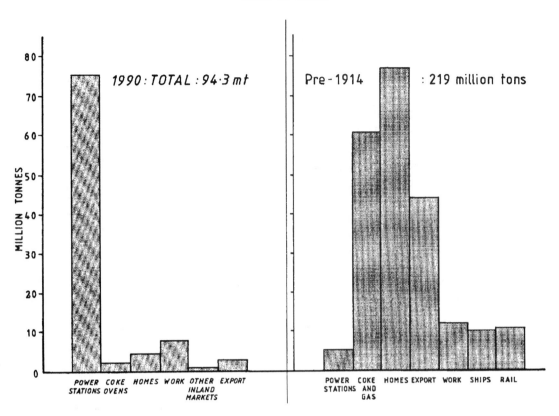

Derivatives of Coal

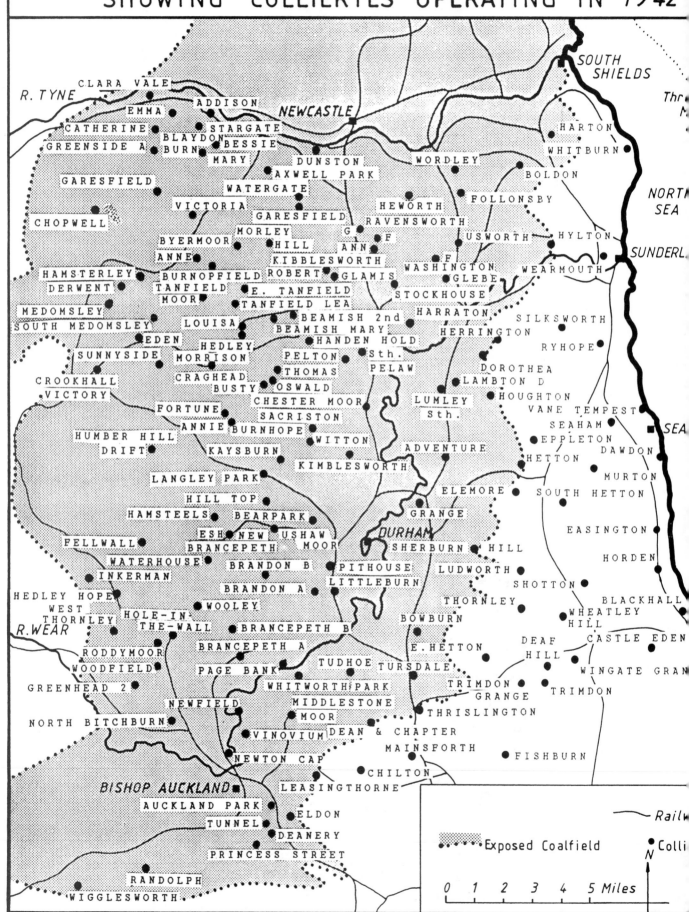

DURHAM COALFIELD
SHOWING COLLIERIES OPERATING IN 1942

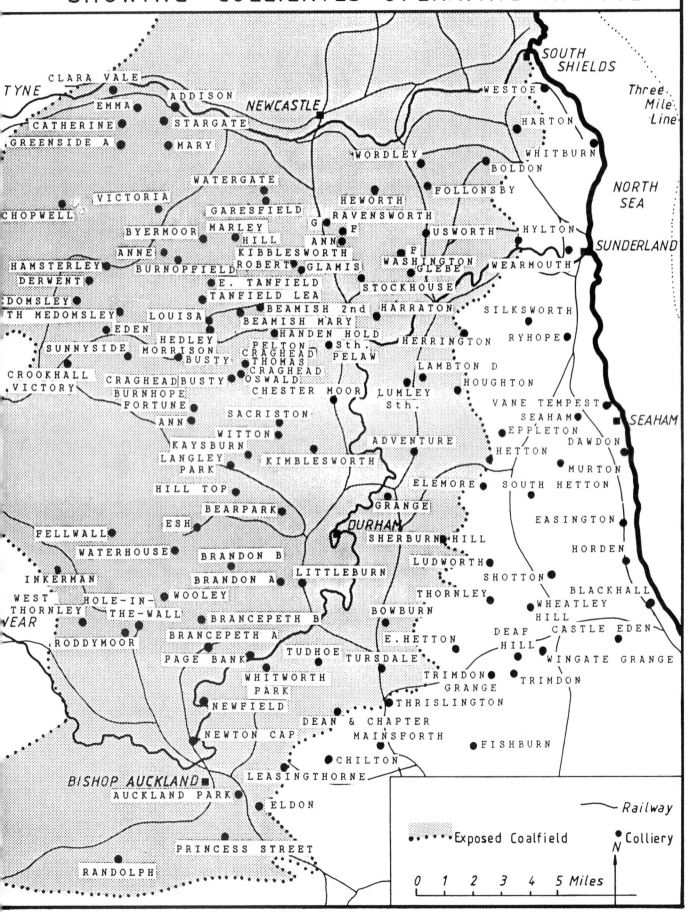

DURHAM COALFIELD
SHOWING COLLIERIES OPERATING IN *1962*

CLARA VALE
TYNE
ADDISON
NEWCASTLE
SOUTH SHIELDS
EMMA
WESTOE
CATHERINE
STARGATE
HARTON
GREENSIDE A
MARY
WHITBURN
WORDLEY
BOLDON
Three Mile Line
WATERGATE
FOLLONSBY
NORTH SEA
VICTORIA
HEWORTH
CHOPWELL
GARESFIELD
RAVENSWORTH
HYLTON
BYERMOOR
MARLEY
G
F
USWORTH
SUNDERLAND
HILL
ANN
HAMSTERLEY
ANNE
KIBBLESWORTH
F
WASHINGTON
WEARMOUTH
BURNOPFIELD
ROBERT GLAMIS
GLEBE
DERWENT
E. TANFIELD
STOCKHOUSE
DOMSLEY
TANFIELD LEA
TH MEDOMSLEY
LOUISA
BEAMISH 2nd
HARRATON
SILKSWORTH
EDEN
BEAMISH MARY
HEDLEY
HANDEN HOLD
RYHOPE
SUNNYSIDE
MORRISON
PELTON Sth.
HERRINGTON
CRAGHEAD
Sth. PELAW
CROOKHALL
BUSTY
THOMAS
LAMBTON D
VICTORY
CRAGHEAD BUSTY
CRAGHEAD
OSWALD
HOUGHTON
BURNHOPE
CHESTER MOOR
LUMLEY
VANE TEMPEST
FORTUNE
Sth.
SEAHAM
SEAHAM
ANN
SACRISTON
EPPLETON
DAWDON
WITTON
ADVENTURE
HETTON
KAYSBURN
MURTON
LANGLEY
KIMBLESWORTH
ELEMORE
SOUTH HETTON
PARK
HILL TOP
GRANGE
EASINGTON
BEARPARK
DURHAM
HORDEN
ESH
SHERBURN HILL
FELLWALL
LUDWORTH
WATERHOUSE
BRANDON B
SHOTTON
BLACKHALL
INKERMAN
BRANDON A
LITTLEBURN
THORNLEY
WHEATLEY HILL
WEST
HOLE-IN-
WOOLEY
BOWBURN
THORNLEY
THE-WALL
CASTLE EDEN
WEAR
BRANCEPETH B
DEAF HILL
RODDYMOOR
BRANCEPETH A
E. HETTON
WINGATE GRANGE
PAGE BANK
TUDHOE
TURSDALE
TRIMDON
WHITWORTH
TRIMDON GRANGE
PARK
THRISLINGTON
NEWFIELD
DEAN & CHAPTER
NEWTON CAP
MAINSFORTH
FISHBURN
CHILTON
BISHOP AUCKLAND
LEASINGTHORNE
AUCKLAND PARK
ELDON
Railway
PRINCESS STREET
Exposed Coalfield
Colliery
RANDOLPH
N
0 1 2 3 4 5 Miles

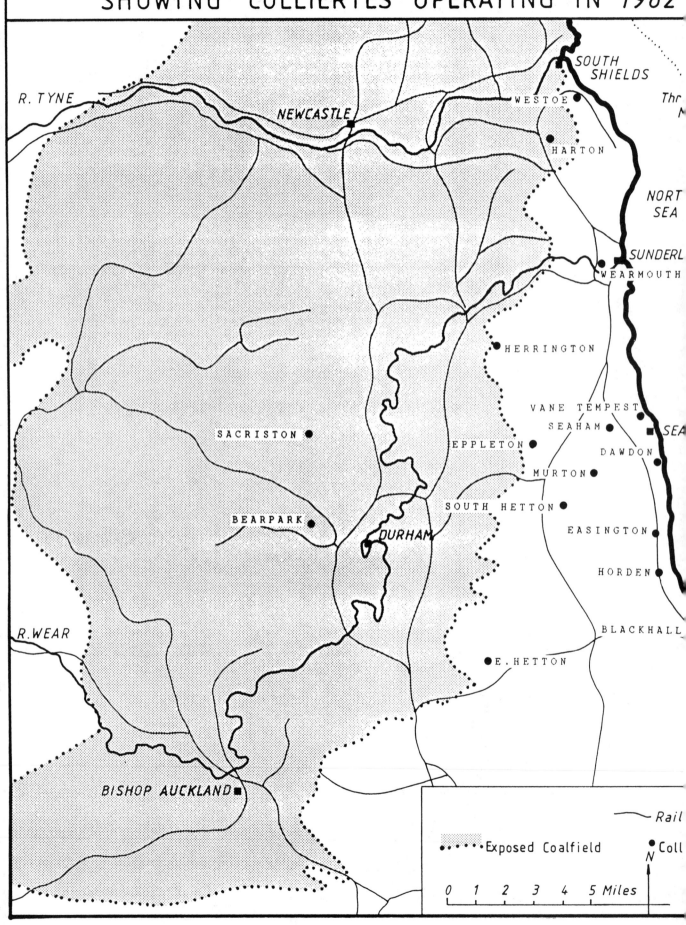

DURHAM COALFIELD
SHOWING COLLIERIES OPERATING IN *1982*

R. TYNE

NEWCASTLE

SOUTH SHIELDS

WESTOE

HARTON

Thr
N

NORT
SEA

SUNDERL
WEARMOUTH

HERRINGTON

VANE TEMPEST
SEAHAM
SEA

DAWDON

EPPLETON

MURTON

SACRISTON

SOUTH HETTON

EASINGTON

BEARPARK

DURHAM

HORDEN

BLACKHALL

R.WEAR

E.HETTON

BISHOP AUCKLAND

Rail

•••••• Exposed Coalfield   • Coll

N

0   1   2   3   4   5 Miles

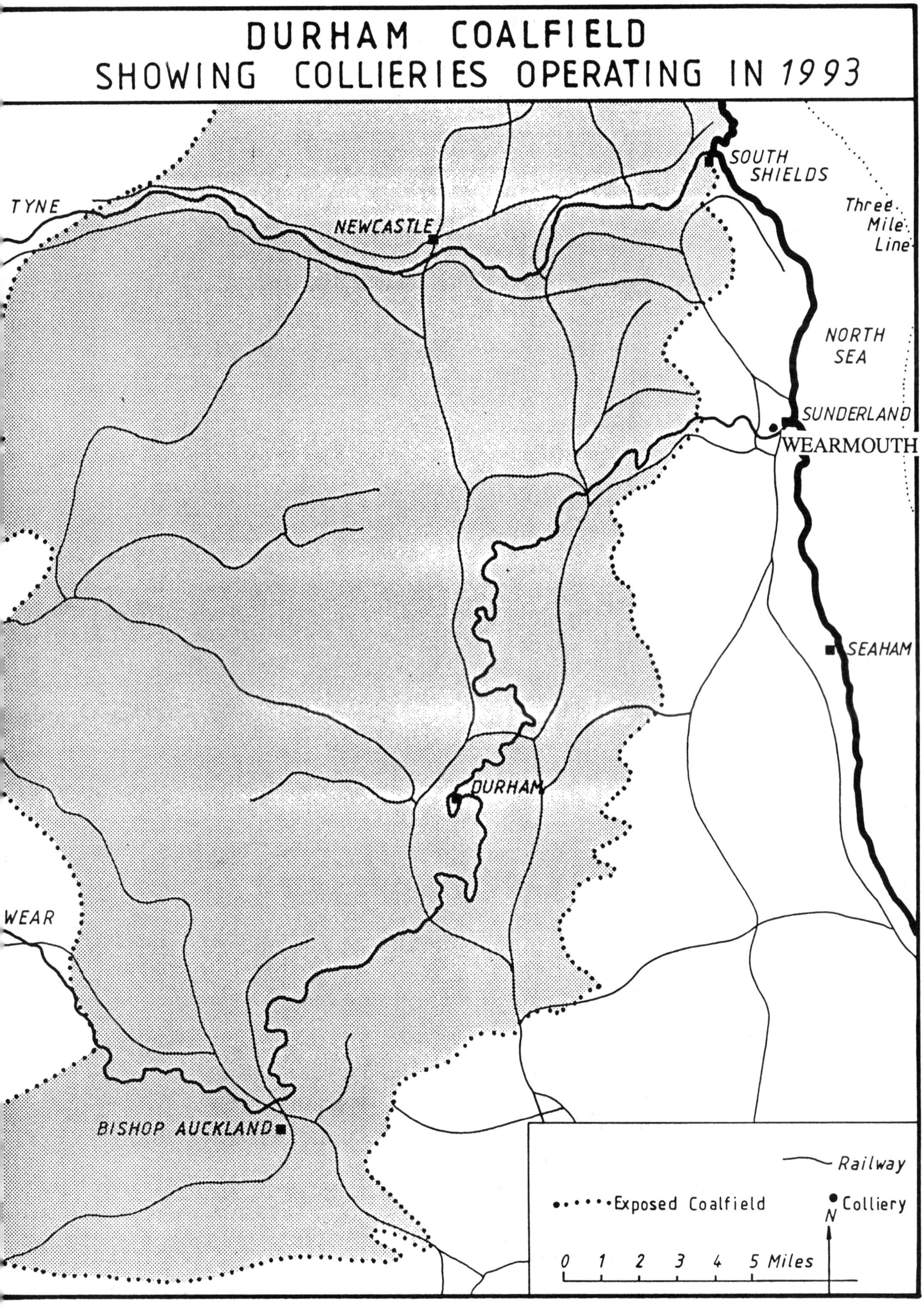

DURHAM COALFIELD
SHOWING COLLIERIES OPERATING IN 1993

TYNE

SOUTH SHIELDS

NEWCASTLE

Three Mile Line

NORTH SEA

SUNDERLAND

WEARMOUTH

SEAHAM

DURHAM

WEAR

BISHOP AUCKLAND

Railway

••••••Exposed Coalfield

Colliery

N

0 1 2 3 4 5 Miles

COLLIERY NAMES

● Don Wilcock takes us through a series of interesting names

The colliery to the west of Shildon was always known to me as **Datton** colliery and the level crossing across the Darlington to Bishop Auckland road, used by coal trains from this colliery was **Datton Gates**. It wasn't until the colliery had closed, had been dismantled and had almost disappeared that I found that its correct name was Shildon Lodge colliery; Datton was its nickname and how it got this name has been forgotten. It has been said that one of its Irish miners told an enquirer who had asked him at which colliery he worked, said 'Over der at datt'un'!. This story and others gleaned from correspondence in the Northern Echo aroused my interest in colliery names in general and local names in particular.

Another Shildon colliery was called **Dabble-duck**, and so too was a small pit along the Wear between Bishop Auckland and Escomb, these were probably named from the fields in which they were sunk being boggy and marshy and fit only for ducks.

Seaham colliery was known as **The Knack** or **The Nicky-Nack**, it took its name from the nearby Mill Inn; the landlord, one Tommy Chilton was skilled at repairing spinning wheels, and earned the soubriquet 'Tommy Nicknack' presumably because of the clicking sound the wheel made. The Inn became the Nicky-Nack and when the colliery was opened the name was attached to it.

There are other collieries which were given pub names, Tudhoe colliery was known as **Black Horse** after the nearby pub. Other local names included **Five Houses** for Trimdon Grange and Tursdale was known as **Hogger's Gate**. Nearby Cornforth colliery was called **Doggy**, so too was the village. The name comes from the fact that Cornforth Lane had two railway stations very close to each other on the two lines which ran through the village, to distinguish between them one station was known as Cornforth Dog Lane, corrupted to Cornforth Doggy!

Many names were derived from nearby villages, even if they were at some distance away, **Cornsay Colliery** for instance is now the name of the village, and so too is **Esh Winning**, both Cornsay and Esh villages being about two miles away; as are **Trimdon Grange** and **Trimdon Colliery** from Trimdon village. At Westerton the owners went back nearly 2,000 years in naming their colliery **Vinovium.**

Names were given to pits and drifts which were either functional or descriptive, **Engine Pit** at Beamish, or **Chain Engine Pit** at Lumley. Ventilation of the pit was often regulated by having an underground furnace with the shaft performing as a chimney and drawing fresh air through the workings, hence **Furnace Pit** at Blaydon and at Shildon, with the introduction of mechanical ventilation one finds **Fan Pit** at Gateshead. Descriptive names such as **Damp Pit** at Kip Hill or **Water Pit** at West Auckland, and **Watergate** appeared as a colliery name long before the infamous American hotel! Where the workings came to the surface you had a **Dayhole Pit**, as at West Auckland and Birtley.

As the sinking of a shaft to reach a profitable seam was, in the late C18, not a certainty, there is a **Chance** at Birtley, North Biddick and Burnopfield; **Lucky** and **Prosperous** also at Birtley, but only **Speculation** at Blaydon. Some one tried hard at Hutton Henry with the **Perseverance** , and while others recovered at Gateshead and Burnmoor with **Restoration**, someone came to a **Conclusion** at Bushblades. Naturally there were difficulties, it was a **Haphazard** at Cockfield, a **Hazard** at North Hetton, a **Hazzard** at Elvet, Durham City but a **Misfortune** at Chester-le-Street!

It is possible to construct a family tree of certain coal-owners from names they give to their workings, with ladies to the fore. **Anne, Bess, Dolly, Dainty**, and **Julia** were all to be found in the Gateshead area. East Howle near

Closed: Burnhope Colliery in 1933. It closed four years after the war in 1949.

Ferry Hill had **Annie, Catherine** and **Marion; Lizzie** was to be found at South Derwent. There was a **Magdalene** Pit at Woodland and a **Virgin** at Cockfield. Titled ladies were remembered; **Lady Adelaide** near Carrville, **Lady Ann** at Burnmoor, **Lady Alice** at Littletown and **Lady Seaham** at Pittington with **Lady Durham** at Sherburn House. The **Queen** was recorded at South Moor and Kip Hill; **Victoria** was to be found at Garesfield, Sacriston and Tow Law.

The gentlemen included the **Black Prince** at Tow Law, **Lord Auckland** at Greenfield and **Lord Lambton**, as was to be expected at Littletown. Eldon had a **John Henry** while **William Henry** appeared at Burnmoor. **George Willie, John** and **Rodney** at Heworth and among its many pits Blaydon Burn had **Edward** and **Knobby**. Hamsteels had **Taylor** and **Clifford**.

National figures are recalled by **Nightingale** (Florence?) at West Auckland and Hebburn both pits being sunk during or after the Crimean War. **Inkerman** is remembered at

Tow Law, while **Victory** is celebrated at North Beechburn. The only foreigner appears to be **Hindenburg** at Grange near Durham. Friends and relations are not forgotten with **Nanny** at Chopwell and at Etherley with an **Aunty** at Cockfield.

Chopwell village was known throughout the coalfield as Little Moscow, a reflection of the militancy of its residents, yet Chopwell colliery had shafts named the **Duke**, the **King** and the **Earl**!

Many of the pits were sunk in rural areas and names reflect this with **Garden** pit at Washington, **Potato Garth** at Cockfield; **Blueberry, Birds Nest, Ashtree, Jay** and **Stag** all in the Gateshead area. **Ash** at Collierley; **Fattening Pasture** at Lambton, Kibblesworth had **Hare, Oat, Pasture, Wheat** and **Whin**. Truly rural were **Fox, Hedge, Pea, Lamb** and **Rose** at South Moor. Birds were mentioned, **Cuckoo** near Burnopfield, **Fryar's Goose** at Gateshead and my favourite **Whistling Bird** at Blaydon Burn.

My thanks to all the correspondents who replied to my query and to the National Coal Board, as was, and the Durham County Record Office for their help in the search.

Friar's Goose

Colliery

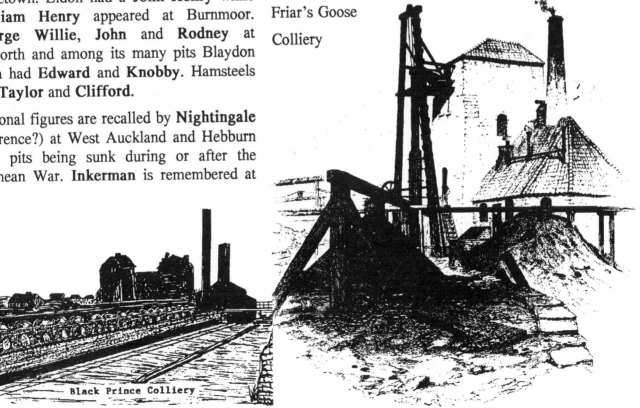

Black Prince Colliery

COASTAL COLLIERIES – DEVELOPMENT AND DECLINE

● D. Winter of Edenhall Junior School, Peterlee describes the growth and decline of Easington, Horden and Blackhall Collieries.

This area comprises, from north to south, the collieries of Easington, Horden and Blackhall. Only Easington is still in operation, whilst Blackhall ceased production in April 1981 and Horden in February 1986. The coal from these three collieries has proved to be of good quality and versatile - it could be used for raising steam, gas making, as coking coal for steel making and as good household coal.

The coal seams exploited by this group of pits lie under a layer of Permian Limestone, the porous nature of which has been the constant cause of serious water problems through percolation from feeder streams which are at their most formidable about 250 metres beneath the surface.

The cost of holding back or pumping out the water has always been a major item of expenditure. At Horden, prior to closure, it came to £3.5 million a year - without doubt a significant factor in the decision to close.

Easington was the first of the three collieries to be sunk and, together with Horden and Blackhall, formed the last part of the Durham coalfield to be developed for deep extraction.

The Easington Coal Company began sinking the first shaft on April 11th 1899. It was not an easy task due to the resistance to excavation presented by the 400 metres or so of water-bearing limestone that overlies the upper coal seams.

Contractors were brought over from Germany to apply their expertise at using newly developed freezing techniques and the sinking of the North Pit was finished on September 17th 1909.

The sinkers lived in crude wooden shacks that had none of the facilities of running water, sanitation, heating or lighting that we take for granted today.

On November 6th 1900, a year and a half after excavation began at Easington, work on the North Pit shaft at Horden, the first of three,

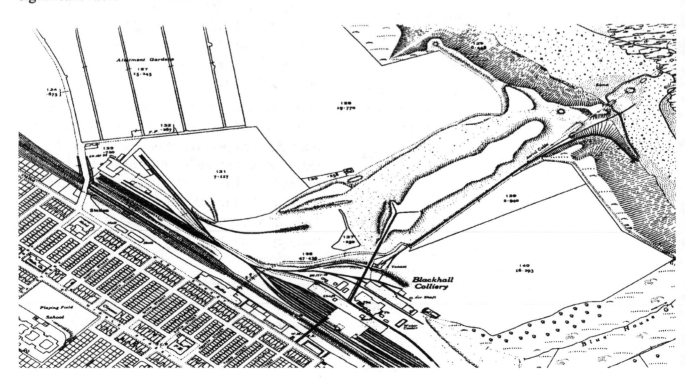

£12,000 to rebuild, the cost being borne by the Company and the Council.

Operations at Blackhall, also undertaken by the Horden Coal Company, began with the commencement of shaft sinking in 1909. The sinkers froze the water as they came to it and operations were completed in 1913 when the first coal was drawn.

Electric winding gear meant that there were no chimneys belching smoke and steam into the air and Blackhall was at that time the most modern pit in Britain. It had one other advantage, too, albeit a dubious one from the environmental point of view. It didn't take long for the owners to realise that its proximity to the shore meant that it could dump much of its waste via a tip on to the beach for the tide to dispose of. There was, therefore, in the long term. no need for the ubiquitous mountain of a heap that typified other collieries.

The tragedy was that one of the most beautiful stretches of sand in Britain was soon to become a desolate wasteland. Easington and Horden were quick to follow this obscene practice to the detriment of their own coastal environment, and indeed Easington continues to do so to this day.

(*A recent proposal by the environmental lobby that the colliery's waste should be transported by rail for dumping into Thrislington Quarry was rejected by the Coal Board who argued that it would cost £60 million over a twenty year period and would add to the cost per ton of the coal produced with the subsequent loss of jobs and possible closure.)

Initial housing provision for the labourers who prepared the land prior to the commencement of operations proper was appalling. They, and also the sinkers and their families during the preliminary period, lived in wooden shacks that were knocked together any old how. Some even lived in tents on the beach and in caves. Their progeny came into the world in deplorable conditions.

With the opening of each pit, life began in earnest in its respective community. The first drawers of coal lived in comparative luxury in solid brick terraced streets. These streets were

commenced. It took the Horden Coal Company nearly four years to complete and it was sunk to a depth of 380 metres. In this instance, cast iron cylindrical mouldings (*tubbing*) were used to keep back the large volume of water. The first coal was drawn in 1904.

Horden quickly became the largest mine in Britain, with three shafts, and the surface operations eventually included a washery, a brick works and a coking plant.

Luckily, Horden escaped disasters of the scale of the one at Easington, but is infamous for the riot that took place there in 1910. How it started no one knows for sure, but the closure of the pit due to a dispute over the Lloyd George Budget, the non-payment of wages owed, together with the volatile nature of the immigrant Cornish and Staffordshire miners and excess of alcohol.

The result was the ransacking, looting and burning of the Workmen's (*Big*) Club. An article in the Northern Daily Mail alleged that J. J. Prest, the agent of the colliery, had brandished a gun by way of protecting himself from the advancing horde who had followed him to his home at Hardwick Hall after a rumour had been mischievously started alleging that he had shot a local youth. Arrests were made and the ringleaders were given custodial sentences of up to five years. The Club, reduced to a shell, cost built by the colliery owners as close as possible to the pithead in order to ensure a ready supply of labourers who didn't need to commute to work and who could be expected to be punctual.

The housing stock consisted mostly of three-bedroomed terraced dwellings, each with its own internal water supply and lavatory (*netty*) in the back yard. In contrast to the settlements that had arisen around pits that had been sunk in the middle of the nineteenth century.

Poor communication patterns generally in East Durham meant that although the three villages were in close proximity to each other and were linked by rail (though not by road until 1924) and movement between them was not a major problem, they were as a group of settlements somewhat isolated from other parts of the county and the colliery owners had, therefore, what amounted to a monopoly over the labour supply. They could decide who would work and who would have to uproot his family and seek employment elsewhere.

Amenities in the villages were limited at first. *Shops* sprung up in the front parlours of the terraced houses, selling everything from food-stuffs to clothing and hardware. *Tin* schools, chapels and churches made out of galvanised steel were the first large buildings. These were crude by modern standards but provided focal points for village life.

Despite the many hardships, a strong community spirit built up in each of the villages with a commitment to mutual help. They were lively places to live in with an ethos of togetherness and sharing.

The establishment of the colliery *welfare* societies as a result of the Mines Industry Act of 1920 went a long way to fostering and sustaining this community spirit. Provision was made in each village for the establishment of a fund to improve social conditions. A levy was made on the coal companies and a small sum of money (1d initially but later rising to 2d) was deducted at source from each miner's wage and paid into the fund for the upkeep of playing fields, a park and a communal hall in the centre of each village.

These welfare grounds were referred to locally as *recs* - short for *recreation grounds*. They comprised swings and roundabouts for the children, a band-stand for recitals by the local colliery-sponsored brass band, tennis courts and excellent turfed playing surfaces for soccer, cricket and bowls.

Between the wars, in each of the villages, new housing schemes were developed, some on the initiative of private developers and others as a result of Council enterprise. The majority of the new dwellings in Easington and Horden came into the latter category.

The new *Council House* estates were built to a much higher standard than the original terraced miners' homes. They were mainly semi-detached with gardens front and back. They had amenities such as indoor bathrooms and lavatories. They were, however, always rather inferior in appearance and quality to the *private* dwellings, particularly those at Blackhall Rocks and Easington. Very few of the miners, apart from some well-paid colliery officials, could afford to take on a mortgage to purchase these. They were more likely to be occupied by professional people such as doctors and teachers, and by families whose breadwinners had good jobs in the local co-operative store. There was a clearly recognisable division in status between private house owners and council house tenants.

This situation was remedied somewhat by the introduction, on the initiative of the coal companies, of *scheme* housing. Encouragement was given for new dwellings to be built by private developers and assistance was made to the miners in arranging mortgages and carrying out the legalities of purchase.

These *scheme* houses were built in neat terraced estates, were well looked after by their proud occupants, and added a degree of smartness to the general ambience of each village.

In the period between the two World Wars, the three collieries were amongst the most productive in Britain with many records being broken. 1947 saw the Nationalisation of the coal mines which meant that the three pits were thereafter to be run by the National Coal Board under the watchful eye of the Ministry of Fuel and Power.

The 1960's and 70's brought increasing competition from oil, natural gas and nuclear fuel. For the first time, doubts about the viability of all three pits surviving began to enter the minds of the local workforce.

The *Plan For Coal*, which at one time had appeared to be a life-saver for the three collieries in that it required them to supply the new blast furnace at Redcar with high-grade coking coal, was now being treated with suspicion.

By 1980 the British Steel Corporation was importing 25% of its coking coals. There was a sudden and dramatic revision downwards of demand for locally produced coking coals. Coal was being imported from Australia, U.S.A., Canada, Poland and South Africa. Coal brought all the way from Australia was £10 a ton cheaper than that produced at the three local pits and was of a quality better able to meet the more demanding requirements of the new blast furnaces at Redcar.

In 1980, supplies of coking coals to Redcar were as follows:- Locally produced = 244,000 tons; Imported = 1,252,850 tons. In 1984 they were:- Locally produced = 48,955 tons; Imported = 2,105,000 tons.

Locally drawn coal was uncompetitive in price and quality. This, together with an overall reduction in demand for household coal and coke, led to a rapid decline in the fortunes of the three pits from 1978 onwards.

They were forced out of necessity in order to maintain their very existence to tender for supplying the steam-raising market of the Central Electricity Generating Board - with the consequent much lower revenues.

Up to 1983. Easington supplied Ferrybridge, Eggborough and Drax. but with the introduction of the new pits at Selby, the C.E.G.B. switched to the North Yorks coalfield for its supplies - a bitter pill to swallow for the local pits!

After the 1984 - 85 Miners' Strike, Horden and Easington were called upon to replenish stocks at the North Yorks power stations, but this only provided a brief respite, particularly for Horden.

Between 1979 and 1984 Horden had lost £55 million pounds. At the time of its demise, the pit had not made a profit for ten years. Severe water problems and geological faults, together with reduced demand, lowering prices and more cost-efficient competition from abroad, had taken their toll.

With the closing of the collieries at Blackhall and Horden, the long-standing bond between pit and village life came to an abrupt end. Each worker was given the choice of accepting redundancy compensation or of being offered employment in a mine further afield.

When Blackhall closed

732 were transferred to other collieries.
- 167 went to Horden,
- 157 to Easington,
- 132 to Murton,
- 90 to Seaham
- 186 to elsewhere in the county.

586 men accepted redundancy their choice was threefold.
- To find other employment elsewhere in the area.
- To seek employment in areas further south.
- To eke out an existence on Social Security benefits - an option which many feel is the only viable one open to them.

The sites of these two former collieries, together with their large deposits of dumped colliery waste, have been processed and transformed into landscaped industrial plots for lease to light industry which will relieve in a small way the massive unemployment problem that exists in the area.

SAFETY

This information was gathered by Frank Burns

Of the many dangers faced by miners that which has always posed the greatest threat to life and limb is the explosion. Methane gas, commonly known as fire damp is trapped, under great pressure, inside coal seams, and is released into the work area when the coal is cut. The methane gas was produced naturally by decaying vegetation when coal was being formed 250,000,000 years ago (see page 120). Methane, by itself, is not explosive, but when mixed with air will explode violently if ignited by a flame. Methane has a density half that of air and will therefore form a layer in the roof of mine workings. Before the invention of the safety lamp men worked underground by candle light. To try to prevent big explosions a man was employed to burn off the methane before it could collect in large amounts. What a dangerous job he had. This was a very haphazard method of protecting the men and explosions and deaths were common.

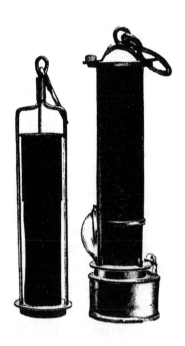

Sir Humphrey Davy's experiments proved that a wire gauze, placed around a flame, spreads the heat of the flame so that it is not hot enough to ignite the gas. Other facts also emerged from his experiments, 15% or more of methane in the air simply burned without exploding but any percentage of methane between 5 and 15 exploded with varying degrees of violence. Its most explosive form being 88%-89% air with 11%-12% methane. Pure fire damp is not dangerous and Sir Humphrey noted that if it penetrated the gauze the flame of the lamp turned blue. This discovery became a vital safety test, carried out by all miners before starting work. To this day miners are searched for matches lighters and tobacco before they are allowed to enter the cage.

Several attempts were made to invent a method of lighting which did not cause an explosion. The Spedding Steel Mill was one such invention. Spedding discovered that sparks would not ignite fire damp and he invented a wheel which when turned threw off sparks which gave a meagre light. This and other attempts at producing a safe light proved unreliable and it was not until 1815 when Sir Humphrey Davy's safety lamp was invented that a reliable safe light was found.

FIGURE 53—*One of the first Davy lamps to be taken underground, 1816.*

The Davy Lamp is commemorated in Durham by the Public House and community of that name near Kelloe. (See page 150)

If an explosion occurs, the violence of its force, concentrated in the narrow seams and tunnels is devastating. Supports, rails and tools are hurled about, and smashed. Men who survive the blast and flames are then in danger of death by suffocation. After Damp or Choke Damp (Carbon Dioxide) is a by product of the explosion and fills the workings. Anyone without breathing apparatus dies from lack of oxygen.

Canaries in cages were carried by rescue teams as a test for choke damp. If the canary died there was a potentially dangerous concentration of the gas. Thus the bird gave its life to warn the men.

Even after taking every safety precaution accidents still happen through the ignition of methane. The 1951 Easington disaster when 83 men were killed, was caused by sparks from the cutter striking iron pyrites in the seam.

The presence of large quantities of coal dust in the air underground was found to be an explosive mixture, which spread the explosive effects of methane over a large area of the workings. In modern mines coal dust control in the form of water sprays and stone dust minimises the risks, while efficient ventilation removes the methane before dangerous pockets can accumulate.

The great pit disasters have always brought

forth great waves of public sympathy with large sums of money being donated to the disaster fund. Every day though men were being killed and injured by accidents with tools, haulage, and rock falls. The graph shows dramatically the fall in accidents which has taken place over the years through the modernisation of the industry and attention to safety.

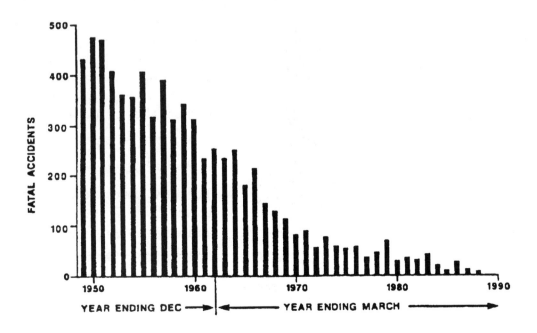

Figure 34 Fatal accident trends

BACKGROUND INFORMATION ON THREE LARGE COLLIERIES

MURTON

Sinking began 19th February 1838 and soon after encountered serious water problems. Pumps capable of extracting 5000 gallons of water per minute made no impression on the inflow. Freezing had to be employed in order to pass through the saturated zone.

Underground - haulage is by 23 English Electric battery powered locomotives each of 65.5 HP. They haul trains of 2 ton capacity mine cars to the rotary hopper at the bottom of Hawthorn shaft. Stones are separated at loading points underground and drawn up at Murton. The whole haulage system is controlled by a Westinghouse signal system using sectioned track on which only one locomotive is allowed to travel at any one time.

Winding - There are three shafts at Murton. The Koefe winding gear was installed in the West Pit in 1924, the first of its kind in the country. Its engine is 750 HP and is used for winding stone waste.

Middle Pit winding gear is 630 HP and is used for men and materials.

East Pit has two speed winding gear of 100 HP and is the ventilation down shaft.

Drainage - There are two 800 gallons/minute pumps in the shaft bottoms plus one standby capable of pumping 540 gallons of water per minute.

Power - 17,500 HP is needed to keep the pit working. 3,700 on the surface and 13,800 underground for lighting, batteries and machinery.

HORDEN

At one time the biggest pit in Britain. Horden was completed in 1904 after only 45 months of work. The cost was £450,000 for three shafts and all the surface and underground equipment. Within 25 years a community of 1400 pit houses and 10,000 people had grown up on the coast. The pit soon produced 6,000 tons per day for gas and steel production. There was a coke works on site and gas from this was used to produce electricity at both Horden and Blackhall pits. Gas coal was sold in London, Berlin, Paris and other continental cities between the two world wars. The pit worked both Bord and Pillar and Longwall methods and had man riding trains 60 years ago. The High Main, Main and Yard seams were extensively worked.

Regulations for working under the sea bed.

1. No mining when there is less than 60 metres to the sea bed.

2. Only partial extraction of coal by Bord and Pillar methods between 60 and 105 metres of cover.

3. No Longwall methods if less than 105 metres to sea bed or less than 60 metres of carboniferous rock above.

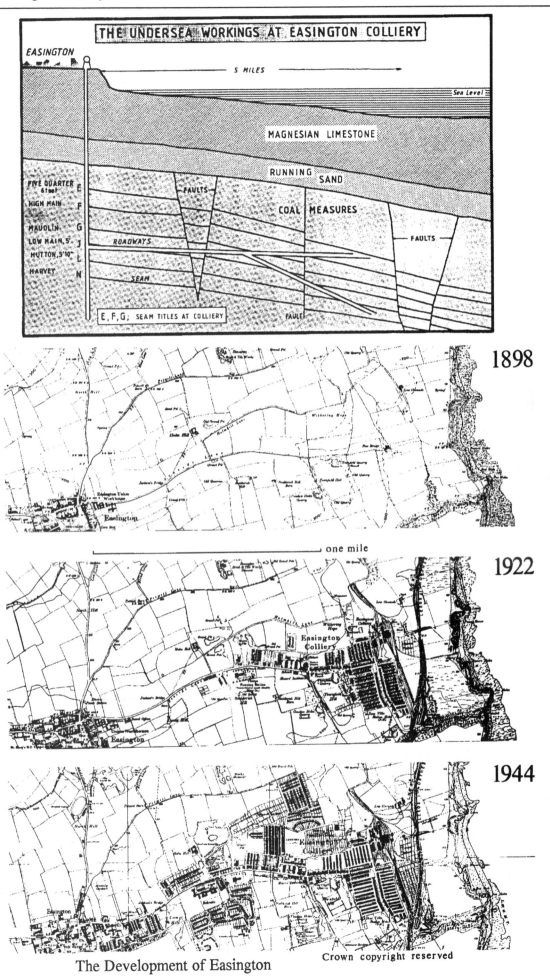

THE UNDERSEA WORKINGS AT EASINGTON COLLIERY

The Development of Easington

Crown copyright reserved

● Information taken from *Men in the Pits* by F. Zwerg, published by Victor Gollanz Ltd. 1948 to whom gratitude is expressed

PIT PONIES

THE PIT PONY'S PRAYER

To thee, my master, I offer my prayer

Feed me with food clear of dust, properly mixed with bran and rolled oats, so that I can digest my food, also water and care for me, when the day's work is done provide me with shelter, a clean dry bed and a stall wide enough for me to lie down in comfort. Talk to me. Your voice often means as much to me as the reins. Pet me sometimes, that I may serve you the more gladly and learn to love you. Do not jerk the reins and do not whip me when going up hill. Never strike, beat or kick me when I do not understand what you mean, but give me a chance to understand you. Watch me and if I fail to do your bidding see if something is not wrong with my harness or feet. Examine my teeth when I do not eat, I may have an ulcerated tooth, and that you know, is very painful. Do not tie my head in an un-natural position, or take away my best defence against flies and mosquitoes by cutting off my tail. Finally oh my master, when my useful strength is gone do not turn me out to starve or freeze or sell me to some cruel owner to be slowly tortured and starved to death, but do thou master take my life in the kindest way and your God will reward you here and hereafter. You may not consider me irreverent if I ask this in the name of him who was born in a stable. Amen.

The ponies are brought into pits at the age of four, and stay there their whole life up to eighteen or twenty. At first they are of little use, and fret easily. It takes a pony about two years to get used to the underground conditions and to develop its full pit-sense. The best ponies are those in the age group of ten to eighteen. Middle-aged ponies, and even those who are getting on, are more appreciated than the younger ones - a feature which has a parallel in the work of the miners.

Many ponies have a better pit-sense than men, and they refuse to go to unsafe places. In fact, I heard many stories of how ponies had saved men from being killed.

A pony fully trained - i.e. after two years - knows the roadways by heart, and can walk alone unguarded, and even open the doors by pushing them. At the end of the shift it returns by itself to the stables.

They work a full shift, then they are fed and

cleaned in the stables underground, which of course show a great range of conditions. Some stables are very good and clean and well-lit. others have a stone floor, covered with dirt, and in dim light. A pony kept clean, often washed, works better; this is the general opinion one hears from the men who work with the ponies. It is not only because it will have less trouble with its skin, but its gait and whole bearing will be different. It will feel better and will have more self-confidence.

The poor creatures usually stay in the pit their whole life-time, because winding them up presents difficulties. A few collieries bring them up to the surface for a week's holiday and let them graze there. During the August week holiday they enjoy the fresh air, rolling over the grazing grounds, galloping and jumping. When they first see the light they can hardly look around, and become a little wild. But in most collieries the ponies stay their whole working life underground and are brought to the surface only when sick or to be destroyed or disoposed of. Some go blind in the course of years, but I was assured that this happens to only a few. It may be that two or three per cent lose their

eyesight. The best ponies often have a chance to get out on the racing grounds, because there is a lot of racing of pit-ponies in the mining areas.

How do the ponies work after a week's holiday? At first they are frisky and stiff, and it takes them a couple of days or a week to get over this. A certain stiffness can be observed even after a weekend's holiday. Habit is the most helpful adaptation, and whenever habit is broken or interrupted it takes time to re-establish it.

Which ponies are the worst? The highly strung ones. There are some nervous types, highly strung, which are no good, and cannot adapt themselves to underground conditions. In that respect horses share the experience of men. Highly strung, nervous types have no place in the pit. They fret too easily, are frightened all the time, have a horror of being enclosed or a fear that the roof is falling on their heads.

Highly strung ponies are very dangerous to the

men who work with them, and often cause derailing of the tubs or other troubles. There is a small percentage of mischievous ponies who bite and kick and injure the men. "There are good and bad in every class, so also among ponies," I was told.

Another very interesting feature about the work of ponies is that they work better for men whom they are used to than for newcomers. They also work better for some men for whom they have an affection than for others. Probably the same is true of men, who work better for some managers or overmen than for others. Some leaders can inspire enthusiasm for work and some cannot. Even the ponies respond to love and kindness. Who doesn't?

It may interest the reader to learn that the ponies also have their limit. If they are used to drive two tubs, and you tried to impose on them an extra burden, they would refuse to move.

In the stable every horse has its name inscribed on a cartboard on the wall, sometimes with the name of a prize won at the races, and when the old horse-keeper comes to it and calls it by its name and pats it on the back, you can see joy and delight in its eyes.

"Are the ponies happy in the pits?" I asked the old horse-keeper, who had served them for more than forty years. "Why not?" he replied. "If you feed them, clean them and treat them properly, they are happy. They are used to the pits, and they don't mind working in them. As a matter of fact, when they are used to the pits they do not mind coming down. After a week's holiday the older ones would go willingly by themselves to the winding-cage, and you don't need to force them to go down. But there can be a lot of trouble with winding the younger ones."

A manager told me, "In a way the ponies made sure by their height that the roadways were reasonably high, and good roadways make for good ventilation, and you know what good roadways and good ventilation means in a pit. You see, the ponies have served well, and not in one way only."

Poor ponies! I do not know whether to regret their disappearance from the pits or to be glad on their account. Anyway, an integral part of old-time mining will be missed by those who have seen in mining not only a profession, but also a way of life not deprived of a certain romance and fancy, linked with mountaineering in the bowels of the earth.

In 1937, County Durham employed 10,336 pit ponies. By 1960 their numbers had fallen to 3,275 and by 1980 there were 50.

The seven at Sacriston were the last remaining pit ponies in the Durham Coalfield.

Here is what happened to them:-

- *Sandy transferred to Ellington Colliery*
- *Smokey transferred to Ellington Colliery*
- *Darkie transferred to Ellington Colliery*
- *Pip - transferred to Beamish Museum*
- *Bobby - retired to Carlisle*
- *Topper - retired to Carlisle*
- *Matt - to private home after RSPCA inspection*

(From NCB Press Brief 15th November 1985)

MINING IN THE SOUTH WEST DURHAM AREA PRIOR TO 1948

The first mining of coal in South West Durham was probably done by landowners and Religious Houses before the general shortage of wood made coal a domestic necessity. Prior to the nineteenth century the shallow or outcropping seams in the western area were the first to be worked. This type of working was confined to opencast operations and bell pit workings employing a small number of men. The coal produced was used either locally or transported overland to Darlington and villages in North Yorkshire. Later, as production increased coal was transported to Newcastle in panniers carried by pack horses, and later, to Stockton for despatch to London by sea. Output was limited and dependent on the transport then available and it was not until the nineteenth century brought swift and easy transport in the form of railways that production of coal increased. The real exploitation of this sector of the Durham coalfield did not indeed come into being until the construction and operation of the Stockton and Darlington railway in 1825 which modernised means of materials transport and created an impetus to industrial development in branches other than mining.

Improvements in mining techniques led to the extension of mining development, and activity as the industry spread eastward towards the concealed coalfields near the coast.

The introduction of electricity into mining operations and better selection and classification of coal together with a new process of making steel led to the sinking of new pits further east to seams at greater depths.

The additional demand for steel and coke used

● Information supplied by MGCW Wheeler

in its preparations led to the closure of the old type of Beehive Coke Oven so common at one time in the western area. Witton Park Steel Works, once a thriving economic industrial unit, was superseded by more up to date plants situated on Teeside.

The increased demand for coal led to employment of more labour and at one time demands could not be met. Locally, in the 19th century, the expanding industry led to extensive immigration into the Durham Coalfield from all parts of the British Isles. At first it was mainly redundant lead miners from the neighbouring dales of North Yorkshire and Durham. These families settled on the western fringe of the area and they combined small scale farming with mining, as they had done in the Dales. The establishment of iron works at Witton Park, Tow Law and Consett attracted a labour force of Irishmen, Welshmen and Scotsmen to take up residence in West Durham.

This steady immigration became a virtual tidal wave in the prosperous 1870's. The Welshmen in general preferred mining whilst Irishmen and Scots preferred employment in the ironworks. Agricultural labourers came from as far afield as Norfolk and Essex and being suited to an open air occupation were best suited to work on the coke ovens.

The cosmopolitan mixture of new labour was augmented by men from Cornwall, Lancashire and Leicestershire and truly it can be said the typical West Durham Man of today is

descended - From the "Land of Britain".

In the early days of mining in the area west of Bishop Auckland numerous pits were working including - Quarry and Diamond Pits at Butterknowle, New Copley - Cockfield, Storey Lodge and Lands Pits near Cockfield, Evenwood

(Cragwood) Ramshaw and Tees Hetton.

The Harvey, Busty and Brockwell Seams were worked; the workings were complicated by the presence of appreciable faulting and underground water. The water problem worsened as workings became deeper.

Later sinkings took place at:- Rush Pit - West Auckland, Jane Pit - Witton Park, Gordon House - Cockfield, Randolph - Evenwood, Coppycrook - Shildon, Woodland and Copley, Rowntree - Cockfield.

Bord and Pillar opened up by Opencast working

Further sinkings took place at - St. Helens - West Auckland, Brusselton, Adelaide - Shildon Eldon and Middridge and most recently, at Chilton.

The majority of the older pits are now abandoned: the resources having been exploited to the limit.

Over the past forty years mining development in the area has been influenced more than ever by the varying and changing economic conditions and industrial relations.

The economic slump after the 1914 - 1918 war led to loss of markets and consequent unemployment, and closure of collieries which became waterlogged. These conditions were aggravated by the 1926 Industrial Dispute when some operative mines became waterlogged.

After 1926, a further difficult period in mining was experienced; efforts were made to reclaim

1857

BUTTERKNOWL
BLACK DIAMOND
COPLEY
WIGGLESWORTH
LANDS
EAST BUTTERKNOWL
R. Gaunless
CRAGGWOOD
LANDS
COCKFIELD FELL
DEAN
Cockfield

● colliery   ⊙ pit, shaft or drift   • old pit, old shaft, air shaft   ⌐ houses

one mile

Chilton Colliery

lost foreign markets culminating in the introduction of the Coal Mines Marketing and Selling Scheme in 1930 when it was realised that the marketing and selling price of coal would have to be thoroughly overhauled.

During this period of unemployment and insecurity a large proportion of the workforce drifted away from mining, and this, together with the absence of long term planning, had its effect in later years when there was an increased demand for coal. As a consequence increased output of coal was delayed and only obtained ultimately at high cost.

From 1926 to 1935 efforts were made to produce coal at a profitable price: this was difficult to attain in face of competition from foreign countries in our export markets. This caused a glut in home markets and consequent unemployment in the South West Durham Coalfield where mines were old and not designed for up to date economic production.

The economic conditions led some of the major mining companies to amalgamate and thereby formulate schemes whereby the more economic units could be worked profitably.

To complicate matters over this period, the thick or more profitable seams became exhausted leaving only the seams of inferior quality coal to be worked. It was realised that to produce coal at a competitive market price it was necessary to introduce machinery into mining development on a large scale.

In 1935, the South West Durham pumping scheme was inaugurated under the constitution of the South West Durham Development Board. The Board's purpose was the relief of unemployment in the mining industry and a co-operative effort between mining companies to deal with waterlogged mines and to safeguard the existing working mines to stem a general exodus of skilled workers from the mines.

From 1935 to 1939 there was a gradual improvement in coal production and conditions of employment and the more secure outlook gave confidence for future planning and stopped the drift of labour from the mines.

Immediately after World War II broke out in 1939 there was an increased demand for coal. This was difficult to attain as many of the proposed long term mining schemes had not been put fully into operation and the mines were not equipped for a quick increase of output. There was a dearth of skilled labour due to recruitment for H.M. forces and many skilled men had drifted into other occupations after 1926. This led to a recruitment campaign for mining trainees.

The Ministry of Fuel and Power came into being in 1941 and was the authority for the control of the mining industry. The outcome of this organisation was to regularise wages, organise the industry and introduce short and long term planning with the view to stabilising the future economic position of the industry. This process was carried out and gave slow but definite results.

In 1942 the Opencast Executive was inaugurated for the purpose of furthering coal production by opencast operations. In this respect numerous sites in Bishop Auckland area were opened out and made an appreciable contribution to coal output during and after the war.

In spite of the exhaustion of the thicker seams numerous isolated areas of coal remained, these areas are at a shallow depth from the surface, suitable for drift mining projects and are comparatively small units .

On 1st January 1947, (Vesting Date) the National Coal Board was established to control the efficient development of the mining industry.

Now it was possible to view the planning of areas for production in a much wider field and to formulate short and long term planning to increase output at lower cost.

Accordingly, much work and effort was put into planning schemes and putting into operation plans for underground and surface re-organisation of collieries. The Durham Division of the National Coal Board comprises of five areas; Bishop Auckland area and westwards (S.W.Durham) is included in No. 4 area and some details of mining activity in this area are outlined below.

The area is traversed by a major fault from Bishop Auckland to Etherley and Lands (Cockfield) running in a south westerly direction. From Lands the fault assumes a westerly direction towards Butterknowle (Copley) and thence to Woodland and the west of Woodland.

At Etherley the throw or displacement of this fault called the Butterknowle Fault (see map page 124) is approximately 650 feet, displacing the various coal seams vertically by that amount. On the north or upthrow side of the fault the upper seams are denuded.

These coal seams lie within the middle Carboniferous Series and the area is overlain with boulder clay, with sand and gravel deposits in the vicinity of the Gaunless Valley.

Travelling westwards from Bishop Auckland the seams outcrop in sequence to the base of the boulder clay and to the surface. Thus in the extreme west of the area the lowest seams Marshall Green and Cowley come practically to the surface in the Woodland district. Immediately east of Bishop Auckland the district in overlain with Magnesian Limestone; the limestone escarpment can be seen at Park Head Bank Top on the road leading from Coundon Gate to Spennymoor.

SEAMS OF SOUTH WEST DURHAM
● Information supplied by MGCW Wheeler

West Durham coals are mainly used for the production of metallurgical cokes. A large percentage of output is carbonized in coke ovens.

The best high grade foundry cokes are made from blends of the Victoria, Brockwell and Busty seams together with smaller amounts of other seams worked which are often not of such good quality.

Generally speaking, seams above the Busty are not particularly suitable for the manufacture of foundry coke but they possess sufficient strongly caking qualities to allow them to be blended with Victoria, Brockwell and Busty for the production of blast furnace coke.

Gas coals are chiefly mined from seams above the Harvey and are generally of a higher volatile content than the true coking coals such as Victoria, Brockwell and Busty.

West Durham coals sold for household use are fairly strongly caking. The major portion mined for this purpose is sold locally.

A brief description of the seams

Main Coal outcrops west of Etherley. The seam section usually includes a dirt band.

Low Main is of low section and in places the seam contains one or more dirt bands. This has probably precluded its more extensive mining.

Hutton is a well known seam extending westwards to north of West Auckland and Cockfield. The section is variable but the coal is clean. In the south east corner of No. 4 area the seam splits into Top and Bottom Hutton and the thickness of the intervening band then necessitates the two seams being worked separately.

Harvey, is worked extensively over the area. it is not quite such a clean seam as the Busty and its sulphur content in particular areas may be higher than either Busty or Brockwell.

Tilley or Beaumont is a banded and rather variable seam; its quality is uncertain.

Busty is extensively worked. In certain localities east of Bishop Auckland it splits into two sections termed Top and Bottom Busty the intervening band varying between 3 and 20 feet.

Brockwell is the lowest seam of the Middle or Main Productive group of coal measures. It is extensively worked over the whole of the area, and west of Bishop Auckland, the seam is practically everywhere free from dirt bands. As this seam approaches its southern outcrop south and west of Bishop Auckland it attains its maximum thickness 7'0" at West Auckland.

Victoria is the lowest of the principal coal seams of the main Durham Coalfield and is the only important seam in the Ganister or Lower Coal Measures which lie between the Millstone Grit and the Brockwell Seam. Little of this seam appears to be workable in the area and it has been worked only on a small scale north west of Toft Hill.

Marshall Green found below Victoria, was worked on the south west outcrop at one colliery only. Further west, where the seam outcrops to the subsoil, a small area has been worked under license. It is generally between 20 and 30 inches thick and resembles the Victoria in coking properties though its ash is considerably higher.

North of the river Tees at Winston the **Yoredale** seam is worked. This seam is at shallow depth and is not associated or correlated with the coals of the lower carboniferous but is included in the Mountain Limestone series.

KELLOE

OWNERS

1836 - 1880 East Hetton Coal Co. Ltd.

1880 - 1935 Walter Scott Ltd.

1935 - 1946 East Hetton Collieries Ltd.

1947 - National Coal Board

KELLOE - EAST HETTON COLLIERY

Reference to a coal mine being worked at Coxhoe in the 14th, century can be found in McKenzie's ''History of Durham'' published in 1834. In the latter half of the 18th. century, numerous boreholes were put down to prove the Five Quarter seam in the Kelloe, Quarrington and Coxhoe areas. The results of these bores led to the sinking of a number of shafts in these areas.

In 1836 a shaft was sunk at East Hetton to the Main Coal seam, and in 1837 the mineral railway leading to Coxhoe Bridge was leased. The colliery being about 14 miles from Hartlepool and 23 miles from Middlesbrough had a ready outlet for shipping coals to the home and export markets. The colliery now has 3 shafts at East Hetton, the North and South Shafts which are 11ft. (3.6m.) diameter are sunk to the Harvey Seam and the Pumping Shaft 6ft. (2m.) diameter is sunk to the Tilley Seam.

● In Cassop Primary School Jim McManners has gathered together much information about the colliery and some of this is presented here

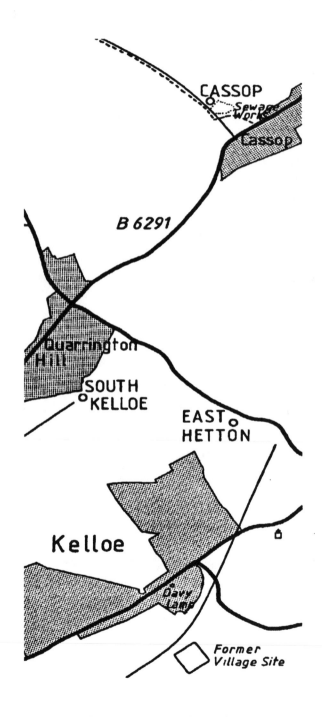

SEAM DEPTH THICKNESS REMARKS

Five Quarter 342 3ft.6in. worked out by 1870

Main Coal 387 4ft.3in. worked out by 1887

Low Main 536 2ft.6in. worked 1883-1914

Top Hutton 637 2ft.2in. worked 1908-1960

Bottom Hutton 672 3ft. worked from 1889

Harvey 808 3ft.6in. worked 1870-1933

Tilley 852 3ft.9in. Commenced working 1938

Bottom Busty 927 3ft commenced working 1937

ROYALTIES

Kelloe Glebe leased when mine started.

Town Kelloe leased in 1843.

Garmondsway leased in 1871. Garmondsway Colliery finished in 1845

Coxhoe leased in 1890. Coxhoe Colliery finished in 1877.

Cassop leased about 1895. Cassop Colliery finished in 1867.

GENERAL INFORMATION

1855 Kelloe Winning Shaft sunk to Main Coal to pump limestone water encountered in East Hetton workings. Began pumping in 1859.

1880 50 Coke Ovens, Gas Works and Brickworks.

1882 Explosion in Harvey Seam at Trimdon Grange, killed 6 men working at East Hetton.

1883 Inrush of water from Cassop Harvey workings in which 10 men were drowned.

1900 101 Coke Ovens

1933 Dry Cleaning Plant in operation.

1934 All coal mechanically cut.

1937 All ponies withdrawn and all coal mechanically cut and hand filled on to conveyors. New Screening Plant erected .

1939 Pit Head Baths and Canteen erected.

1954 Medical Centre opened in March

1959 Power Loading introduced.

1960 New Headgear on South Shaft.

1962 New Winder for South Shaft.

1965 All coal power loaded. New surface tub circuit.

1968 All coal loaded into tubs near shaft bottom from new belt system.

1975 New Winder installed in North Shaft. All coal conveyed to South Shaft (Skip Winder installed). North Shaft now men and materials only.

Last Shift at East Hetton

HOW THE END CAME (From an interview with Mr Dunbar - Manager 1983)

On the 24th March 1983 the pit was working normally. Most of the winnable coal had been extracted from all 8 seams. However, two miles North East of the shafts, under the village of Thornley, there were untouched areas of the Busty seam which promised to keep East Hetton in production until 1989. The development work was done, the roadways made and everything was prepared to open the new face. However, on 25th March, 1983, officials in the Busty seam became suspicious of the presence of water above them. This area of the Busty lay 90 feet below the old worked out Tilley seam of the now closed Thornley Colliery. In 1960 when that seam was worked it had been dry so no water problems were anticipated.

It was decided nevertheless to drill up to this old seam and on 29th March the drilling began with a 15mm drill. The hole was drilled forward at an angle to protect the drillers making the distance to be drilled 112 feet.

On 19th April they made contact with the Tilley "Goaf". Immediately water began to flow but the narrow hole soon blocked. The drill hole was then reamed out and the engineers fitted a pressure gauge. The reading was 68 lbs/sq inch, it astonished the officials. Mr Dunbar ordered a replacement water Gauge, convinced that such a high reading would turn out to be incorrect. The second gauge confirmed the reading. To their horror the engineers calculated the implications of the readings; 162 feet head of water, this meant that the entire Thornley Tilley seam **and** the Harvey above it were filled with water. They were standing 90 feet below **173 million gallons** of water.

The men were withdrawn and the pit was finished.

TOW LAW
-an abundance of mines

● Dave Farms has collected this information about one of the oldest mining areas

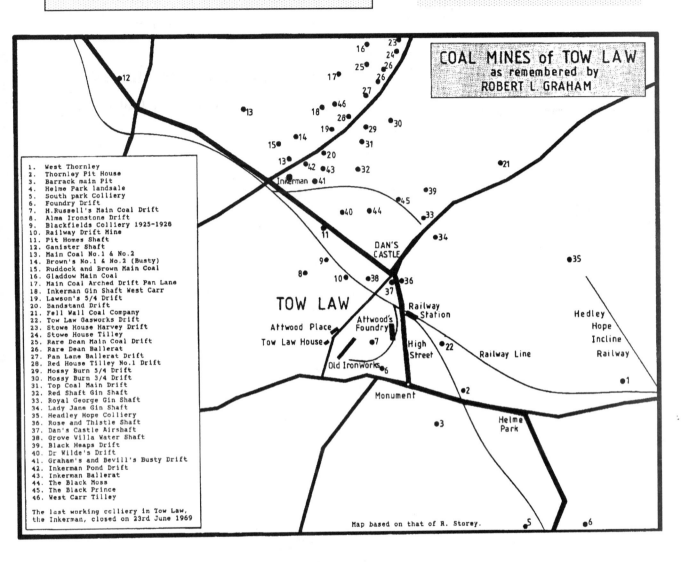

COAL MINES of TOW LAW
as remembered by
ROBERT L. GRAHAM

1. West Thornley
2. Thornley Pit House
3. Barrack main Pit
4. Helme Park landsale
5. South park Colliery
6. Foundry Drift
7. H.Russell's Main Coal Drift
8. Alma Ironstone Drift
9. Blackfields Colliery 1925-1928
10. Railway Drift Mine
11. Pit Homes Shaft
12. Ganister Shaft
13. Main Coal No.1 & No.2
14. Brown's No.1 & No.2 (Busty)
15. Ruddock and Brown Main Coal
16. Gladdow Main Coal
17. Main Coal Arched Drift Pan Lane
18. Inkerman Gin Shaft West Carr
19. Lawson's 5/4 Drift
20. Bandstand Drift
21. Fell Wall Coal Company
22. Tow Law Gasworks Drift
23. Stowe House Harvey Drift
24. Stowe House Tilley
25. Rare Dean Main Coal Drift
26. Rare Dean Ballerat
27. Pan Lane Ballerat Drift
28. Red House Tilley No.1 Drift
29. Mossy Burn 5/4 Drift
30. Mossy Burn 3/4 Drift
31. Top Coal Main Drift
32. Red Shaft Gin Shaft
33. Royal George Gin Shaft
34. Lady Jane Gin Shaft
35. Headley Hope Colliery
36. Rose and Thistle Shaft
37. Dan's Castle Airshaft
38. Grove Villa Water Shaft
39. Black Heaps Drift
40. Dr Wilde's Drift
41. Graham's and Bevill's Busty Drift
42. Inkerman Pond Drift
43. Inkerman Ballerat
44. The Black Moss
45. The Black Prince
46. West Carr Tilley

The last working colliery in Tow Law, the Inkerman, closed on 23rd June 1969

Map based on that of R. Storey.

The earliest record of coal mining in the Tow Law area shows that an old mine known as "TOLLAWE" existed in 1424. An old lease referring to the coal mine was granted by Bishop Langley in 1424 to William de Eure when mines at Raby, Caldhurst, Toftes (Toft Hill?) and Hartgyll were leased by the Bishop to Robert Walker.

In 1427 the same Bishop leased to Thomas Wilton the mines at Raby, Toftes, Caldhurst, Hartkild, Heatherclough otherwise Tollawe, Morapitt and Wollawe. Thomas Buk was appointed surveyor and Ralph Gyllaw was appointed clerk. In 1496 Leonard Forester was appointed surveyor.

Even in the past the tracing of this mine was a difficult proposition, but evidence produced from old workings is claimed to substantiate the existence of an "early mine". Mr James Portney a former undermanager of East Thornley stated that in 1895 he found chalked on a stone, "Looking for the Old Mine". He also found in one of the old boards a "barrow" fitted with wheels, one of which had a cutting edge. This was submitted to the College of Mining which dated it as C1760. Wooden picks and sledges were also found showing evidence of early mines.

The first recorded pitman in Tow Law district was Ralph Davison of Lark Cottages. He was born in 1774 and died at the tender age of 86. He worked with others at a bell pit situated in Dan's Castle. it was to this shaft that donkeys were lead from Weardale to get coals.

In the first quarter of the 19th century there existed a great many mines of the "bell pit" type. A shaft was dug down and coal was worked outwards in a bell shape, until it was on the point of collapse. Then another shaft was sunk nearby. The only machinery in use was a windlass and basket, known as the "swill basket".

In 1845 a transformation occurred in Tow Law. Charles Attwood commenced his Iron producing operations. This naturally lead to an increase in both the number and the size of the local mines. In all there are records of 46 pits of varying size in the Tow Law area at this time.

The larger mines were as follows:

NAME	SUNK	OWNERS
Elm Park	1836	Wingate Grange Coal Co.
Hedley Hope	1836	Bearpark Coal Co.
Lady Jane	1845	
Black Prince	1846	Mrs. Lawson
Inkerman	1873	Wm Callan Esq.

In addition beehive coke ovens existed at the following sites:

NAME	OWNERS
Inkerman	Ferrens and Love
Black Prince	Weardale Coal Co.
Hedley Hope	Sir B Samuelson & Sons
Elm Park	Weardale Steel, Coal & Coke
West Thornley	Weardale Steel, Coal & Coke

The Beehive Coke Oven shown above is at Inkerman and can be visited if the correct approaches are made to H J Banks and Co. Ltd.

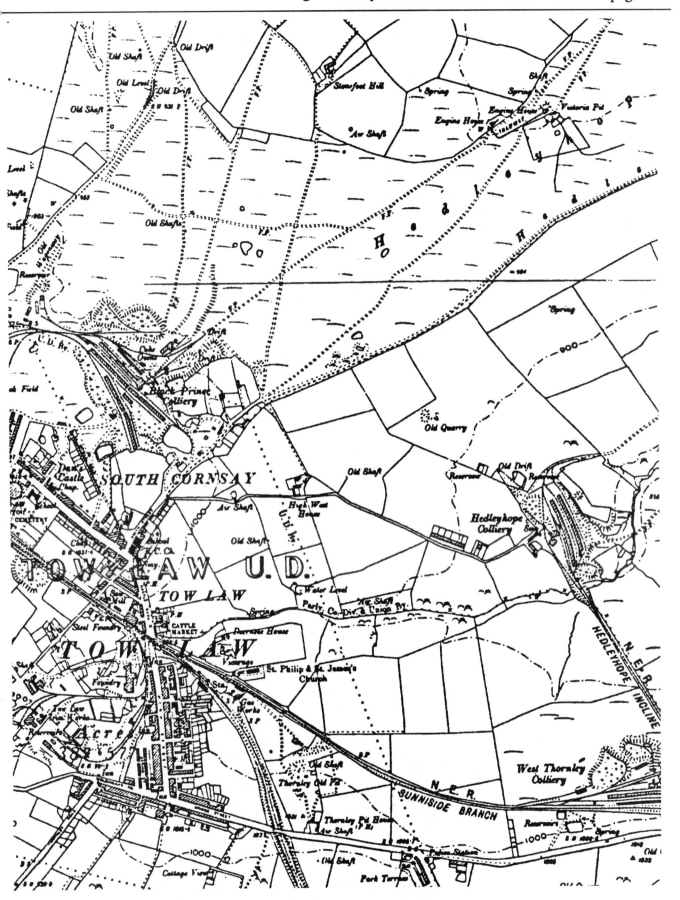

Map of the Tow Law area in approximately 1930

SACRISTON COLLIERY - CLOSURE DETAILS
NCB (North East Public Relations) PRESS BRIEF ISSUED
15 November 1985

SACRISTON COLLIERY:

County Durham

Closure Background

Coal production will end at Sacriston Colliery on Friday 15th November 1985. The Colliery closes officially on Friday 28th December 1985.

Agreement was reached in October between the Board and the mining unions that because of abnormal geological conditions coupled with dwindling reserves, the pit would close before the end of the year.

Sacriston is the thinnest seam pit in Britain and one of the complaints from the men was that conditions on one of the two faces had deteriorated so much that the working height had been reduced in some sections to only 17 inches.

It is the last hand worked pit in County Durham where men cut the coal by pneumatic pick from longwall faces and then shovelled it onto belt conveyors.

The present mine dates fom the 1880's but the locality has associations with mining dating back centuries.

Manpower

Although the last coal will be drawn on Friday 15th November, underground and surface salvage work will continue for some weeks. In the mean time men will start transferring.

Out of a total workforce of 201, 68 men will transfer to Vane Tempest/Seaham Colliery, 5 to Wearmouth, 2 to Dawdon and one to Tursdale Workshops and 134 - mainly older men - will leave on voluntary redundancy terms.

Manager

Mr Tom Hardy, Sacriston's Manager for the past six years, will retire next month, aged 59, after spending 45 years in the mining industry.

He started at the former Deaf Hill Colliery at the age of 14. He was appointed a technical assistant at Easington Colliery in 1953 and later went to Morrison Busty as Under Manager. He was Deputy Manager at Herrington and Manager at Hylton before moving to Sacriston.

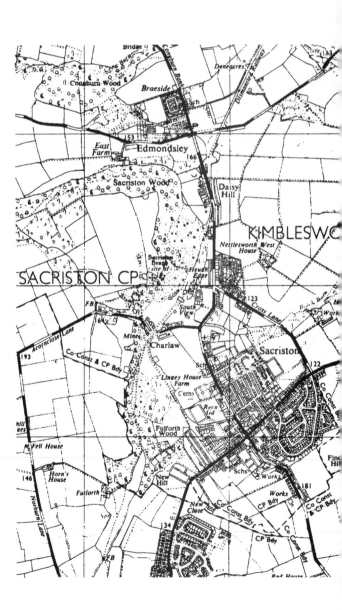

ALLIED INDUSTRIES - dependence on coal

CONTENTS

BY WORD OF MOUTH
COLLIERY RAILWAYS

● Information gathered by CHA Townley in the 1950's photographs loaned by Million Makepiece.

BUTTERKNOWLE MARSFIELD COLLIERY RAILWAY - JUNE 1950

The colliery closed about 1910 but Butterknowle was able to provide a lot of information about the railway system.

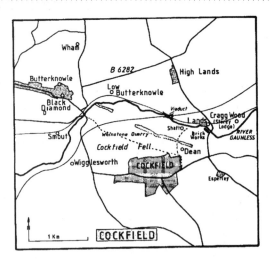

There were three locomotives. Butterknowle, Shotley and Copley which had been built in the 1870's. All were four coupled saddle tank engines. Prior to this horses provided the motive power. There was also a narrow gauge engine Firefly which worked on the top of the beehive ovens. The railway system started at the level crossing adjacent to the Stockton and Darlington station and went in two branches through the two valleys. There were beehive coke ovens all the way down the Marsfield Valley. Coal was taken to a washing plant at the top and led from the Hoppers by the narrow engine which worked on the oven tops. Coke was drawn into standard gauge trucks. The standard gauge locomotive shed was down in the valley about 200 yards west of the Stockton and Darlington terminus at the end of the rows of houses. Mr. McKay produced two sales catalogues relating to the new Butterknowle Colliery Company in liquidation. The first was for a sale on Tuesday, July 21st 1910. This included lot number 234, locomotive Butterknowle. A second sales catalogue of the same period gave details of the locomotive Firefly.

WOODLAND COLLIERY - June 1950

Mr. Kit Blackett of 8 Whitwell Terrace, Woodland, was interviewed. He was then aged about 73. He had started work at the age of 13 for the Butterknowle Marsfield Colliery first as a level crossing keeper and then at the age of 16 he went on to the locos.

He came to Woodland Colliery in 1896. He confirmed Mr. McKay's version of the history of the Butterknowle railways. On the subject of the Woodland Colliery railway he was unable to say when the line was opened. It had originally

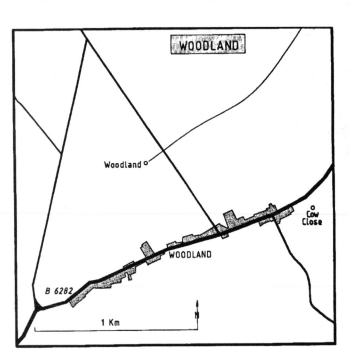

been worked by the North Eastern railway until the arrival of the locomotive Nelson. When the Woodland Colliery Company obtained their own engine they began to work the line right through to the connection with the North Eastern railway Bishop Auckland to Barnard Castle line near the Gaunless viaduct. The wagons always ran down from the colliery by gravity with a locomotive following. There were brakesmen on the wagons to control the speed but they had to run down very fast as it was necessary to have sufficient momentum to get over a level section near Wham. It was usual to run sets of 50 to 60 wagons but Mr. Blackett remembers an occasion when 66 wagons ran

down in one set. The first locomotive to arrive was Nelson, a six coupled saddle tank with inside cylinders built by Kitson's of Leeds. It had come second-hand during the 1880's from a Teesside contractor Charles Nelson. The second locomotive to arrive at Woodland was Eleanor a six coupled saddle tank engine with outside cylinders built by Barclay of Kilmarnock in 1891. During the 1914 - 18 war a six coupled tank locomotive was purchased from South Wales and named George. This was a six coupled saddle tank with inside cylinders. It was in a scrap condition when it arrived at Woodland but nevertheless it was patched up and gave useful service. Towards the end of its history the Woodland Colliery Company was taken over by the Cargo Fleet Iron Company. The Cargo Fleet Company sent a small four coupled saddle tank to Woodland but it was far too small for the work and not very much liked by the

Woodland Cokemen c1900

drivers. The pit closed in 1921 and demolition continued until 1923. The Woodland Colliery had beehive coke ovens but never had a narrow gauge locomotive on them. Some of the coke went to the North Lonsdale Iron Works at Barrow.

WESTERTON AND LEASINGTHORNE COLLIERIES - JUNE 1950

The following notes were obtained as a result of a conversation with an old man who had only been in the district for thirty years or so. He had come to shift the dirt heaps at Westerton and Auckland Park. However he had made himself familiar with a lot of the features of the district.

He was first questioned about the possible connection between Leasingthorne Colliery and Westerton. He confirmed that there was a stationary engine house at the junction of the roads between Middlestone and Coundon and Westerton and Coundon, grid reference 243308. The engine man's cottage was only pulled down four years previously. He could not remember this railway working.

Part of the line from Leasingthorne up to a stone heap at an old quarry, grid reference

246038 had lastly been worked by a locomotive from Leasingthorne. He was of the opinion that when the connection was in between Westerton Colliery and Leasingthorne Colliery wagons went down from the bank head to Leasingthorne on a self-acting incline. On the subject of the connection between the Blackboy and the Auckland Park Collieries and Leasingthorne, he confirmed that he had heard stories about this. There was a stationary engine near the chemist's shop in Coundon. Questioned about the old method of working at Leasingthorne he said there used to be a level crossing at the bottom of the pit yard. A standing engine hauled the wagons to the top of the yard where they gravitated through the screens. This was later re-levelled for loco working. He also said that the old shaft at Westerton Colliery was used as an escape shaft for Binchester. There were ladders up to the shaft with landings every few fathoms. Whenever it had to be used Spennymoor men who came up the shaft were completely lost, they did not know their way home.

TODHILL NEAR SPENNYMOOR - JUNE 1950

Todhill was on the main line of the West Durham railway which was closed for most of its length at a very early date. However the North Eastern railway established a relatively large locomotive depot at Todhill working mineral traffic from the Spennymoor district. This was closed in the 1930's and converted to a brickworks. Much of the building still remains.

An old man aged 73 was questioned about the working of the railways round Todhills. He stated that the incline from Todhill down to Sunnybrow up the other side to Willington finished about 70 years previously, and the stationary engine near Todhill was taken out 60 years ago. There was a passenger service from Spennymoor to Todhill which closed when the new line from Bishop Auckland to Spennymoor through Byers Green was opened. There were no intermediate stations between Todhills and Spennymoor. After the passenger service was

suspended the last engine to shed at Todhill left Spennymoor after the last Bishop Auckland passenger train and on a Saturday night as many as 100 people travelled in the brake van from Spennymoor to Todhills. The engine shed closed 17 or 18 years ago. Nine engines were kept there. In this vicinity there was a long branch which ran down to the Page Bank Colliery. It appears that the branch line was always the property of the Colliery Company not the North Eastern railway. He was questioned about the working on this branch. He stated that it was always North Eastern railway engines which worked the traffic from Spennymoor to Page Bank. There also seems to have been some sort of workmen's passenger service taking the miners from Spennymoor to Page Bank. My informant at Todhills stated that an engine left the North Eastern shed at 2 am and picked up vans presumably to convey the workmen at Spennymoor at about 4 am which took the foreshift down to the colliery. The vans were run up and down the branch between Page Bank and Spennymoor at shift times.

Leasingthorne Colliery – Jan 1950

● Information gathered on site from retired employees.

A fortnight ago coal ceased to be drawn here and is now wound up at the Dean and Chapter. Leasingthorne is still retained for man riding. The two road brick locomotive shed is now disused, the locomotive comes up from Chilton to shunt the brickworks at Leasingthorne.

When the pit was first opened horses were used to pull the black wagons up to the pit but soon afterwards a haulage engine was installed in the pit yard to bring the wagons up from the sidings to the east of the Leasingthorne, Kirk Merrington road. At a later date locomotives were used throughout and it appears that the level of the track was altered at this time. Originally there had been a level crossing over the road but a bridge was substituted presumably with the object of easing the gradients. There were beehive coke ovens at Leasingthorne but none of the informants could remember narrow gauge locomotives on them. They stated that shunting on the ovens was done by horses. However Westerton Colliery is reputed to have had a narrow gauge engine on the beehive ovens. My informant thought only one. There is a suggestion that originally Westerton Colliery sent its coal out over a railway to Leasingthorne and thence down through Chilton Buildings to join the Hartlepool line south of Ferryhill. As this is somewhat doubtful various people at Leasingthorne were questioned about this. There is certainly no local tradition. The general impression is that the Westerton to Spennymoor had

latterly been worked by locomotives but one of the old employees stated that he could remember two stationary engines on this line. Some early maps of Leasingthorne suggest a line to tap the collieries round Blackboy and Eldon with the object of diverting these coals over the West Hartlepool railway for shipment at Hartlepool. Various old people round Leasingthorne were questioned about this. One man stated that he had heard that many years ago the Blackboy coals were in fact led to Hartlepool by Leasingthorne but this was very long before his time. From Leasingthorne there was certainly a branch or siding going off in the right direction but within living memory this has only served a coal depot. There was also a coal depot for the Blackboy Pit and the chemists shop in the main street in Coundon served a railway coming up from the Eldon vicinity. What is not known is if the link line, if such existed, took the course of these two coal depot branches. There is nothing on the ground to suggest that they were linked up and if a line had gone through this way it must necessarily have been worked by stationary engines because of the steep gradients.

RODDYMOOR

● Peter Taylor and the Crook local history group provided the information for this section

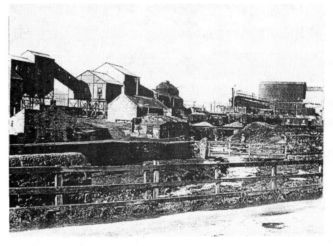

Speed's map of Durham dated 1610 shows "Cole Pits" near Crook, but it was not until the arrival of the railway in 1843 that real development occurred. In 1811 the population of Crook was 176. In 1841 it was 538. Then the Emma, Lucy and Edward drift mines were opened at Roddymoor and by 1851 the population of Crook was 3936.

These drift mines, like the railway, were a part of the Pease family empire and Bankfoot works was established in 1850 because of the high coking quality of the coal. At one time there were 618 beehive coke ovens on the Bankfoot site. They were about 5m in diameter and constructed of firebrick. Coal was piled up inside and ignited. Then the oven was sealed. This was a very wasteful process as many valuable by-products were just burned off.

In 1882 Henry Simon was hired to build the first Otto waste heat by-product ovens in Britain. This was a highly efficient coal distillation process in which all the by products were collected and used. By 1908 there were 120 of these retorts, and they remained in almost constant use until the works were modernised in

1951. Their replacements had lasted in service for a mere 16 years when the works closed down.

Coal for the works came from the Roddymoor drifts directly, or from the Tow Law pits down the Sunniside incline and later the snaking deviation line. On arrival the coal would be washed and fed into the retorts which produced 200000 tons of coke a year. After the recommended time in the retorts the white hot coke was pushed out by hydraulic rams and quenched with water. The water was pumped through two timber cooling towers and stored in ponds for re-use an early example of water conservation.

Three kinds of coke were produced. About 5000 tons per year of a special low ash coke for the manufacture of electrodes for the aluminium industry. This was made from Ballarat coal and was said to be the best coke in the world. The remaining production was either foundry coke or furnace coke cut to size ranging from 30cm to 150cm. All the coke left the works by rail, in 12 ton waggons with characteristic plank rails around the top. These increased the volume carried, so that the same weight of coke was carried as in a conventional coal truck.

As well as the coke many valuable by-products were produced at Bankfoot. A refinery produced benzol which was taken away by rail tankers to be blended into National Benzol Mixture, Britain's first

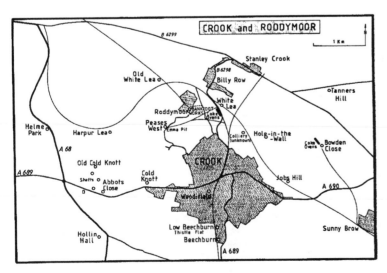

home made petrol. A tar distillation plant produced vast amounts of road tar, which left the works in rectangular tar trucks. This plant also produced extremely smelly fumes and sufferers of whooping coughs went downwind specially for a vapour cure. Sulphur dioxide was collected and used to make sulphuric acid, which again left the works in rail tanks without a trace of acid rain. Other organic chemicals produced were sent to paint works and drug firms.

The Roddymoor drift mines also produced large quantities of seggar clay which was used in the local brickworks to make yellow colliery bricks. These were used to build the colliery "raas" and also the Hownes Gill viaduct near Consett in 1856. At the height of production the Roddymoor drift mines employed 1200 men. There was a Mines Rescue Brigade located in this area, one of only three on the Durham coalfield.

The brickworks closed in 1935. Bankfoot closed in 1965, the reason given was that of exhaustion of local coal supplies. This also lead to the closure of the railway. Ironically the area has since been extensively opencast mined, an operation which extracted vast quantities of coking coal, all of which was transported by road. Now there is talk of reworking the old opencast sites using much more advanced deep opencast mining techniques.

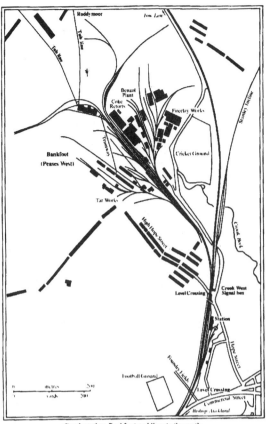

Crook station, Bankfoot and lines to the north

The dual combination of opencast working and the landscaping work of district and county councils have obliterated any evidence of the existence of Bankfoot works or the Roddymoor drift mines. Only the name "Peases West" serves as a reminder of the importance of the area in the past.

BANKFOOT

WAGGONWAYS

● Gravity railways in the Beamish area are examined by Mike Horne

The wealth of Newcastle was built around the coal trade mainly because of the difficulty of transporting this commodity especially in the 18th century when demand for it was rising in London and the South of England. It is interesting that in good weather it took 14 days for a load of coal to travel by sea from Newcastle to London, and this part of the journey was relatively easy.

From the pit the coal had to travel overland to the port. Roads in this time in history were at best dusty or muddy tracks and at worst were a quagmire. As the sources of coal near to the Tyne were worked out the coal had to be carried over progressively longer journeys to arrive at the river and wheeled vehicles had to use these roads with the result that the roads were made worse and worse. Waggon Ways were a method of overcoming the problems caused by the state of the roads.

The Waggon Way was essentially a railway as we would know it today, the main difference being that the rails were made of wood and laid on wooden sleepers. Over these rails passed wooden waggons often using flanged wheels again similar to the railway wheels of today. The motive power available was that of the horse which meant that the ballast or gravel around the sleepers also had to cover them to protect them from the horses hooves. In the end the geography of the area was put to advantage and many of the Waggon Ways used the force of gravity to overcome the major part of the journey, when the waggon was loaded. The horse was used to pull the empty waggons back to the pit for reloading. This meant that the routes covered by the waggon ways had to be chosen with great care. It also meant that the river side depots or staithes were limited in number as they had to be in a place to be served

Coal has been a source of energy for the people of Britain for centuries. The North East and Durham in particular have provided this coal in the main by shipping it through its two major ports Newcastle on the River Tyne and Sunderland on the River Wear. "Carrying coals to Newcastle." is a well known saying.

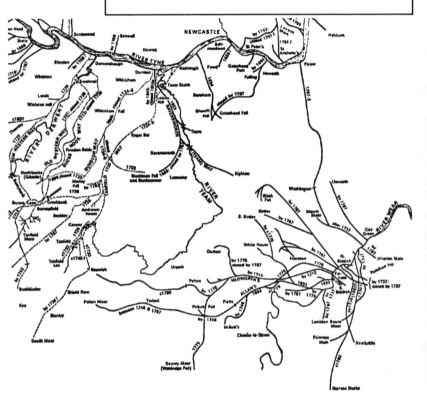

by the gravity lines, inclines. From the map you will see that Dunston was a busy staithe on the River Tyne and Fatfield on the River Wear. The Waggon Ways developed from the Staithes up into the mining areas.

It is difficult to see remains of most of the old Waggon Ways as the routes they took were so good that later rail and or road builders followed exactly the same routes and so have built over the remains. The Tanfield Waggon Way is one that is more easily seen than others due to the restoration work done by Durham County Council in the late 70's and early 80's.

The Tanfield Waggon Way was constructed in 1724/25 to carry the coal from Tanfield pit to the tyne at Dunston. The major obstacle to the line was the Causey Burn (River Team) very near to the colliery end of the line. This had to be crossed twice and the crossings were major civil engineering feats for their time. The first crossing was made using a bridge - Causey Arch, the second crossing used an embankment and culvert system. At the time of its construction Causey Arch was, at 105 feet, the longest single span bridge in the country. The waggon way had wooden rails and consisted of one route for the loaded waggons, the main way, with a separate parallel route for the empties, the bye way. Wooden rails caused many problems especially with wear so the main way was constructed with two rails on each side, one above the other, whilst the bye way consisted of one layer. This method meant that as the top rail of the main way wore more quickly it could be removed without too much disturbance to the sleepers. In any event the rails usually only lasted for about one year before renewal. This must have been costly as well as a hindrance and as soon as technology allowed the rails were replaced with iron rails, on the Tanfield line iron rails were laid in 1839.

Tanfield pit was closed after a major underground fire in 1740. By this time the waggonway had been extended beyond Tanfield and was carrying coal from other pits in the Tanfield Lea area and a spur from the line led to the west of Beamish and eventually to Stanley and South Moor. Horses ceased to be used to move the waggons when steam locomotives were introduced to the line in 1881. The line was eventually closed in 1962 having carried coal down to the Tyne for some 235 years.

The steam age brought a powerful ally to the movement of coal and allowed for it to be carried to its destination more quickly and over more direct routes than had been possible hitherto. The inclines of the steam age are more easily traced than the waggon ways. These were initially built and used steam engines that were in fixed positions pulling the coal waggons by the use of a cable loop or endless belt system. The coal waggons were attached to the cable for uphill journeys and often travelled downhill

using gravity and a braking system to prevent run away waggons crashing and causing damage. As steam technology advanced and locomotives became more reliable and powerful they took over the work of the stationary engines except for the steeper sections of the journey.

If you look at ordnance survey maps you may be able to pick out sections of the routes if you can find areas referred to as "Engine Cottages" or "Engine Bank".

In these two photographs it is possible to see the wire ropes that were used to pull the wagons up the incline and the rollers to allow the ropes to travel easily.

IRON AND STEEL

● Don Wilcock provides this account of Iron and Steel in County Durham

Until the 16th century the most common method of producing iron was to smelt the ore in a shallow bowl furnace with charcoal or brushwood, preferably on an exposed hill side so that the prevailing wind produced the blast necessary to raise the temperature of the furnace. Remains of this type of furnace from the Iron Age have been found at West Brandon (NZ 2013990) by George Jobey. Slag from similar sites has been located at Smith Syke (NY 879284) by D Coggins and K Fairless. Medieval bloomeries have been found at High Bishopley (NZ 012355) and Harthope Mill (NZ108322), the latter after a systematic historical and field search by Dr R F Tylecote; and there is documentary evidence for a bloomery at Gordon, Evenwood (NZ 144267).

Some iron was turned into steel, required for edged tools and swords. From the 17th century the cementation process was used, where iron bars packed in charcoal were heated over a period of 4 to 7 days in a furnace. This produced a 'blister steel' which was then worked in nearby forges. The earliest known site was at Shotley Bridge in 1686, where steel was produced for the Hollow Sword Blade Company. About 1691 Ambrose Crowley established a nail factory at Winlaton Mill, and erected 2 cementation furnaces in 1700 and 1701; while Wilhelm Bertram, a German steel-maker, began operating a similar furnace at Blackhall Mill in 1719, supplying steel to the Germans at Shotley Bridge. The county's only surviving cementation furnace is that at Derwentcote (NZ 131565), probably worked from 1753 to 1898 and feeding steel to a nearby forge.

The primitive bloomery furnaces gradually increased in size from Elizabethan times, and bellows driven by water-wheels were used to create an adequate blast. The Allensford charcoal-fired blast furnace (NZ 098503) on the Durham-Northumberland border was working in 1683, the first such furnace in the Derwent valley. It supplied iron to the cementation furnaces of the area. After 1709 these charcoal-fired furnaces were gradually replaced as coke came into use; the first known coke-fired furnace in County Durham was at Whitehill, near Chester-le-Street, about 1753. The ore came from iron stone seams among the coal measures, supplemented by ore gathered on the shore at Whitby and shipped via the Wear. The three basic ingredients for iron-making, iron, coal (for coke-making) and limestone, were all at hand in the county, and as demand grew in the first half of the 19th century so did the number of blast furnaces. The two furnaces built at Birtley in 1827 continued in blast until the late 1860's using, initially, local ironstone. The Consett Iron Company, established in 1840 as the Derwent Iron Company, built their blast furnaces to use locally mined ironstone with limestone brought by the Stanhope and Tyne Railway from the Weardale quarries. At Stanhope itself a blast furnace was erected in 1854, smelting the spathic (iron carbonate) ores of Weardale and fuelled by coke brought as return loads from north-east Durham by the railway.

In 1846 Charles Attwood, having leased large tracts of ironstone in the Wolsingham and Stanhope areas, built blast furnaces at Tow Law on the edge of the coalfield, and founded the Weardale Iron Company. Later known as the Weardale Iron, Steel and Coal Company, it expanded to take in mines and develop the Tudhoe Ironworks in 1853. The company built a standard gauge railway across the Durham moors from Weatherhill over Bolt's Law and down an incline into Rookhope. Here the line branched into two, one branch running up the valley to the Grove Rake ironstone mines, the other high above the Wear to Middlehopeburn and the Slitt iron mines; and the pathic ores thus collected from Weardale fed the furnaces of Tow Law and Tudhoe.

The Middlesbrough ironmasters Bolckow and Vaughan sought to use Durham ores, and in 1846 built four furnaces at Witton Park to utilise local ironstone. Soon afterwards, in 1850, the Cleveland ores were discovered in the Eston Hills south of the Tees on their own doorstep; thereafter ore was shipped to Witton Park by the Stockton and Darlington Railway, which also carried Cleveland ores to the Derwent Iron-works. Many other smaller iron companies sprang up in the 1850's and 60's on the edge of the coalfield to use the new ores from Eston and Rosedale, with local limestone and coke pro-duced in their own ovens from coal won in their own pits. Bell Brothers appeared at Port Clarence in 1854, the Ferryhill and Rosedale Iron Company (later Carlton Iron Company) at Ferryhill (West Cornforth) in 1858, and the Coxhoe Ironworks in 1856. More furnaces appeared in central Durham, at Washington in 1856, with the nearby Wear furnaces in 1858. At Stockton and Norton furnaces were built between 1853 and 1860, and at Middleton St. George in 1867. Some produced pig-iron for re-sale, others used their iron foundry and forge, as at Darlington, 1854, and Seaham, 1855; while Palmer's of Jarrow used their shipyard from 1857.

Attwood's Blast Furnace at Tow Law

Following the introduction of the Bessemer converter and the Siemens open-hearth process in 1856, and the Gilchrist-Thomas process of 1879, there was a move towards producing bulk steel in integrated iron-and-steel units. But local ores were becoming exhausted by the end of the century, and their winning proved too expensive to compete with Spanish ores; so inland furnaces began closing, and the industry was increasingly concentrated around the Tees. The Weardale Company at Tudhoe (at one time the largest pro-ducer of Bessemer steel in the region) and the Carlton Company (at Stil-lington) continued until the 1920's, while the Consett Iron Company grew in size and output, remaining a major feature of the Dur-ham Industrial land-scape until the 1980's.

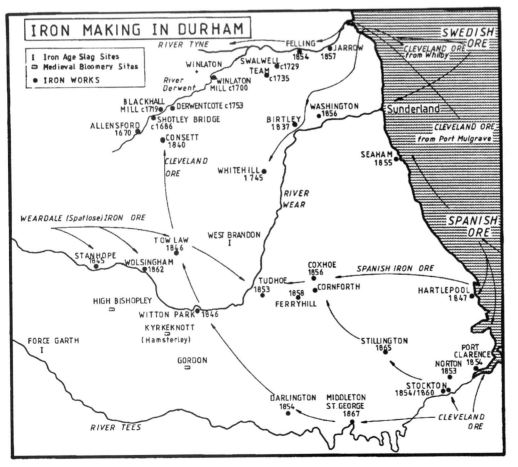

A USE FOR FORMER COLLIERY SITES

● Frank Burns looks at new uses for old sites

In years gone by when a pit closed it was common to see the empty buildings and headstock still standing many years later, with the pit heap gradually cooling and being naturally colonised by plants and trees. These sites progressively deteriorating, became an eyesore in the community. What a contrast today. No sooner has the cage ascended for the last time than the shafts are capped, buildings levelled and the pit heaps landscaped. The sites are valuable land, highly suitable for new industries. New industries to replace jobs lost through the pit closure. New Offices and Factories have to have a pleasant environment with infrastructure and communications of a high standard to attract firms. Financial and other help is available in the form of location grants from Local and National Government and more recently British Coal Enterprises.

One of many such sites around the county is the Dean and Chapter Industrial Estate at Ferryhill. The huge pit heap is now grazing land and woodland while use has been made of the old colliery buildings as small industrial units. The plan shows the site with the former colliery buildings in the centre with new units on the left.

A measure of the problem of replacing jobs lost when a pit closes is graphically illustrated by comparing the 1074 employed at the Dean and Chapter Colliery in 1963 with the figures for employees on the industrial estate in 1991.

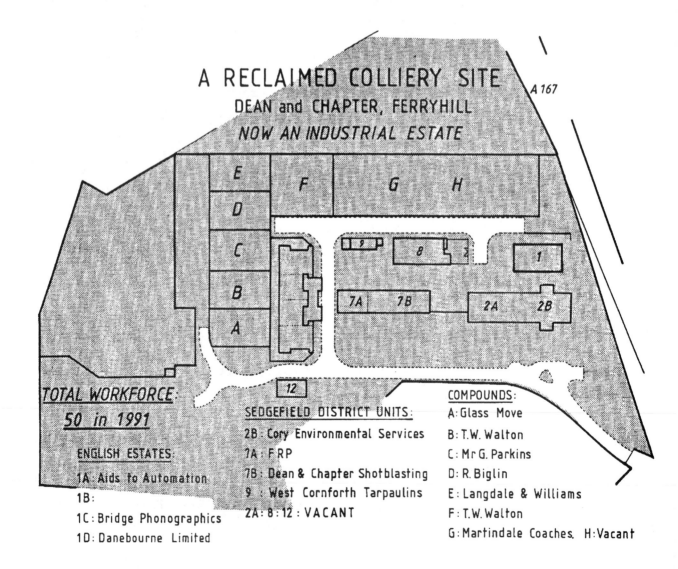

A RECLAIMED COLLIERY SITE
DEAN and CHAPTER, FERRYHILL
NOW AN INDUSTRIAL ESTATE

A 167

TOTAL WORKFORCE:
50 in 1991

ENGLISH ESTATES:
1A: Aids to Automation
1B:
1C: Bridge Phonographics
1D: Danebourne Limited

SEDGEFIELD DISTRICT UNITS:
2B: Cory Environmental Services
7A: FRP
7B: Dean & Chapter Shotblasting
9 : West Cornforth Tarpaulins
2A: 8: 12 : VACANT

COMPOUNDS:
A: Glass Move
B: T.W. Walton
C: Mr G. Parkins
D: R. Biglin
E: Langdale & Williams
F: T.W. Walton
G: Martindale Coaches. H: Vacant

RECLAMATION OF DERELICT LAND TUDHOE COLLIERY, SPENNYMOOR, CO. DURHAM - DURHAM COUNTY COUNCIL PLANNING DEPARTMENT

The site lies immediately to the east of Tudhoe Colliery Village which grew adjacent to the mine. The site can be seen most clearly from the former A1 road (now the A167) from where it presented a considerable visual intrusion in the landscape, extending to the rear of the housing in Front Street. A large allotment area and agricultural land formed the south boundary with a wood and a school on the north side. Some industrial use was made of the former colliery buildings within the site.

The land to be reclaimed consisted of 45.7 hectares of derelict colliery area, waste heaps, the low quality Loggins Wood and some agricultural land required for spreading and soil provision. The design of the reclaimed site included extensive Public Open Space areas adjacent to the housing, rationalisation and screening of the allotments, an extension of the industrial area with wooded mounds as screens, and the remainder of the site becoming agricultural land or woodland. The Public Open Space and Industrial Areas were agreed with Sedgefield District Council and allocated to be taken over by them at an appropriate time. The old shafts were capped and numerous unsuspected coke ovens demolished before earthworks could be completed. Design constraints were placed on the site by the presence of C.E.G.B. pylons and by the existing uses. Fortunately, however, the site was large in relation to the size of the heaps, earthmoving being only 415,000 cubic metres and a satisfactory solution was possible.

The major difficulty was caused by the suspected presence of an unexploded bomb from an air raid during the Second World War and this necessitated sweep searches by the Royal Engineers before each successive cut by the earthmoving machinery. This was a long and frustrating exercise but was fortunately concluded without incident.

After uses for the site are 15.1 hectares pasture land, 3.8 hectares arable land, 4.4 hectares public open space, 1.3 hectares allotments, 17.5 hectares woodland and 3.5 hectares of Service Industry.

Other points of interest in the site are the arrangements made with the local (Tudhoe Colliery Primary) school in the north-west corner of the site for a slight enlargement of the playing fields and the construction of a pond/natural regeneration area for Environmental Studies purposes.

The project expenditure was £153,901, made up of - Land acquisition £40,000, Works grant aided £108,485, Staff and other costs £4,100, Development works Non grant aided £1,316

Income - 85% from the Department of the Environment £101,647 Net cost to County Council (including after value of land at £33,000) £52,254.

The following article published in the Northern Echo 9th December 1992.

PLANS to remove more than 300,00 tonnes of coal from a colliery spoil heap near Murton in East Durham were yesterday approved by councillors.

The five-year programme will clear the way for a new industrial estate to be built as part of an ambitious jobs package in the Easington District which has been ravaged by the demise of the coal industry.

Forty jobs will be created by the plan to recover coal from spoil heaps at Dalton Flatts, south-east of Murton.

The colliery spoil currently forms two large heaps alongside the A19 which dominate the landscape.

Coal will be recovered through an operation of digging, transportation and washing - the washing plant is intended to operate 24-hours a day on site.

Forty-eight lorries will visit the site each day, taking coal up the A19 to South Tyneside.

Durham County Council received six letters of objection from local residents who were concerned the operations would be a hazard for children and would cause disturbance due to dust, noise and extra traffic.

But members of the county council's development control sub-committee yesterday approved the plan, following a site visit.

It is expected Easington District Council will grant permission for the industrial estate which it is hoped would be created once the spoil heaps have been dug away.

BRANCEPETH PITHEAP

Location:

On the north side of the High Street in the centre of **Willington** and alongside the road to Oakenshaw.

Design:

Durham County Council (DCC) as consultants to the Crook and Willington UDC.

Contractor:

J. C. Hayes Limited, Barnsley.

The scheme was started in October 1967 and was finally completed in July 1969.

Description:

The pitheap, 58 metres high, completely overshadowed the centre of Willington and was very prominent in distant views from the A690 road and the B6286 road to Hunwick. The heap covered 12.14 hectares and another 6.07 hectares of demolished housing and semi-derelict allotments lay between it and the High Street. Beyond the heap to the north the fields rose fairly steeply. It was therefore possible to regrade the heap onto these fields so that the heap became an extension of the hillside. This spreading land was used under licence, and therefore soil was not available for covering the heap.

The main after-use was 14.57 hectares of new pasture land (mostly without soil), 1.21 hectares of new woodland and 2.43 hectares of open space alongside the High Street. In 1981/82 a new old peoples' home was built on part of the open space area.

Works:

By agreement with the owners and agricultural tenants the bulk of the 1.37 million m³ was regraded onto 19.42 hectares of agricultural land after soils had been stripped to a combined depth of 1 metre. Only small amounts of soil were available for the heap area which were spread thinly on the High Street side of the heap. The remaining bare shale was treated with 25 tonnes of sewage sludge per hectare. Prior to spreading the heap, under-drainage had to be installed to collect ground water from the hillside.

This was probably the first scheme in the country to tackle a pitheap of this size and apart from experience on opencast schemes little advice was available on the handling of shale, soils, drainage, etc., or on the matter of contract documents. A considerable amount of discussion, site visits and correspondence took place before grant approval was given by the DOE from its London office!

Economics:

Expenditure	£	£
Works (grant aided)	126,252	
Staff costs	10,924	142,

Income		
Grant 85% DOE	116,313	
*Grant from DCC	20,526	
Other income	2,731	139,

Net cost to Crook & Willington UDC   3,
(after-value of land)

*DCC operated a grant aid scheme for District Councils fro 1965 until 100% grant became available from DOE in 1975 s to encourage them to undertake reclamation work. The or cost to the District Council was the after-value of the land. During this period DCC gave nearly £½ million in grant aid 174 schemes covering an area of 852 hectares.

Before

After

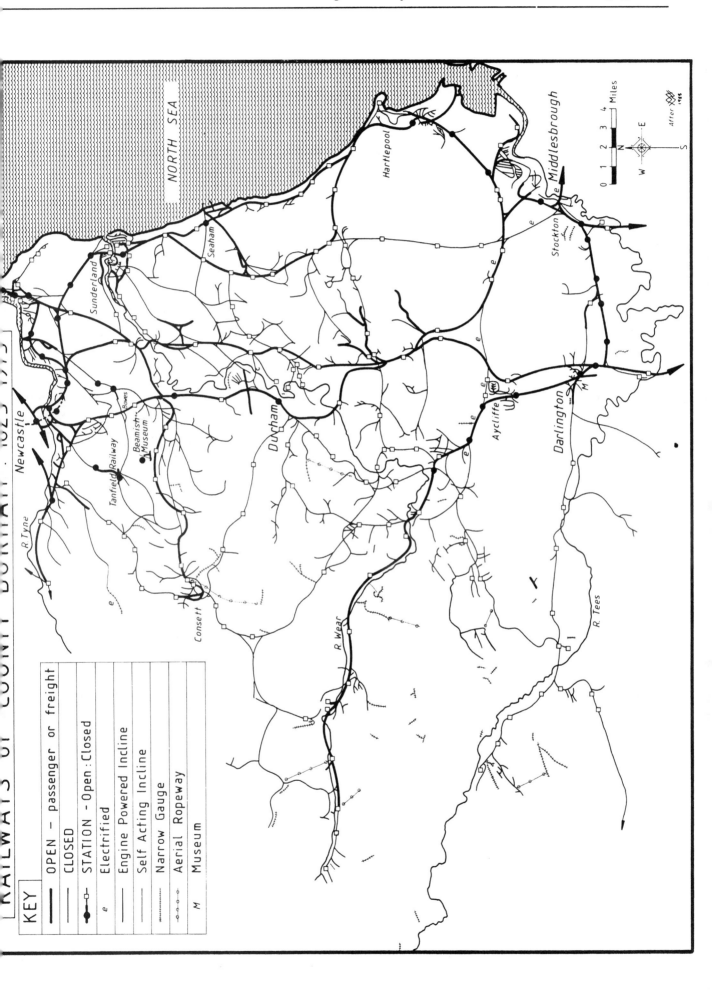

RAILWAYS OF COUNTY DURHAM : 1825-1975

NORTH SEA

KEY

OPEN – passenger or freight
CLOSED
STATION – Open : Closed
e   Electrified
Engine Powered Incline
Self Acting Incline
Narrow Gauge
Aerial Ropeway
M   Museum

Newcastle
Sunderland
Seaham
Hartlepool
Middlesbrough
Stockton
Darlington
Aycliffe
Durham
Consett
Bowes
Tanfield Railway
Beamish Museum
R. Tyne
R. Wear
R. Tees

N
W   E
S

0 1 2 3 4 Miles

After 1985

COKE AND CHEMICALS

● Evenwood Primary School present this data on Evenwood and Randolph Cokeworks following a visit to the school by K Richardson and B Carter - former Randolph workers. Miss Nancy Bell provided additional material.

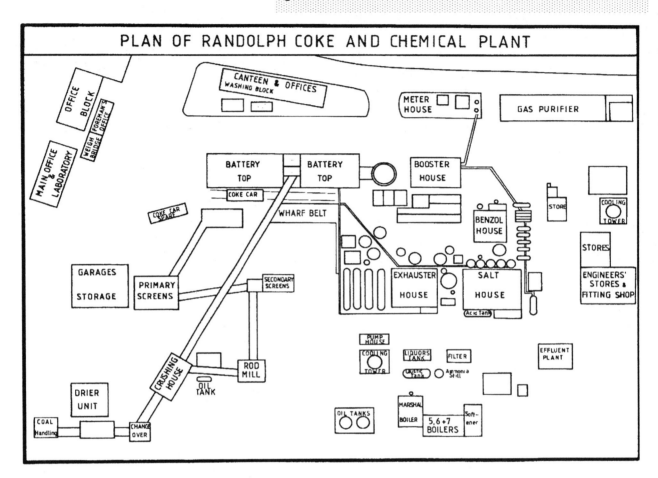

PLAN OF RANDOLPH COKE AND CHEMICAL PLANT

EVENWOOD COKEWORKS

There has been a tradition of coke manufacture in this area, in the 1851 census several men and boys were identified as working in this industry, however, it seems reasonable to assume that the industry was not very well established at this time. Towards the end of the 19th century there was a bank of coke ovens at Norwood Colliery. The production of coke was very crude. Coke was usually produced from large coal. Coking occurred in open heaps commonly known as cinder rows (the older term of "cinders" was commonly used to describe coke) or open topped brick boxes with a central brick chimney to improve the draught. Small coals could not be used with this method as they choked the draught. The coking of small coals grew rapidly

as a result of the development of the iron industry on Teesside. There was a rapid demand for coke and the "beehive" coking technology was perfected. It was a circular brick oven with a sloping floor with crude washers installed to reduce ash content before coking. West Durham was the major producing region up to 1913, and the Gaunless valley contributed to the output of coke throughout the period with coking plants located at many collieries in the area e.g. Woodland, Butterknowle, Evenwood.

Probably the most important feature associated with Evenwood was the cokeworks. In 1895 the North Bitchburn Coal Company began the erection of 60 French "Coppee" coke ovens and in 1897 a second set of 20 ovens were constructed. In June 1909 the Company decided to take down the ovens and replace them with a battery of 50 patent by-product ones. The third battery of ovens was erected after nationalisation in 1948 and extended in 1957. The works were privatised in May 1957 when the Randolph Coke and Chemical Company Limited was formed. The works closed in September 1968 but reopened the following month as a subsidiary of Millom Hematite Ore and Iron Company Limited, Cumberland. Rail transport ceased at this time. A local syndicate of Hope, Evans and Tremewan took over the plant before British Benzole Carbonising Limited, and then finally in 1981 Coalite P.L.C. ran the works. The plant finally closed on the 25th of May 1984, and the huge chimney was demolished on the 19th of December 1984. The site was then sold to Durham County Council who carried out reclamation works throughout 1987.

RANDOLPH COKEWORKS

First coke ovens; 1895 sixty French "Coppee" ovens commissioned by The North Bitchburn Coal Company. 1897 a further set of twenty ovens constructed.

Second ovens; 1909 battery of 50 byproduct coke ovens constructed. Third ovens; 1948 battery of fifteen ovens (11 W-D Becker underjet coke ovens). 1957 a further battery of eleven ovens added.

The works were nationalised 1947 then "privatised" in 1957 when the Randolph Coke and chemical Company was formed. The works closed in September 1968 but reopened the following month. Coalite P.L.C. were the final operators and closed the works 25th May 1984 (the last oven was shoved 15th March 1984). The site was reclaimed throughout 1987 by Durham County Council.

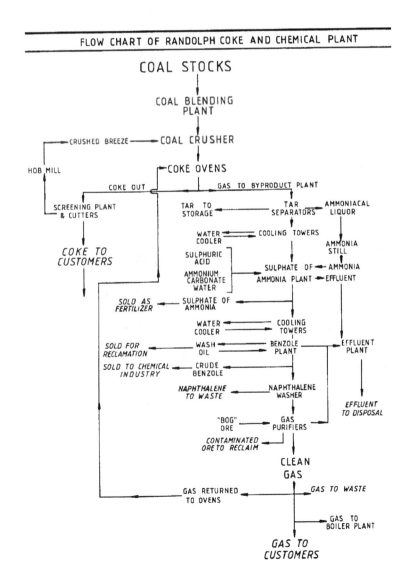

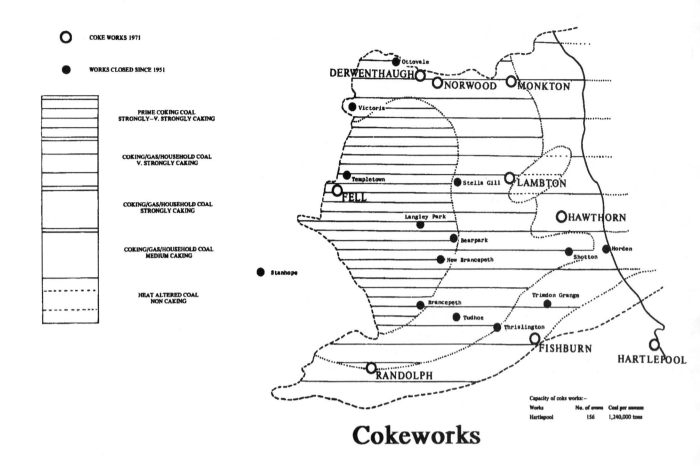

| COKE WORKS 1971 | |
| WORKS CLOSED SINCE 1951 | |

PRIME COKING COAL
STRONGLY—V. STRONGLY CAKING

COKING/GAS/HOUSEHOLD COAL
V. STRONGLY CAKING

COKING/GAS/HOUSEHOLD COAL
STRONGLY CAKING

COKING/GAS/HOUSEHOLD COAL
MEDIUM CAKING

HEAT ALTERED COAL
NON CAKING

Capacity of coke works:-

Works	No. of ovens	Coal per annum
Hartlepool	156	1,240,000 tons

Cokeworks

Almost all coal from Co. Durham is good for coking, steam raising bunkering and general purposes. The volatile content increases in easterly, north easterly and south easterly directions from Mid West Durham where the prime coking coals are found, the lower seams producing better coking coal than the upper seams. Because of closures in the west, most coking coals now come from the east. By-products of coke works include tar, sulphate of ammonia, concentrated ammonia, liquor, crude benzol and gas. Coke is used for local industries, for local domestic consumption and is also transported elsewhere.

Feeding the Coke Ovens

OPENCAST COAL MINING

● This example from the Congburn Valley was completed by
D. Rendell of Edmondsley Primary School

Open Cast Coal Mining is a variant of a type of mining known as surface mining, and practised widely across the world. Over 80% of solid fuels and mineral ores are mined by this method in America and major open-casting operations, for a wide variety of solid fuels, metallic ores and precious stones, extend across South America, Africa, Europe, Australasia and the Commonwealth of Independent States. The study of open-casting in North Durham can therefore be used to illustrate not only changes in the British coal industry but also wider technological, economic and environmental issues.

Surface mining, in its simplest terms us the removal of topsoil and rock (overburden) to recover mineral or fuel product.

When compared to underground methods, surface mining offers several distinct advantages. Surface mining makes it possible to recover deposits which, for physical reasons (such as faulting and flooding) cannot be mined underground, it provides safer working conditions, it usually results in a more complete recovery of the deposit and most importantly, it is generally significantly cheaper in terms of cost per unit of production.

The cost per unit is largely determined by the ratio between the thickness of overburden to be moved to recover a given amount of product and with the increasing size and capability of earth moving machinery this ratio is also increasing, making deeper deposits of product more attractive to surface mining methods. In the case of the Cong Burn valley this has meant that deposits of coal that were considered uneconomic to mine 20 years ago are now of great economic value and sites are often worked and reworked several times, each operation going deeper than before.

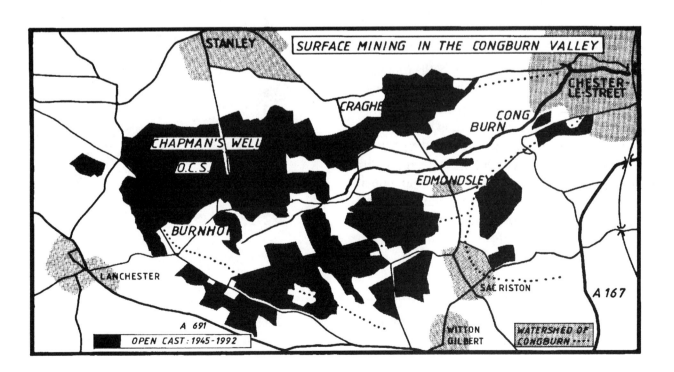

The actual mining process is divided into 2 phases:

1. exploration - to discover, delineate and prove the deposit

2. mining

The landsurface and the configuration of the deposit influence both phases. During the exploration phase a variety of geophysical techniques are used but the commonest, and simplest, method is that of drilling. Surface mining operations can be classified as:

l. Open pit mining - quarry or opencast

2. Strip mining - area or contour

3. Auger mining

4. Dredging

5. Hydraulic mining

Open pit mining is best exemplified by quarried producing limestone, sandstone and granite; sand and gravel pits and the large excavations opened to produce iron and copper. Two distinctive features of open pit mining are that the amount of overburden removed is proportionately small compared to the amount of rock or metallic ore recovered and that, because of the depth of deposit, mining tends to be long term, 50 years or more, producing a deep mine with a relatively small surface area. Because coal seams are comparatively thin, however, surface coal mines have a relatively short life.

Area strip mining is common in both America, Australia and Europe. A trench is cut through the overburden, in a relatively flat terrain, to expose a portion of the deposit, which is then removed. As each succeeding parallel cut is made, the spoil (overburden) is dumped in the previous cut. The final cut leaves an open trench, bounded on one side by the last spoil bank ad on the other by undisturbed highwall. In many regions of the world the resultant landscape resembles a giant washboard, often extending for several miles.

Contour strip mining is usually confined to shallow hillsides. An initial cut is made into the hillside, the spoil being tipped downslope. Subsequent cutting and filling takes the mine into the hillside to that point where the ratio of overburden to product makes further cutting uneconomic. The landscape produced by this type of mining resembles a shelf or bench, bounded by a highwall into the hill and spoil on the downhill slope.

Where coal seams are thick enough to justify the cost, but too thin to justify deep mining or drifts, augers are sometimes used to win more coal from a completed contour strip mine. Completion and abandonment of an auger mine leads to surface subsidence, above the highwall of the contour mine.

Although dredging and hydraulic mining are important methods of extracting sands and gravels, as well as precious metals and stones, they are not used in mining coal.

The surface mines in the Congburn valley use a combination of open pit and area strip mining methods. Clearing and storing the overburden and topsoils and then trenching or 'box cutting' through the coal seams to the physical and/or economic limits of the site. The spoil is then graded and the overburden replaced and graded to conform to the original contours.

MINING IN THE CONGBURN VALLEY

The Congburn valley lies to the west of Chester le Street, along the east-west axis. The southern watershed of the valley is formed by the high ridge of Long Edge and Waldridge Fell, the northern by Pelton Fell, Craghead and Wheatley Hill. Edmondsley lies on the southern side of the valley, below Daisy Hill and adjacent to Waldridge Fell. The present valley occupies an earlier, pre-glacial, valley which lies buried beneath thick glacial drift. The head of the valley lies below Burnhope and Quaking Houses.

Evidence of the earliest Roman coal mines at Benwell, on Tyneside, and in the Forest of Dean suggests that they were simple quarries dug into outcroppings of coal on a valleyside, a practice revived during the early thirteenth century. Records from that period indicate the establishment of surface workings, providing coal for a variety of industrial and agricultural uses, such as limeburning and saltmaking as well as baking and brewing. Sacriston, to the south of Edmondsley, was a manor belonging to Durham Cathedral and contemporary papers indicate that coal was taken from Sacriston and Durham.

Within a relatively short space of time the quarrying of coal seams became uneconomic, as well as being undesirable in terms of land conservation since the land was more valuable for farming and woodland coppices. Thus by the fourteenth century open surface workings were being replaced by day drifts and shallow shafts that required timbering.

Although there is archaeological and documentary evidence of continuous settlement in the Congburn Valley since the late Iron Age, including Roman occupation related to the Fort at Chester le Street, there is no evidence of coal mining until the eighteenth century, when a number of shallow shafts and day drifts are recorded on Edmondsley and Waldridge Fells (as well as stone quarries).

During the nineteenth and early twentieth centuries there were large collieries in the valley; at Waldridge, Pelton Fell, Edmondsley, Burnhope and Craghead. The extent and scale of mining in the area may be judged from the fact that on Waldridge Fell alone, between 1820 and 1975, there were 11 shaft mines and 9 drifts. Many of the smaller workings had a limited life but the larger mines remained in production for several decades.

Each colliery complex contained a large number of coke ovens and a complicated network of waggonways connected the mines to the Pontop and South Shields Branch Line at Stellagill, at the eastern end of the valley near Chester le Street.

Of the deep, modern collieries in the valley; Edmondsley closed in 1929, Burnhope (1949), Waldridge (1963), Craghead (1969) and Sacriston ... just to the south but working into the ridge that forms the southern watershed of the valley ... (1985). Deep shaft mines, such as those in the Congburn Valley, employ large numbers of skilled workers. Open cast mines employ relatively few workers in comparison, but require large numbers of expensive earth moving machines such as draglines and excavators. Because of the shortage of skilled labour during the second world war a number of surface mines were opened and by 1946 were producing about 6% of the national output of coal.

The first surface mine in the valley was opened by the NCB at Waldridge in 1945 and was worked for 2 years. Between 1945 and 1960, 10 sites in the valley were surface mined. No sites were worked in the valley between 1960 and 1973. Since 1973 6 sites have been worked-out and 2 sites are still in production with a third site at Daisy Hill just to the south. In total, including the open-cast mines on the watersheds of the valley, 35 sites have been worked between 1945 and 1991, 5 sites have been refused licences and 4 areas have been declared to be of 'interest' by British Coal. 2 site applications from private companies have gone to appeal with their results pending.

MODERN SURFACE MINES IN THE VALLEY

The two largest open-cast sites in the area are at Daisy Hill, between Edmondsley and Waldridge to the south of the watershed, and Chapman's Well at the head of the valley near Burnhope and Quakinghouses.

Both sites are worked by private contractors (Coal Contractors UK and Wimpey Mining Ltd respectively) for British Coal and follow a mining cycle common to all British Coal surface mines.

DAISY HILL OPEN-CAST SITE (OCS)

Daisy Hill OCS lies on the western edge of Waldridge Fell Country Park, close to the village of Edmondsley. Prior to the opening of the site the area consisted of poor quality farmland and two areas of colliery dereliction, the old Nettlesworth A and B Pits worked between 1850 and 1900.

3 Coalseams being opencasted are:- the High Main (1.8m), the Fivequarter (1.06m) and the Main (1.8m). All 3 seams belong to the Middle Coal Measures series of the Carboniferous Age and are about 250,000,000 years old. The site has already been worked on 4 occasions. Between 1850 and 1900 by the Nettlesworth Colliery, by a drift mine that opened after the closure of the shaft mine; opencasted, between 1949 and 1952, by the NCB and finally worked from the Sacriston Colliery until its closure in November 1985. The underground workings used a pillar and stall method of mining and the opencast is mining the pillars that were left. The site is crossed by a series of faults and a buried glacial channel, these made deep mining complicated and caused large areas of coal to be left.

Excavation and Restoration Cycle (Daisy Hill)

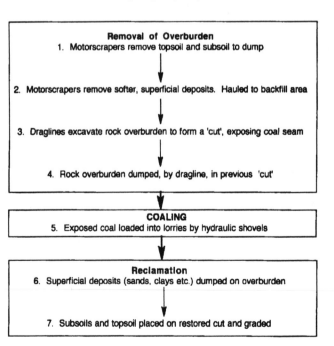

1. **Site Preparation**
    Clearing the site of vegetation and obstructions (including old colliery buildings and plant) Constructing access roads, offices, workshops

2. **Removal of Topsoil and Overburden**

3. **Excavation and Loading of Coal**

4. **Transportation of Coal to Processing Plant**

5. **Reclamation of Site**

Removal of Overburden
1. Motorscrapers remove topsoil and subsoil to dump

2. Motorscrapers remove softer, superficial deposits. Hauled to backfill area

3. Draglines excavate rock overburden to form a 'cut', exposing coal seam

4. Rock overburden dumped, by dragline, in previous 'cut'

COALING
5. Exposed coal loaded into lorries by hydraulic shovels

Reclamation
6. Superficial deposits (sands, clays etc.) dumped on overburden

7. Subsoils and topsoil placed on restored cut and graded

EXCAVATION AND RESTORATION CYCLE (DAISY HILL)

The hydraulic shovels load 20 tonnes of coal into each lorry, 1 tonne at a time, every 15 minutes. From the coal face at Daisy Hill the lorries shuttle direct to Wardley Coal Disposal Point, near Gateshead. There the coal is weighed and blended with coal from other sites and stockpiled. The lorries return to Daisy Hill on a 'merry-go-round' system, so that there is always a lorry waiting to be filled at the coal-face.

From Wardley some of the coal is taken by road (A1M) to Nottinghamshire, where it is blended with deepcast Nottingham coal to reduce moisture and sulphur content prior to being used in one of the Trent Power Stations. Smaller quantities of coal are taken by road to East Coast Ports to be shipped to Greece and Morocco, where it is used in the making of cement. The remaining coal is transported by rail to Blyth, in Northumberland, where it is either shipped south to the large Thameside Power Stations or burnt at Blyth Power Station itself.

At Daisy Hill, as on all British Coal sites, great care is taken to safeguard the environment. Grassed baffle banks have been constructed to reduce noise and noise levels are monitored on a regular basis. In dry weather mine roads are sprayed with water to reduce dust, the local road outside the site (used by lorries) is washed and swept and Coal lorries are washed before they leave the site for Wardley.

Daisy Hill was opened in 1988 and is due to close in 1992. Although the site has been worked before it is expected to yield 600,000 tonnes of coal. The deepest point in the mine is 43m below original land surface and 12,000,000 cubic metres of overburden will be removed and then replaced to reach this point. The site ratio (overburden: product) is 19.8:1. The site covers 100 hectares (250 acres) and employs 55 men, producing 3000 tonnes of coal a week.

When work on the site is complete British Coal intend to restore the site, just over half the site will be restored to agricultural use (56 ha), part will be restored as hay meadow 13 ha) and the rest (31 ha) is to be planted as woodland and heathland. As far as is known, this site is the first Open Cast Site to be restored to heather heath.

The site at Chapman's Well is very similar to that at Daisy. Like that at Daisy it has also been worked before and the opencast will reclaim the pillars from the High Main seam, which is slightly shallower here than at Daisy. The site however, is much larger, covering 283 hectares (698 acres) and will, over 8 years, produce 1.3 million tonnes of coal (site ratio 31:1).

Because of old workings on site the coal cannot be recovered cleanly and must be washed. Because of this the coal from Chapman's Well must be blended with the dry coal from Daisy Hill at the Wardley Disposal Plant to reduce moisture content before use.

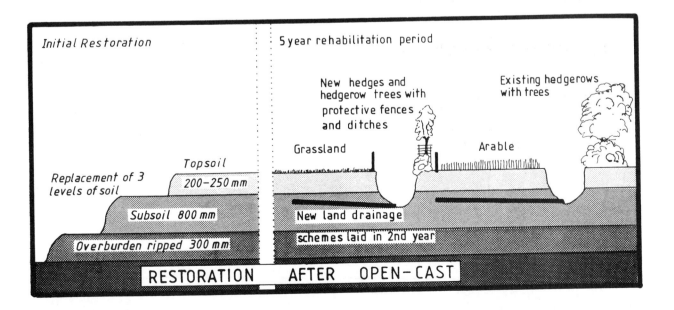

OPENCAST THE CONGBURN VALLEY, WIDER ISSUES

Before an Open Cast site is opened and worked, planning permission has to be granted by Durham County Council; or, should it be refused by the Council, by the Secretary of State for the Environment.

During recent planning appeals over sites in the valley, the following arguments (for and against surface mining) have been made by the site operators and the County.

Arguments against Surface Mining in the Valley	
Quality of life of residents :	dust noise visual amenity vibration lowering of property values
Road traffic: (Increase in volume)	road and pedestrian safety noise vibration dust
Tourism:	visual amenity (valley on direct route between Durham and Beamish) *see also Regional Image.* restricted access to countryside
Agriculture:	short term loss of farm land
Water:	pollution changing drainage patterns
Wildlife:	loss of natural habitats
Regional Image	**Open Cast Mines and spoil heaps conflict with the image of a 'New North'**

Arguments for Surface Mining in the Valley	
Employment:	creation of employment in area of high unemployment
National energy needs:	open cast coal is needed to provide a better quality of coal-mix for the production of electricity; cleaner, drier with a lower chemical content than deep mined coal
Balance of Trade:	reduces dependence on coal imports
Restoration of derelict land:	because surface mines are frequently located on or near old workings, areas of dereliction are cleared and restored during the mining cycle ..... without cost to the community
Environment:	the use of open cast coal reduces acid rain restored open cast sites are landscaped and often contain 'wildlife areas'
Continuity of tradition:	the Valley is a former mining area, there are still strong links and ties with the past which are strengthened through new mines
Community:	the mining contractors and British Coal play an important role in the local community; as ratepayers, employers and their support of a wide range of activities within the area

BRICK, PIPE AND TILE MANUFACTURE

● The material for this article was gathered by **P Davison** for his thesis on 'Brick and Tile makers in Co. Durham' which is deposited in the County Record Office.

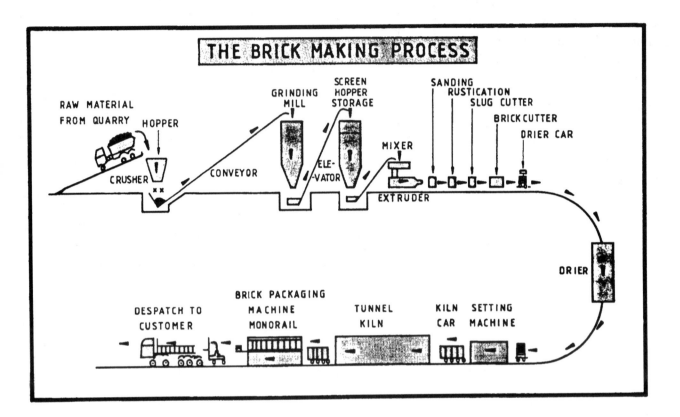

Most of us live in a house made of bricks with a tile roof with drains taking away waste water and sewerage. All of these products are made from clay or shale deposits which occur widely throughout the County, either at or near the surface, or are a part of the coal seams below ground. With the growth of towns and villages in the 19th century, the need for bricks, tiles and pipes was enormous and hundreds of brick and tile works were built throughout Durham to satisfy this demand.

Iron and steel works, coke ovens and furnaces required specialist refractory and fire bricks. The extensive deposits of gannister and fire clay, usually located immediately below coal seams, provided a raw material easy to obtain, at economical cost, close to the point of use.

There are several kinds of bricks, each having their own specialist use:-

Refractory and Fire Bricks - Heat resistant bricks.

Industrial (Engineering) Bricks - Very hard bricks for structures like viaducts and bridges.

Paving Bricks - A short lived substitute for stone or concrete paving stones in the 1920's. Now enjoying a revival for pedestrian shopping centres and patios.

Facing Bricks - High quality bricks visually attractive sometimes with a pattern or rustic finish. Used for the outside of houses.

Common Bricks - These are used for inside work or side walls where appearance is not important.

Bricks sometimes have the name of the manufacturer impressed upon them. Find out the kind of bricks used to build your house and school.

In addition to brick works there were many specialist tile and pipe works making roofing and ridge tiles, drain pipes for houses and farm land. They sometimes made a variety of other products, chimney pots, sinks, toilet fixtures, cattle troughs and garden ornaments. The toilet fixtures, sinks and troughs would be glazed for hygienic reasons using a salt glaze in the firing process.

Bricks are a standard size as shown on the illustration. This is the result of machine manufacture in the 19th century. Prior to this period, bricks were hand made, much slimmer in appearance and often irregular in shape.

Old bricks made in moulds often have a hollowed out portion on the upper face. This is called a frog. It is filled with mortar by the brick layer and helps hold the bricks together. Modern bricks often have three holes bored through them top to bottom serving the same purpose. Sanding and rustication is done on one face and both ends of facing bricks only, as these will, be the only surfaces to show on the outside wall.

Brick, Pipe and Tileworks on the Durham Coalfield

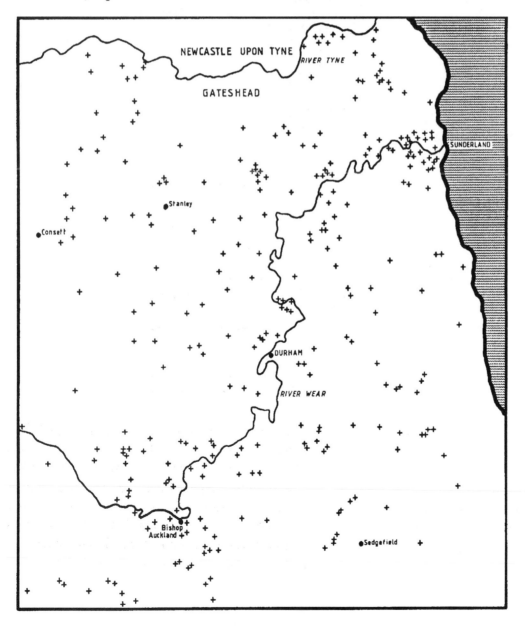

TEMPLETOWN BRICKWORKS

These were built in 1922 on the site of the old beehive coke ovens. Harold Boot was the works engineer who designed the new yard. The Manager was Tom Jemison who came here, along with some of his workforce, from Villa Real brickworks, which had just closed. Silica bricks were made at Templetown.

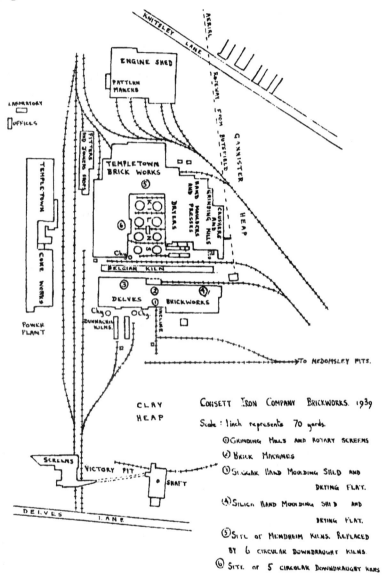

The Fell coke ovens, built in 1924, were lined with these bricks, as were the Derwenthaugh coke ovens in 1929. By 1964 half the bricks and special shapes used in lining coke ovens throughout Britain were made at Templetown. Refractory bricks were exported to India, Australia and the U.S.A.

The local gannister, a kind of sandstone, contained 97.5% silica. The main quarry was at Harthope in Weardale, between St. John's Chapel and Langdon Beck, 2,050 feet above sea level. In 1960 800 tons of gannister was quarried every week at Harthope. The Butsfield quarry became disused in 1953. Gannister was also obtained at Allenshields near Blanchland.

The gannister went through a primary crusher and then a cone crusher which produced 1.5 inch size 'nuts'. Two Brightside grinding mills pulverised the gannister nuts into graded particles of dust. This was mixed with 2% lime, used for a bonding agent, 0.5% sulphate lye for strengthening the 'green' brick prior to burning, and a measured amount of water.

The 'silica clay' was hand moulded into a large variety of shapes, 30,000 in all, that went into the construction of gas retorts and coke oven batteries. Gannister expands 0.5 inches per foot and allowance was made for this when the pattern moulds were made. The hand made silica bricks of normal size were made in a tray of 6 steel lined moulds. The special shapes were made in wooden moulds. The moulder threw handfuls of the silica clay into the corners of the mould and nudged it firmly down. Then he filled the mould, using a small shovel, and then beat it down on the mould to ensure a uniform density. The top was smoothed out and excess silica removed by a wooden slicker.

In the 1930's 60 hand moulders worked at Templetown but in the 1950's this number dropped to 35 when, first, a Sutcliffe machine press was bought, to make standard size bricks, and then an Aebi press was used. The shapes were dried for 36 hours in 6 tunnel dryers which were supplied with hot air from the 19 circular down draft kilns (those kilns that were cooling down). The silica bricks were burned in the beehive kilns, the temperature being slowly raised to a heat of 1450 degrees centigrade, over a period of 12 days. White seger cones inside the kiln told the burner the approximate temperature during the firing and samples of the bricks were withdrawn from the kiln to be tested for the amount of expansion the bricks had undergone to judge if they were properly burned. The seger cones were in later years replaced by visual pyrometers. 10 days were allowed for the kilns to cool down.

In the 1950's 350 people worked at Templetown. The silica bricks were also used for lining Open Hearth and Electric Arc steel furnaces, and for glass smelting furnaces. From 1948 to 1951 some insulation bricks were made.

SACRISTON COLLIERY BRICKWORKS

16 people worked here. In 1936 segar clay from the Brockwell seam in Sacriston colliery was made into firebricks, and 'stone' shale from the Shield Row drift made red coloured bricks. 3 hand moulders made 2.5 inch thick firebricks and special sized lumps. Quarls were made for the coke ovens at Sacriston colliery. A Bradley & Craven machine could make up to 10,000 3 inch firebricks or common red bricks a day. Some of the firebricks went to Consett Ironworks and to collieries in the Doncaster area. The firebricks were dried on a floor made of fireclay tiles and heated by warm air from the Belgian kiln. This continuous kiln had 16 chambers, each chamber holding 8,000 bricks. An electric fan helped to pull the draught through the kiln. From 1945 only red common bricks were made. The yard closed in 1958.

LONDONDERRY BRICKWORKS

At the Londonderry brickworks, Seaham, only common bricks were made, though selected commons were sold and used by the local builders as facing bricks. The bluestone shale that came out of Dawdon and Seaham collieries made a good red coloured brick. Before the First World War the Company had worked a clay pit in one of the fields next to the Nack pit. In the 1920's very fine dust was collected from the floor beneath the grinding mill, put into sacks and taken to the coal face workings underground to help prevent firedamp explosion.

In the late 1920's as many as 16 women worked in the yard, taking bricks off the machines and wheeling them to the setters at the kilns. By 1945 the women had left for better jobs.

DATA BASES

CONTENTS

COLLIERIES Supplementary Information

KEY

NAME	LIFE
OWNERS PRIOR TO 1947 IF KNOWN	SEAMS WORKED IN 1940s — 1960s. TYPE OF COAL. H HOUSEHOLD G. GAS. C COKING. S. STEAM M MANUFACTURING.
EMPLOYEES. 1930 1940 1950 1960 1970 1980	ADDITIONAL INFORMATION. IF AVAILABLE.

RAMSHAW NO1, NO.2. — 1959.

RAMSHAW COAL Co. 1930	BROCKWELL. HARVEY. HUTTON. BUSTY. C. H. S.
1930 18 1940 39 1950 242	

RANDOLPH   1893 — 1962

NORTH BITCHBURN COAL Co 1905- 1933 RANDOLPH COAL Co,	HUTTON HARVEY BUSTY BROCKWELL C. H.
1930 824 1940 77 1950 491 1960 221	CLOSED DUE TO EXHAUSTION.

GORDON HOUSE   1933 1930 — 1950

NORTH BITCHBURN COAL Co. 1905-1930	HUTTON HARVEY BUSTY. BROCKWELL C. H.
1930 504 1940 472	MERGED WITH RANDOLPH 1950

ARNGHYLL COPLEY. 1852 — 1951

BISHOP OF DURHAM ROYALTY	TOWNLEY. BUSTY. C
1950 95	DRIFT MINE NO EARLY RECORDS AVAILABLE

GREWBURN (BUTTERKNOWLE) 1850s - 1950	
BISHOP OF DURHAM ROYALTY BUTTERKNOWLE AND MARSFIELD COLLIERIES.	HARVEY H. M. S.
1930 18 1940 4 1950 41	COPLEY LANE BUTTERKNOWLE.

COCKFIELD FELL 1850s - 1950	
DUKE OF CLEVELAND H. BROWN 1930-50	BROCKWELL S
1930 ? 1940 ? 1950 3	

WIGGLESWORTH (COCKFIELD) 1900-1957	
A. TEASDALE AND SON	HUTTON G.
1930 ? 1940 20 1950 22	

BRUSSELTON 1834 - 1968	
SIR GEORGE MUSGROVE 1852 BRUSSELTON COAL CO 1930s	BUSTY. HUTTON HARVEY. H . S.
1920 45 1940 120 1950 262 1960 366	

BRUSSELTON TOWER ? 1965	
BRUSSELTON TOWER COAL CO. 1930-1947	BUSTY. H. S.
1930 ? 1940 25 1950 30 1960 20	

SOUTH SHILDON 1929 - 1958	
SOUTH SHILDON COAL CO. 1930s	TOP AND BOTTOM BUSTY. H. M. S.
1930 ? 1940 43 1950 102 1960 0	

OLD ELDON DRIFT. 1914 - 1962	
RT. HON THE EARL OF ELDON	FIVE QUARTER MAIN H. M.
1930 ? 1940 163 1950 258 1960 277	CLOSED DUE TO EXHAUSTION

PRINCESS ST 1 AND 2 1958	
PRINCES COAL CO 1930s.	FIVE QUARTER LOW MAIN H. M. S.
1930 1940 27 1950 88	

TUNNEL DRIFT	
JOSEPH HETHERINGTON AND CO.	MAIN S
1950 9	

SHINCLIFFE 1860 - 1877	
JOSEPH LOVE AND PARTNERS FERENS AND LOVE LTD.	

BOWBURN. 1908 - 1967	
BELL BROS.	TILLEY BUSTY. HARVEY BROCKWELL LOW MAIN C. G. H. M. S. FIRECLAY.
1930 636 1940 2358 1950 2353 1960 2102	CLOSED. UNECONOMIC. MERGED WITH TURSDALE 1931.

BEAMISH "JAMES & MARY." 1784 - 1966	
LAMBTON. HETTON JOICEY.	BUSTY. HUTTON. BROCKWELL C. G. FIRECLAY.
1930 665 1940 518 1950 495 1960 768	UNECONOMIC.

HEDLEY HILL	1936 — 1966
BELL'S HOUSE COAL Co.	BALLARAT THREE QUARTER C. H. FIRECLAY
1930 1940 26 1950 22 1960 22	

EAST HEDLEY HOPE	1870s — 1959
SIR B. SAMUELSON AND Co. 1905 PEASE AND PARTNERS 1930s BEARPARK COAL Co. 1936	BALLARAT MAIN THREE QUARTER FIVE QUARTER HARVEY C
1930 ? 1940 ? 1950 468	COAL EXHAUSTED

MOSSY BURN	1937 — 1969
INKERMAN COLLIERY Co. TOW LAW.	BALLARAT FIVE QUARTER THREE QUARTER S
1930 1940 17 1950 27 1960 18	EXHAUSTION OF COAL.

WEST THORNLEY	1940s — 1965
	HARVEY C. H.
1930 1940 64 1950 50 1960 18	UNECONOMIC.

EAST HETTON	1836 — 1983
WALTER SCOTT (NEWCASTLE) 1905 EAST HETTON COAL Co. 1930s	BUSTY HUTTON MAUDLIN TILLEY. C. G. H. M. S.
1930 1200 1940 1200 1950 1278 1960 1083 1970 903 1980 870	DANGER OF FLOODING SO CLOSED 1983.

CASSOP	1840s — 1877
THORNLEY COAL Co 1840s R.P. PHILIPSON 1854 ROBSON & Co 1875	
	KNOWN SOMETIME AS CASSOP VALE CASSOP MOOR.

PAGE BANK   1855 — 1931

BELL BROS. BRANCEPETH COAL CO.	HUTTON HARVEY.
1930 378	

WHITWORTH PARK. 1839 - 1974

WHITWORTH PARK COAL CO.	HARVEY C. H.
1930 11 1940 280 1950 291 1960 315 1970 291	COAL EXHAUSTED.

MIDDLESTONE MOOR   —   1965

SPENNYMOOR COAL CO.	HUTTON H. S.
1930 – 1940 24 1950 31 1960 24	

WESTERTON   1932 BINCHESTER 1932-6?

BOLCKOW AND VAUGHAN DORMAN LONG.	
1930 214 1940 1950 1960 51	RE OPENED AS BINCHESTER 1932.

RODDYMOOR   1844 — 1963

PEASE AND PARTNERS.	BALLARAT HARVEY, TILLEY THREE QUARTER FIVE QUARTER MAIN C. H, CLAY. WITHERITE.
1930 1037 1940 1055 1950 1027 1960 742	COAL EXHAUSTED

FELL WALL   ? — 1950s

FELL WALL COAL CO	BALLARAT HARVEY THREE QUARTER C
1930 12 1940 27 1950 20	

SHOTTON	? — 1972
SHOTTON AND EASINGTON COAL Co.	THREE QUARTER MAIN LOW MAIN HIGH MAIN C. G.
1930 2050 1940 1837 1950 1830 1960 1128 1970 783	UNECONOMIC

MURTON	1843 — 1991
SOUTH HETTON COAL Co.	HARVEY., TILLEY. FIVE QUARTER. HUTTON LOW MAIN THREE QUARTER C G H M. S.
1930 3332 1940 3032 1950 2880 1960 2303 1970 1506 1980 1003	UNECONOMIC GEOLOGICAL DIFFICULTIES.

SOUTH HETTON	1833 — 1983
SOUTH HETTON COAL Co.	HUTTON THREE QUARTER MAIN , TILLEY LOW MAIN FIVE QUARTER. C G H M. S.
1930 1395 1940 1119 1950 1245 1960 953 1970 609 1980 607	MERGED WITH MURTON 1983.

ELEMORE	1825 — 1974
LAMBTON, HETTON AND JOICEY COAL Co.	HUTTON HARVEY LOW MAIN MAIN FIVE QUARTER. G. H. S. FIRECLAY.
1930 1476 1940 1481 1950 1525 1960 904 1970 509	DANGEROUS WORKING CONDITIONS

EPPLETON	— 1986
LAMBTON, HETTON AND JOICEY COAL Co.	LOW MAIN MAUDLIN BUSTY. FIVE QUARTER G. S.C. FIRECLAY. H
1930 2094 1940 1955 1950 1946 1960 1710 1970 1354 1980 901	MERGED WITH MURTON 1986

WINGATE GRANGE	1839 — 1962
WINGATE GRANGE CULLY. Co. WINGATE COAL Co. 1930s.	HUTTON BUSTY LOW MAIN MAIN C. G. H. M.
1930 1412 1940 1412 1950 910 1960 675	DIFFICULT TO WORK

VANE TEMPEST	1929 —	
LONDONDERRY COLLIERIES LTD	FIVE QUARTER MAUDLIN HUTTON LOW MAIN G. H. M. S.	
1930 393 1940 1460 1950 1820 1960 1681 1970 1628 1980 1500 1990 845		

EASINGTON	1895 —	
EASINGTON COLLIERY CO.	HIGH MAIN FIVE QUARTER LOW MAIN HUTTON MAIN	
1930 3199 1940 2759 1950 2880 1960 2752 1970 2447 1980 2412 1990 2000		

HORDEN	1913 — 1986	
HORDON COAL Co.	LOW MAIN HUTTON HIGH MAIN FIVE QUARTER. G. H. I. S.	
1930 4428 1940 4048 1950 3880 1960 3172 1970 1975 1980 1891	UNECONOMIC. WATER PROBLEMS. LARGEST COLLIERY IN BRITAIN FOR MOST OF IT'S LIFE.	

BLACKHALL	1909 — 1981	
HORDEN COAL Co.	FIVE QUARTER HUTTON MAIN LOW MAIN G. H. M. S.	
1930 2255 1940 2300 1950 2490 1960 2047 1970 1709 1980 1438	UNECONOMIC WATER PROBLEMS	

CASTLE EDEN	1840 — 1894	
CASTLE EDEN COAL Co. LTD. HORDEN COAL Co 1910	FIVE QUARTER HUTTON. MAIN.	
	CLOSED DUE TO FLOODING. PUMPING CONTINUED TO KEEP WATER FROM BLACKHALL.	

HASWELL	1835 — 1896	
HASWELL, EASINGTON SHOTTON COAL Co. HASWELL COAL Co.	THREE QUARTER MAIN FIVE QUARTER.	

MAINSFORTH	1904 – 1968
CARLTON IRON Co. 1905 – 1930 DORMAN LONG	BROCKWELL HARVEY. HUTTON BUSTY. LOW MAIN C. G. H. M. S.
1930 1957 1940 2249 1950 2181 1960 1546	UNECONOMIC. LOW MAIN FLOODED

THRISTLINETON	1835 – 1967
DORMAN LONG.	MAIN LOW MAIN BUSTL FIVE QUARTER HUTTON HARVEY TOP BUSTY BOTTOM. C.G. H. S. M.
1930 1005 1940 986 1950 1124 1960 805	EXHAUSTION OF SEAMS.

WITTON AND SACRISTON BUSTY 1839 – 1985	
CHARLAW AND SACRISTON COLLIERY Co. LTD. 1905 – 1947	BRASS THILL BUSTY BROCKWELL VICTORIA.
1930 560 1940 580 1950 483 1960 478 1970 279 1980 272	EXHAUSTION OF SEAMS AND WETNESS.

SACRISTON SHIELD ROW	– 1942
CHARLAW AND SACRISTON COLLIERY Co. LTD	SHIELD ROW
1930 330 1940 210	EXHAUSTION OF SEAMS.

SEAHAM	1852 – 1987
LONDONDERRY COLLIERIES LTD.	MAIN MAUDLIN HUTTON FIVE QUARTER G. S. CLAY.
1930 2776 1940 1540 1950 1570 1960 1423 1970 1035 1980 633	MERGED WITH VANE TEMPEST 1987. "NICK NACK"

DAWDON	1902 – 1991
LONDONDERRY COLLIERIES LTD.	LOW MAIN MAIN MAUDLIN HUTTON G. H. M. S.
1930 3809 1940 2375 1950 2596 1960 2348 1970 2311 1980 2340	UNECONOMIC.

BEAMISH "SECOND" & PARK 1784-1962	
LAMBTON, HETTON AND JOICEY.	HIGH MAIN HUTTON — WEAR — PONTOP G.
1930 550 1940 — 1950 367 1960 119	MERGED 1930s WITH BEAMISH "STANLEY" COAL EXHAUSTED.

CROXDALE 1875 — 1934	
WEARDALE COAL Co. TUDHOE PARK COAL Co.	
	CLOSED FIRST 1915. THEN RE-OPENED.

TUDHOE PARK 1864-1935 1941 - 1969	
TUDHOE PARK COAL Co.	HUTTON — TOP — BOTTOM. M.
1930 847 1940 — 1950 134 1960 236	FORMERLY TUDHOE COLLIERY

TUDHOE MILL DRIFT 1954 - 1965.	
1960 207	

DEAN AND CHAPTER 1904 — 1965	
DORMAN LONG	BUSTY BROCKWELL HUTTON MAIN FIVE QUARTER C. G. M. S. H. FIRECLAY.
1930 2585 1940 2978 1950 2510 1960 2125	UNECONOMIC. MERGED WITH LEASINGTHORNE 1949.

EAST HOWLE 1871 — 1905	
CARLTON IRON Co.	BROCKWELL BUSTY HARVEY. C
	CLOSED DUE TO FIRE. REPLACED BY MAINSFORTH.

THORNLEY.	1970
	TILLEY HUTTON BUSTY C. G. S.
1930 1659 1940 1659 1950 1380 1960 1340	UNECONOMIC. HEAVY FINANCIAL LOSSES.

FISHBURN	1911 — 1973
HENRY STOBART AND CO. LTD	BROCKWELL BUSTY HARVEY
1930 899 1940 1340 1950 1536 1960 1422 1970 710	LARGE COKING PLANT ATTACHED. SERIOUS WATER PROBLEMS

TRIMDON GRANGE ? 1968	
WALTER SCOTT (NEWCASTLE 1905 EAST HETTON COLLIERIES LTD. TRIMDON COAL CO.	BUSTY TILLEY C. H. S.
1930 800 1940 350 1950 767 1960 796	UNECONOMIC.

DEAF HILL	1870 — 1967
TRIMDON COAL CO.	HARVEY HUTTON BUSTY C. H. M
1930 966 1940 966 1950 580 1960 593	EXHAUSTION OF COAL.

LIST OF COUNTY RECORDS OFFICE DOCUMENTS

This is a collection of documents chosen to cover as many aspects of the topic as possible. It would be feasible to make a personal selection from them which, with suitable editing and preparation, could be used with children of primary and secondary levels, both for classroom and project work.

The indexes and catalogues of the County Record Office can be used for further examples of similar documents with a view to fitting such material into local study projects.

GENERAL

D/Lo/C 739 (2) - Letter from Lord Londonderry to N. Hindhaugh Esq. stating his attitude towards the miners and his plan for educating the miners' children. See transcript.

D/Lo/B 327 (8) - An account of coals shipped at Seaham Harbour, in 1842.

D/Lo/B 306 (14) - An account of the expense of leading coals from Rainton Bridge to Seaham Harbour..., 1838.

D/Lo/B/306 - List of men employed leading coals from Rainton Bridge to the bottom of Seaham Incline, 1839.

D/Lo/B 332 - A comparison of coal & coke shipped at Seaham and Sunderland for eleven years. (Only ten years completed)

D/X 248/3 - Lambton Colliery paysheet, giving names of workmen and their wages, 1866.

D/X 80/2 - Letter from Durham Miners Association to Ludworth Colliery and the reply, 1867. See transcript.

D/X 80/3 - A list of officials and their salaries, Seaham Harbour, 1873.

F. PAR 16 - Extracts from Parliamentary Reports on the Employment of Children, 1842.

S/X 148 - Notice about allowances to be paid during the First World War. Harton Coal Company, 1914.

NCB 3/105 - 4 Photographs, Harton Coal Company.

D/X 260/1 - Statistical tables of the engines, ventilation, screens and sales etc., and of the pitmen and the strata of nine principal collieries in the County of Durham. Engraving of Sunderland coal drops.

SOCIAL CONDITIONS

D/Lo/B 327 (6) - Petition from the tradesmen of Seaham Harbour to John Buddle, Lord Londonderry's viewer, complaining that Mr Henzel Clark, who had already a good job in the harbour office, was dealing in seamen's requisites and cornering the market.

D/Lo/E 517 - A report to Lady Londonderry on the Colliery Schools set up by her in 1846 at Pensher, Rainton, Pittington, Old Durham and Houghton-le-Spring, August 1861.

D/Lo/B 256/49 - Results of John Buddle's enquiries into the literacy of the pitmen at Pittington Colliery, September 1840.

D/X 115/6 - Rents paid by the workmen at Pontop Colliery, in 1842.

NCB/4/219 - Extracts from the Committee Meeting Minutes of the Waterhouses Miners' Institute from May 16th to July 4th, 1922, showing the sort of business dealt with.

D/Ph 98/1 - Extracts from Frederick Charlton's journal for January 1871. He was a Colliery Joiner and Engineer, and lived in various towns in the county, Spennymoor, Shildon, Bishop Auckland, South Hetton and Pittington. He was involved in Chapel and Sunday School activities, (See Transcript).

F/PAR 75 - Some pages from a Parliamentary Report on Mining Districts, 1855, mainly concerned with the employment of children under 10 years in the mines.

NCB/3/102 p 29 - Drawing from the Illustrated London News of May 10th 1899 of colliers playing pitch and toss.

D/Ph 92/1 - Copies of photographs from Esh Winning, c1910.

   (i) The Pigeon Fanciers' Club.

   (ii) The Cycling Club

   (iii) The Football Team

   (iv) The Tennis Club

D/X 115/13 - A petition from the inhabitants of Burnopfield asking the Marquis of Bute's trustees for their assistance in improving the water supply to their village, August 7th, 1868.

D/Ph 92/1 - Photographs of back to back houses at Marley Hill.

F/PAR 75 - Parliamentary Report on the colliery settlements at Gilesgate Moor, 1865.

D/Lo/B 260 - Letter to Lord Londonderry about the required improvements to the water supply at Rainton, 1871.

STRIKES

NCB1/Sc 583 - Request from the workmen of Townley Colliery for more money and setting out the rates of pay requested for working under various conditions.

NCB3/102/p 28 - Cutting from the Illustrated London News, May 10th, 1879. The great colliery strike in Durham.

NCB3/102/P 102 - Cuttings concerning the Boldon Dispute, February, 1896.

D/Lo/B6 - Notice from the Coal Trade Office to Lord Londonderry about miners who are on strike, 1854.

D/Lo/C 142 (659) - Letter from John Buddle, colliery viewer, to Lord Londonderry about an impending strike, 1838.

D/Lo/X45 - An open letter from Lord Londonderry to his employees following a strike in Silksworth Colliery, 1891.

NCBI/JB/616 - Letter from Thomas Hall to John Buddle concerning a dispute at Black Boy Colliery, June 1851 (See Transcript).

ACCIDENTS

EP/Wa 55 - Page from the Northern Weekly Leader for February 29th 1908, dealing with the aftermath of the Washington Pit Explosion.

D/Lo/X54 & D/Lo/X56 - Pages from the Illustrated London News for September 18th 1880 about the Seaham Colliery disaster.

NCBI/SC/574 - A subscription list for the relief fund set up after a disaster at Townley Colliery, not dated.

NCBI/SC/572 - Notice of a meeting to discuss the arrangements for spending the Benevolent Fund, 1861.

NCB 3/102 - Newscuttings about a fire at Boldon Colliery, October 1889.

NCBI/JB/2079 - Extracts from the Lambton View Book, June 1817. This is an example of a day book kept by a Colliery Viewer, in this case, John Buddle (See transcript).

F/PAR 61 - Extract from a Parliamentary Report on accidents in mines, discussing preventative measures, 1835.

F/PAR 66 - Extracts from the Parliamentary Report of the Inspectors of Coal Mines, 1852, giving statistics of accidents.

D/X 188/6 - Memorial booklet produced on the West Stanley Colliery Explosion of February 16th 1909.

EP/NS/52 - Statement of accounts of the Seaham Permanent Relief Fund - the men killed, and the allowances paid to their dependants following a disaster in September 1880.

NCBI/SC 628/40 - An account of accidents to men and boys employed underground at Townley Colliery in 1851. The nature of the injury and the number of days off work are given.

D/X391/1 - Commemorative Poem written by W C Bickle on the deaths of Richard Carr, Thomas Carr and John Defty at Kimblesworth Colliery, 1885.

D/Lo/B282 - Seaton Colliery - Minutes of a meeting to discuss safety measures and ventilation in mines, 1861.

D/X 126/2 - Notice issued by the Hetton Coal Company about forming a relief fund to which the coal company will contribute, 1834.

Bibliography
Some further Reading

Coals from Newcastle	R. Finch	Terence Dalton
A New Look at the Collieries of Northumberland and Durham	GL Atkinson	NCB North East
British Coalminers in the 19th Century	J Benson	Gill & McMillan
Mining and Social Change (Durham County in the 20th Century)	M Bulmer	Croom Helm
The Collier's Rant Song and Culture of the North East	R Colls	Croom Helm
The Pit Children	E Forster	Frank Graham
Views of the Collieries of Northumberland and Durham	TH Hair	David & Charles
To the Miner Born, Life in a Durham Pit Village	M Wade	Oriel Press
The General Strike 1926	P Renshaw	Eyre Methuen
Durham Miners 1919 - 1960	WR Garside	Allen & Unwin
The Banner Book	WA Moyes	Frank Graham
Mostly Mining	WA Moyes	Frank Graham
Contracting Coalfield	WA Moyes	Frank Graham
The Great Northern Coalfield	F Atkinson	University Tutorial Press
Coalmining	AR Griffin	Longmans
An Introduction to the Coalmining Industry	CJ White	Colin Venton
Environmental Impact of Coalmining	M Chadwick	Pergammon
The Death Pit (West Stanley 1909)	E Forster	Frank Graham
Miners of County Durham	Keitch	
The Coal Miners of County Durham	Emery	Sutton

Contributors

This project began in July 1990 as a part of the Environmental Education Curriculum Group's on-going programme of publications for use in schools. The group wish to thank Durham County Education Committee, the Director of Education and the Chief Inspector for Schools for their support and for the opportunity to produce this resource. Contributions were invited from many sources and the response was magnificent.

W. A. Moyes.

Particular thanks are due to the editorial group which collated, arranged and presented the material. The editorial board was led by W.A.Moyes, retired Senior Education Adviser, who worked many hours voluntarily. Frank Burns, Head of Earl's Orchard Field Study Centre, co-ordinated the project with great enthusiasm and chased up the contributors. Mike Horne, Deputy Warden of Beamish Hall painstakingly put the project onto computer and prepared the material for reproduction. The Editorial board is especially grateful to T M McKeon B.Sc. M.Ed., Warden of Beamish Hall who kindly allowed the use of the Hall as a meeting place and to Jean Ambler and Christine Brown of the Beamish Hall secretarial staff gave invaluable assistance on many occasions. The board were helped enormously by David Noble, Head of Witton Park Centre whose maps and diagrams added to the quality of the finished product. John Coatswith produced some attractive illustrations. John Nelson toured the county taking photographs. Final production was in the capable hands of the Northern Echo.

Individual contributions are acknowledged within the body of the text and the complete list is most impressive.

Mr P Hodgson	Teacher Evenwood C.E. Primary School
Mr D Snell	Head Teacher Henknowle Primary School
Mr J Nelson	Teacher Spennymoor King Street Junior
Mr D Wallace	Deputy Head Gurney Pease Primary School
Mr J McManners	Head Teacher Cassop Primary School
Mrs V McCourt	Teacher Sacriston Junior School*
Mrs J Heseltine	Teacher Haswell Primary School
Mrs E Williams	Teacher Dean Bank Primary School
Mr D Wilcock	Retired Teacher
Mr D Farms	Head Teacher Wearhead Primary School
Mrs C Kirkwood	Science Support Team
Mr M G C W Wheeler	Curator Schools Museum Service
Mr D Miller	Head of Centre, Seaham Coastal Centre
Mrs A Henderson	Teacher Murton Jubilee Primary School
Mr D Winter	Teacher Eden Hall Junior School
Mr D Rendell	Head Teacher Edmondsley Primary School
Mr C Edwards	Retired Miner
Mr W Dowding	Retired NUM Officer, Red Hills Durham
Mr C H A Townley	Historian
Mr P Andrew	New College lecturer
Mr W A Moyes	Retired Senior Adviser, Durham Education Authority
Mr M V Horne	Deputy Warden Beamish Hall
Mr F Burns	Head of Centre, Earls Orchard Field Study Centre

Acknowledgements

The Environmental Education Curriculum Group wish to record their thanks to those named below for the right to use their work. Every effort has been made to trace the copyright holders of work and photographs used in this book To any one we have been unable to trace we offer our sincere apologies. Every effort has been made to contact all copyright holders the publishers would like to hear from any copyright holders not mentioned in the acknowledgement.

J C Curry	Photographs "Troubled Seams" McCutcheon
J Pears	Photograph "Troubled Seams"
Methuen Publishers	"Coal mines and Miners" Miles Tomelin
Northern Echo	Photographs 1984/5 Miners Strike and printed material
P Davison	"Brick and Tile makers in County Durham", County Archive
N Cowans	"Of Mining Life and Aal its ways"
D W Patterson	Diagrams of Seaham Harbour
J Harrison	Drawings of Beamish 2nd Colliery Engine North Eastern Industrial Archeological Society Bulletin 11. 1970
Alan W Stobbs	"Memories of LNER"
Durham County Record Office	Contributions and assistance on numerous occasions
G M Hall	"Murton, its development from hamlet to industrial village"
Easington D.C.	East Durham Heritage Trails and Walkways and Photographic Archives
Sedgefield D.C.	Photographs
Colliery Guardian	Reproduction of Colliery information
British Coal	"Coal Information Pack for Schools"
Colin Mountford	"Industrial Locomotives in County Durham"
Waltham and Holmes (North East England) Cambridge University Press	
Wharncliffe Press Barnsley	Photographs
Million Makepiece	Photographs and Information on Butterknowle
Durham NUM	Archive Material
Gaunless Valley Historical Society	Maps and Photographs
Gilesgate Primary School	"In them Days" Claire Martin
G.H.A. Townley	Oral History 1950-51 S.W. Durham
Gollantz Publishing	Men and the Pits by F Zwerg
Beamish Museum	Photographs and information
Austin of the Guardian	Cartoon
Frank Graham Publisher	Photographs and diagram
Jack Waltham	Slides and photographs
Colin Gibson	Material from Trimdon and Fishburn Local History Society
Brian Layfield	Woodham Burn Junior School - Bevin Boys
W A Moyes	Excerpts from "Wingate", "Mostly Mining", "Contracting Coalfield" "The Banner Book"
Ordnance Survey	
F Mason	Practical Coal Mining for Miners Virtue & Co. Ltd.

Miners Past and Present and their families who wish to remain anonymous.
Martin Wainwright and McAllister of the Guardian
Matt of the Daily Telegraph
John Welsh - Blackhall
Durham University Business School
Lynesack and Softley Parish Council
The GUARDIAN

Durham County Environmental Education Curriculum Group Members

Mrs J Baker	Mrs V McCourt
Mrs J Beard	Mr J McManners
Mrs P Bell	Mr D Miller
Mr F Burns - Chairman	Mr J Nelson
Mr J Crossland	Mr D Noble
Mr R Higgs	Dr J Palmer
Mr M Horne - Secretary	Mr G Smithson
Mrs V Hughes	Mr D Snell
Mrs H Hyde	Miss M Sykes
Mrs B King	Mr M Tones
Mrs C Kirkwood	Mr D Wallace
Mr P McGuire	Mr A Westerman
Mrs C Martin	Mrs E Williams

Previous Publications

1. Making an Environmental Trail
2. A Step in the Dark (Mini Beasts)
3. Flowers in the Environment
4. Parks Ponds and People
5. About Trees
6. Animals in the Environment

Fieldwork from Durham Schools No 1 1985
Fieldwork from Durham Schools No 2 1987
Fieldwork from Durham Schools No 3 1989

A FEW MORE PHOTOGRAPHS

Alphabetical Index to Collieries in the Book

Alphabetical Index to Collieries in the Book

Alphabetical Index to Collieries in the Book

Alphabetical Index to Collieries in the Book

They're Closing Down the Pit

They are closing down the pit I've always worked in
And saying "Go elswhere and make your pile".
They are closing down the pit I've always worked in
And everybody's leaving with a smile
I started in the Brockwell two's,
It's not the place you'd choose
The coal was canny but the ramble was four foot high,
The face was on the siddle
With a big fault in the middle
And a grit big stone came down and broke my thigh.
Another awful place
Was that Brockwell fourth east face.
It had water, ramble, gas and trouble and strife.
But the worst bit of all
Was that rotten exit stall
When the cutter shortened Ishy Jowet's life.
Then I cut up top coal
An, I'll say upon my soul,
What a place to work, the coal was one foot eight,
Belly flopping all the way,
And the Overman wouldn't pay.
You hardly dared stop to get your bait.
I'm in the Busty now,
Another stinking cow.
One foot ten of coal, I can find no more.
It's clarts, from end to end,
Enough to drive you round the bend.
But I'm leaving it, its there for ever more.

by Bert Draycott